SOME VITAL ASPECTS OF PEACE EDUCATION

SOME VITAL ASPECTS OF PEACE EDUCATION

Ravindra Kumar

GYAN

ISBN: 978-81-212-1293-9

Price: ₹ 900

First Published, 2015

Published by

Gyan Publishing House
23, Main Ansari Road
Daryaganj, New Delhi-110002
Phones: 23282060, 23261060
Fax : 91-11-23285914
E-mail: books@gyanbooks.com

Laser Typesetting: Dinesh Kumar, Meerut

Printed at: G. Print Process, Delhi

Cataloging in Publication Data—DK
Courtesy: D.K. Agencies (P) Ltd. <docinfo@dkagencies.com>

Some vital aspects of peace education / Ravindra Kumar.
pages cm
Contributed articles.
Includes bibliographical references and index.
ISBN 9788121212939

1. Peace—Study and teaching. 2. Nonviolence. I. Kumar, Ravindra, 1959-, editor.

DDC 303.66071 23

Foreword

Peace originates from non-violence, which, therefore, is the key to bliss. Peace builds a congenial environment for a large-scale co-operation wherefore the welfare of everyone becomes tenable. Further, in a state of peace, harmony, love and unity flourish leading humankind a step forward on pathway to progress. Human beings realize importance of coexistence and make collective endeavours to ensure that they thrive even in an adverse and the most challenging situation.

Thanks to the stellar importance of peace in life! It has always been the nucleus of preaching, teaching and endeavours of great teachers all over the world. Peace has been in the centre of thoughts of all those who have striven for the development, prosperity and welfare of humanity. The significance of peace remains upbeat even in current perspective and it will remain so in all times to come. It is a universal law embodying co-operation, co-existence and wellbeing of all.

Dr. Ravindra Kumar is a well-known scholar. As an eminent peace-educator, he has his own identity and recognition around the world. For years, he has been making laudable efforts in propagating and espousing peace education. The present work is a valuable addition in this regard. Taking inspiration from this valuable and timely work, it is hoped, people associated with the process of education, especially teachers, professor and peace educators, will come forward in creating a environment conducive for peace studies at different levels of education. They will, hopefully, work to execute, in letter and spirit, the following message of Mahatma Gandhi:

"Let the first act every morning be to make the following resolve for the day: I shall not fear anyone on Earth; I shall fear only God. I shall not bear ill will towards anyone. I shall not submit to injustice from anyone; and I shall conquer untruth by truth, and in resisting untruth, I shall put up with all suffering."

For a wonderfully significant work like this, I welcome and salute to Dr. Ravindra Kumar. I also wish a grand success for this body of work.

Ela Gandhi

Introduction

Peace is not only important, but an indispensable basis of a pleasant and secure life. Co-ordination and co-operation, the two foremost conditions required for common welfare and development, are possible only in a state of peace. Without an atmosphere laden with peace, no concrete step towards real progress and prosperity is conceivable. That is why; peace cannot be shoved away to the margin. It is always centrally significant.

What is peace? Familiarity with the basic spirit at the root of peace and appropriate knowledge about its purpose is of utmost importance. State of peace is generally taken to be the situation of the status quo, or a state of as it is, or of inactiveness. However, this is not correct interpretation of the real peace. It is rather contradictory to both, the meaning and the purpose of peace.

Peace is undoubtedly a state free from hostility and retribution. It is a state liberated from violence and fight. Besides this, peace is opposite of the situation of war, or a warlike state. In this, there is a keen longing for mutual respect and goodwill and a strong revulsion to use of arms. But, it is surely not a situation of the status quo or passive perpetuity. There is no room for inaction in it.

Peace is, in fact, a state fully dedicated to dynamism. It is a continuous pro- active state calling for broad co-ordination and collation among people to pave the way for progress of one and all. It inspires to move forward with unity for the welfare of humanity as a whole. Moreover, the importance and worth of the state of peace can be well appreciated in its uncanny ability to foster courage for making situations conducive for the desired constructive purpose.

In realizing the state of peace, education can play a vital role. The process of education can contribute significantly in conditioning one to work for the progress, welfare and development of all on the basis of wide-ranging co-ordination and co-operation. It is the community of teachers or educators, indeed the fulcrum of the whole process, who can be the real torch-bearers and guiding force for peace blitz. Each one in the community of teachers can contribute tremendously, as Gautama Buddha has rightly said, ***"Thousands of candles can be lit from a single candle, and the life of the candle will not be shortened."***

It is, therefore, highly expected of teachers and educators that they come forward to make peace studies an essential part of education, and they impart it at different levels of the pedagogy as per the need of time and space.

This expectation from them multiplies many folds today when the process of globalization is increasing rapidly and mega scale welfare and progress schemes fall in want of co-ordination and co-operation of people at all levels and in all walks of life.

Keeping the significance of peace education in the centre, many scholars, professors and peace educators from India and other countries of the world have contributed their articles on the vital aspects related to it. They have gone in depth of the core issues related to peace education and have made worthy suggestions. Some of them have based their surmise on well illustrated case studies.

This work will, hopefully, draw the attention of those who have interest in peace education. It will also be found useful by those who think about necessity of peace education and desire to work for it.

I am thankful to all those who have contributed for this work. I express my gratitude towards Mrs. Ela Gandhi for writing a foreword to this. Finally, I convey my heartfelt thanks to Ms. Seema Sharma, Ms. Megha Arora and Dr. Bir Singh Yadav for their substantial help in reading the manuscript of this work before sending it to the press.

Ravindra Kumar

Contents

A: Peace Education

1. PEACE EDUCATION: A VIEW

Ravindra Kumar*

Peace [*Shanti* in *Sanskrit*] a word signifying the state of harmony in a holistic perspective, calls for peak of human dynamics and proactive co-operation of all fellow-beings. Bliss, calmness, serenity and tranquility are the words synonymous to it. Thomas Stearns Eliot [1934-65] a US born eminent English lyricist, social critic, Nobel laureate [1948] and composer of famous poem, The West Land, wonderfully opines that *Shanti* is the state to accord understanding that is worth consideration. But, which type of understanding? It is, in one way or the other, the understanding of co-operation. Therefore, the state of peace is the source of origin of mutual understanding, of co-operation, and a clarion call for prosperity of one and all in the larger interest of humanity. Hence, it is not an ordinary state. Rather, the state of peace is extraordinary.

---

* Indologist Dr. Ravindra Kumar is a former vice chancellor of CCS University Meerut; he is the editor-in-chief of Global Peace International Journal.

That is why; *Shanti* occupies pride of place in the *Vedic* prayers, which is well illustrated in the *Shanti Prakaran* [peace-perception], as a predominant maxim [*Mool-Mantra*] calling for peace in every nook and corner of the universe:

"Om Dyau Shanti Rantariksha Gwam
Shanti Prithvi Shanti Rapah
Shanti Roshadhayah Shanti Vanas Patayah
Shanti Vishwe Devah Shanti Brahma
Sarvag Wam
Shanti Shanti Reva Shanti Sa Ma Shanti Redhi
Om Shanti Shanti Shanti Om"

"Unto the Heaven be peace, unto the Sky and the Earth be peace; peace be unto the Water, unto the herbs and trees be peace; unto all the gods be peace, unto Brahma and unto all be peace; and may we realize that peace."

Doubtless, peace is vitally important in life. It is indispensable for creating atmosphere of mutual understanding and harmony for common development. It is, therefore, a crucial link in the chain of life.

II

Education is a process that continues till the end of life. It is a lifelong process leading a human being to realize and develop virtues already present within his genome, and achieve prosperity in life on the basis of these intrinsic virtues.

Epithets like knowledge, skill and talent, frequently eluded to education, are, in fact, in-born qualities, which remain dormant in man for continuous exploration and enhancement. For the realization and proper development of these qualities direction and guidance are necessary and only a teacher [Guru] can do this. The indispensability and importance of education in life are known to all. It is the education and education only, which accords identity to man makes him a true human being.

III

Peace and education must go forward simultaneously. Both of them aim all-round development of human beings. Education brings out what already exists within for the unfolding of personality while the state of peace creates atmosphere and accords certainty to this act. Further, both of them call for proactive co-operation and manage to gather it. Such is the vibe and virtue of peace and education.

It is for this reason that various aspects related to peace and education [peace education] are being discussed and analyzed regularly through symposiums and seminars at different levels national and international, particularly in colleges and universities and at social forums all over the world. Scholars of repute and subject specialist are discussing the way and means to make it an essential part of educational process and about pedagogies to be adopted for the same. In many institutions work has been started. But, a lot has to be done in this regard. The process must go on continuously and in a planned manner.

Although scholars and subject specialists are in agreement for inclusion of peace education in syllabi, they also cede to its urgency, yet they have not been able to suggest a cogent action plan for the same.

In this regard I am of the opinion that the work of imparting peace education should start from the higher secondary level. It is for the simple reason that peer pressure, interpersonal jealousies and competitive rivalries amongst students begin building up at this level of education giving rise to acrimony, disputes and sharp differences of opinion culminating in chaos and disharmony.

Therefore, initiative must be taken from this stage and as first lesson students should be familiarized with life, works and views of leading lights of world peace that brought harmony in society through love, compassion, non-violence and practicing in their own personal lives what they preached to others. Along with this, initiatives should be taken by the community of teachers to train students to settle their differences and resolve disputes by way of arbitration in primary stage itself. In this regard, the following suggestion would be helpful:

1. Realizing the value and significance of peace education, teachers must take it up as their personal responsibility;
2. Keeping practices of peace messengers as nuclei, they should prepare students for self-settling of their disputes, or if necessary, teachers may themselves play role of arbitrator in resolving disputes; and
3. Having the intent of developing the spirit of peace, teacher should convince students that living in harmony with each other and their environment is their social, national and global responsibility.

As the higher secondary level is the most important phase of the entire educational process, it can, therefore, play a vital role in a fundament change in the education system. More than one million higher secondary schools impart education all over the world. In India the number of such schools is more than 1,20,000 [one *lakh* twenty thousand] in which approximately 2,00,00,000 [two *crores*] students are enrolled.

Further, at higher level of studies, in colleges and universities, there is a need of special pedagogy-based curriculum. Both theoretical and practical aspects should be the essential part of that curriculum and it should appear as a combination of art and science subjects. In addition, the course curriculum could be prepared as per the demand of space and time of national-regional and global contexts.

As a whole, there is a need to take the work for peace education relentlessly in a planned way, as top end responsibility. There is no other way available to accomplish this task. The task is not difficult, but it demands sincerity and commitment, sacrifice and above all a holistic outlook for the welfare of all beings.

2. PEACE EDUCATION: AN EFFECTIVE APPROACH FOR THE CULTURE OF PEACE

BR Dugar* and Vandana Kundalia**

In the present scenario, there is an urgent need for new strategies of peace based on the common fundamental interest of mankind, rejecting the use of force, and aimed at creating a new world order. Recognizing the close interrelationship between culture and peace, and the extension of international interdependencies in reducing economic disparities, emphasis must be given to develop positive attitudes to inculcate peace in the minds of all men. The dangers inherent in the arms race require that education for disarmament be an integral part of

* Professor BR Dugar and **Dr. Vandana Kundalia are from the Peace Research Centre of the Jain Vishwa Bharati [Rajasthan], India.

peace education. Likewise, the connections between peace and other international objectives such as development and human rights need to be stressed. Peace education should lead not only to a greater awareness of problems but also to a sense of responsibility. This is an active involvement in efforts towards promoting equal rights, economic and social development, and mutual respect and understanding among nations. The power of informed public opinion, internationally, in influencing governments towards peace and disarmament should not be underestimated; therefore, greater attention in peace education needs to be given to identifying and overcoming the structural, conceptual and cultural obstacles to peace. As the GCPE [Global Campaign for Peace Education] puts, "***A culture of peace will be achieved when citizens of the world understand global problems, have the skill to resolve conflicts and struggles for justice non-violently, live by international standards of the human dignity and equity, appreciate cultural diversity, respect the Earth and each other.***"

Humankind needs to take lesson from its past in order to build a new and better tomorrow. One lesson learned is that, to prevent our violence –ridden history repeating itself, the values of peace, non-violence, compassion, tolerance, human rights and democracy will have to be inculcated in every group, woman and man. Today's world, its problems and challenges are becoming increasingly more interdependent and interconnected. No time is more appropriate than now to build a culture of Peace.

Culture of Peace: A culture of peace aims at the transformation of values, attitudes and behaviors within each individual, leading to a culture shaped by peace, rather than by war and violence. A culture of peace is one where the definition of security will have changed from just national security to include human security. The criteria for the agenda and success of our leaders will have shifted from wealth, power and domination to harmony, inclusiveness, respect, integrity and healing. There will be a shift away from low citizen political involvement, combined with powerful non-democratic institutions, including the military, information industry and corporations, toward regular, well subscribed elections, a code of ethics for government, a comprehensive justice system, public participation sustainable global economy based on localism, education for everyone, and a compassionate health and welfare system. We will have redefined the value system from power as a reference point to community as a reference point, with the well-being of all citizens coming before the self-interest of the few. The concept of community will have expanded beyond people to include: animals, fish, birds, plants, air, water, earth and wind, all seen as interconnected, interdependent, cooperative and mutually supportive.

A culture of peace represents an everyday attitude of non-violence and determination to defend human rights and human dignity. Peace will be a permanent feature of all social institutions, especially schools, the economy, and the political scene. The media, sports and relationships will all be premised on peace. Hope, persistence, solidarity, inclusiveness and morality will be the norm. Principles of tolerance, open mindedness, sustainability, participation and democracy are paramount. A global awareness and perspective, co-operation and a deep respect for interdependency are key features of this culture. Responsibility and accountability, the sharing and free flow of information and notions of empowerment and emancipation are central tenets of a culture of peace.

Intercultural understanding leading to sustainable dialogue, cross-cultural exchanges and a shared vision of peace are cornerstones of a peaceful culture. Mutual support, empathetic listening and unwavering respect for human rights and dignity are solid anchors for peaceful cultures. Constant striving for justice, freedom, non-violence, equity, equality and ongoing, rigorous critique of the status quo are the roots of a culture of peace. Respecting the role of history, the arts and peoples' lived stories is central to creating a peaceful culture

In accordance with the United Nations Declaration and Programme of Action for a Culture of Peace [A/RES/53/243], the culture of peace in practice means actions:

- To foster a culture of peace through education;
- To promote sustainable economic and social development;
- To promote respect for all human rights;
- To ensure equality between women and men;
- To foster democratic participation:
- To advance understanding, tolerance and solidarity;
- To support participatory communication and the free flow of information and knowledge; and
- To promote international peace and security.

Nobel Peace Laureates developed this idea for the UNESCO by listing six important things for people to do that can make a difference to the whole planet. These following Peace Principles were first proclaimed unanimously by the United Nations General Assembly in the year 2000:

Respect All Life: Respect the life and dignity of each human being without discrimination or prejudice.

Reject Violence: Practice active non-violence, rejecting violence in all its forms: physical, sexual, psychological, economic and social, in particular towards the most deprived and vulnerable such as children and adolescents.

Share with Others: Share my time and material resources in a spirit of generosity to put an end to exclusion, injustice and political and economic oppression.

Listen to Understand: Defend freedom of expression and cultural diversity, giving preference always to dialogue and listening without engaging in fanaticism, defamation and the rejection of others.

Preserve the Planet: Promote consumer behavior that is responsible and development practices that respect all forms of life and preserve the balance of nature on the planet.

Rediscover Solidarity: Contribute to the development of my community, with the full participation of women and respect for democratic principles, in order to create together new forms of solidarity.

In order to systematize the idea of a culture of peace, Rivera has taken the aspects articulated in the UNESCO documents and General Assembly resolution, and organized the aspects into a model of a culture of peace that reflects some sociopolitical theory. He has arranged them into some interrelated clusters according to whether the desired aspect primarily involves changing societal norms, transforming sociopolitical structures, or promoting governmental policies that help establish an environment that nourishes a culture of peace. Following table presents some aspects of a model of a culture of peace with comparison to aspects of culture of violence.

Comparative Models of Cultures of Peace and of Violence:

Culture of Peace	Culture of Violence
Conflicts should be resolved by dialogue, negotiations and non-violent action. People should cooperate for common goals.	Conflicts settled by superior force.
Women's voices are as important as those of men. Children and nurturance are valued.	Men dominate. Domination valued more than nurturance.
Societal cohesion based on unilateral tolerance, solidarity, and mutual obligations.	Cohesion based on images of an enemy.
Democratic participation with a civic society enabling freedom of advocacy so that needs can be met.	Authoritarian hierarchical society.
Open communication with transparency, accountability and pure journalism.	Control of information through secrecy and propaganda.
Assurance of human rights and inclusion of all groups.	Exclusion of minorities.
International security.	Competition for armed superiority.

The model establishes an ideal goal. Although this model rests on the Universal Declaration of Human Rights, it may be objected that both the declaration and the model reflect Western liberal ideals rather than universal values.

Education towards Culture of Peace: The most significant way of promoting a culture of peace is trough peace education. Peace education needs to be accepted in all parts of the world in all societies and countries as an essential element in creating culture of peace. To meet effectively the challenges posed by the present complexity of our time, the young of today deserves a radically different education ***"one that does not glorify war but educates for peace, non-violence and international cooperation. They need the skills and knowledge to create and nurture peace for their individual selves as well as for the world they belong to."***

Montessori mentioned earlier that those who want a violent way of living prepare young people for that but those who want peace have neglected their young children and adolescents and that way are unable to organize them for peace. However, the last decades of violence and human insecurity had led to a growing realization in the world of education today that children should be educated in the art of peaceful living. As a result, more and more peace concepts, attitudes, values and social skills are being integrated into school curriculum in many countries. It is being increasingly realized that over emphasis on cognitive learning in schools at the cost of developing children's emotional, social, moral and humanistic aspects has been a costly mistake. Peace education does not simply mean learning about conflicts and how to resolve them peacefully. It should also involve participation of young people in expressing their own ideas and cooperating with each other in order to eliminate conflict. Peace education is an essential component of quality basic education. It is concerned to develop an awareness of the process and skills that are necessary for achieving understanding, tolerance and goodwill in the world today. It should be a participatory process which aims at changing society's way of thinking and which promotes learning of peace. Education should be put on issues that may lead to conflict well such as gender studies, speaking the language of non-violence and creation of proper international relations.

Education for Peace Means:

- Examining and discussing our values and attitudes towards diversity, cultural differences, tolerance and human dignity and directing our efforts towards achieving fundamental changes within societies;
- Developing language and social interaction skills to promote peaceful relations among people, among nations and between human beings and the natural environment; and
- Learning to solve problems and to think critically regarding issues of conflict and violence.

Peace education is more effective when it is adapted according to the social and cultural context and the needs of a society. It is enriched by that society's cultural and spiritual values along with universal human values. For example, these same published and yet-to-be published materials for Indian schools are based on what are termed universal human values such as love, reciprocity, empathy and concern for others, and justice and fairness. Such values can be included in peace education for schools throughout the world. But at the same time this curriculum, being developed in India, reflects Indian social problems, Indian culture, its strong religious beliefs, and the country's needs especially as the curriculum moves up to higher age levels. So it is enriched by certain widespread Indian spiritual and cultural values as ahimsa, that is, non-violence and non-killing. As to a definition of peace education, there are several, but a good one is from Dale Hudson, who rests his definition on certain basic principles. He states, ***"Peace education can be defined as: education that actualizes children's potentialities in helping them learn how to make peace with themselves and with others, to live in harmony and unity with self, humankind and with nature."***

Conclusion: Today humanity faces challenges of unprecedented proportions such as the continued development of weapons of mass destruction, conflicts between states and ethnic groups, the spread of racism, community violence, the huge widening gap between the rich and the poor throughout the globe, massive violation of human rights and the degradation of the environment. These issues are a stumbling block to the attainment of world order. In order to tackle these complex and interwoven problems, there is a need to make the preventive measures and solutions to these problems deeply rooted in the minds of the populations. This justifies the need for peace education, which should focus on human security and how to live in a world infested with diversity. Besides, the fact that what culminate into global conflicts originate at community level in a particular nation and the subsequent appeal to the notion of state sovereignty especially where the conflict involves the military, has posed great problems. The UN charter I Article 2 [iii] contains the clause on state sovereignty, which restricts the situation in which domestic affairs of a nation can be questioned. The campaigns for peace education at community level can therefore better serve as an ultimate solution where international intervention cannot be a reality. This is because the methodology of peace education encourages critical thinking and prepares learners to act on their convictions.

We need peace education for ourselves, our relationship with other human beings to promote respect for oneself and respect for others on individual level as a prerequisite for the prevention of violence and conflict at society level and to raise people's consciousness about their rights whilst promoting international understanding between the people of different worlds. Thus in present scenario peace education is a best tool for developing the culture of peace.

Bibliography:

- Adams, D [Ed.]. 1997. *UNESCO and a Culture of Peace: Promoting a Global Movement.* Paris: UNESCO Publishing [Culture of Peace Series].
- De Rivera, Joseph. 2004. *Assessing the Basis for a Culture of Peace in Contemporary Societies* in the Journal of Peace Research [Volume 41, Number 5], pp. 531-48
- De Rivera, Joseph. 2004. *A Template for Assessing Cultures of Peace, Peace and Conflict* in the Journal of Peace Psychology, 125-46
- Galtung, Johan. 1975. *Peace, Research, Action, Education* [Essays in Peace Studies: Volume 1] Copenhagen: Christian Ejlers.
- Galtung, Johan. 1996. *Peace by Peaceful Means.* New Delhi: Sage Publication.
- http://cultureofpeacehamilton.com/
- http://sites.google.com/site/peaceeducationsnp/
- http://www.peace.ca/whypeaceeducationbycovell.htm
- Reardon, B. A., Human rights education for the twenty-first century ,PA: University of Pennsylvania Press, Philadelphia,.1997,pp. 255-260
- UN Resolution, A/RES/52/13, A /RES/52/15, A /RES/53/25, A/RES/53/243, 1999

*****

B: Non-Violence and Peace Education

1. NON-VIOLENCE AND PEACE EDUCATION

Muhammad Suleman Kakar*

Here I want to quote Badshah Khan, the companion of Great Mahatma Gandhiji, who has said, ***"Today's world is travelling in some strange direction. You see that the world is going toward destruction and violence. And the specialty of violence is to create hatred among people and to create fear. I am a believer of non-violence and I say that no peace or tranquility will descend upon the people of the world until non-violence is practiced, because non-violence is love and it stirs courage in people".***

Actually, in our today's world it is hard to imagine a place or situation without violence, fear or war. Every day, we experience new conflicts; we hear new reports of escalating tensions and violence and old grievances. What does violence

---

* Mr. M Suleman Kakar is a former minister from Afghanistan. He is currently a BM of CPAU.

bring to us? Destruction, killings, calamity, poverty, fears, hatred and distrust, darkness or even no future!

Parallel to what happens to the humanity today, we also witness a new trend where an incomparable number of men and women, from around the world, take actions to stop violence. They increasingly work hard to promote peace as a response to violence. We also notice a gradual increase in the number of people and organizations who take the courage to come closer with a new commitment to combine their energy and resources for the promotion of culture of non-violence and peace. No matter how small in number they are or how little their efforts are, but together with their small or large constituencies they make significant contributions to the societal and global peace.

As we observe, violence, discrimination and exclusion cause suffering for millions of people across the world today. Violence, discrimination and exclusion affect people in every corner of the globe, endangering health, lives and livelihoods and limiting human potential. While their effect is most severe on the vulnerable, no one is immune.

Differences of opinion and disagreements are a normal part of humanity, but the question is: how can we deal with these in a constructive way? Violence, discrimination and exclusion are often looked at in isolation, as separate issues. However, they are intertwined and have common root causes. By looking at these common root causes, we can seek common solutions. The promotion of a culture of non-violence and peace is not just about the absence of war. It is not an end or final goal, but a process. It is about creating an enabling environment for dialogue and discussion and finding solutions to problems and tensions, without fear of violence, through a process in which everyone is valued and able to participate. Going even further, the promotion of a culture of non-violence and peace is about prevention and minimization, as much as possible, of the sources of tensions. A culture of non-violence is not a Utopian ideal. There are concrete actions we can take to work towards a more non-violent, humane and equal society. We have seen non-violence work as a foundation of a number of social and religious movements.

Changing a culture of violence into a culture of peace requires a transformation of problems to creative and constructive solutions that answer the needs of those involved. When we think about violence, discrimination and exclusion, the challenges may seem impossible. However, these challenges are fundamentally connected. Ignorance and misunderstandings and assumptions based on a lack of communication and mistrust, feed discrimination and violence.

These all influence and reinforce one another. Vulnerability to violence, discrimination and exclusion can also be linked to a number of common social determinants, such as poverty, inequalities of income, gender or power and misuse of power. Seeing these connections, it becomes clear that it is essential to systematically address common root causes.

Just as there can be common roots of violence, discrimination and exclusion, there can be common solutions. Successfully addressing these three humanitarian challenges requires a change of mindsets, attitudes and behaviors.

We need a global mind and behavior shift from the way we currently think and interact: from being locked into differences to valuing diversity and pluralism; from adverse reaction to joint response and even further to proactive prevention; from exclusion based on fear to connection based on our common humanity; and from resorting to verbal or physical violence when feeling threatened to constructive dialogue and trust.

We need a values-based transformation of human behavior. We need to start with ourselves. We all carry bias and prejudice. Awareness, questioning and critical self-reflection can help break conditioning or correct bias learned through schooling, media and upbringing.

We live in a world with enormous diversity: there are many different perspectives and ways of thinking. Rather than being perceived as making us richer and stronger, differences or diversity are causes of tension and problems all too often, especially when not approached from a culture of non-violence and peace perspective. The key to creating a culture of non-violence and peace is to develop the ability within individuals and communities to deal with and respect these differences, rather than to reject them. As discrimination is frequently born out of fear of the unknown, it is important to foster active listening and communication between communities in order to lead to mutual understanding, respect for diversity and a willingness to explore solutions together.

Here again, I quote Badshah Khan who says, ***"the best way to find yourself is lose yourself in the service of others. Earth provides enough to satisfy every man's need, but not every man's greed. In gentle way, you can shake the world."***

Values and skills-based education is key to overcoming discrimination. Learning and cultivating open-mindedness and understanding will help us to accept those around us and to respect their differences. When we respect others, we can avoid tensions from forming and, where they do exist, to resolve them peacefully without resorting to violence. With self-reflection, we can identify our own biases and work to erase them by developing skills such as active listening, empathy, dropping bias and non-judgment.

As we all know, peace seems to be humanity's fondest dream. Almost everyone claims to be in favour of peace, but it can be used to mean many different things. A situation that is peaceful for one group may be oppressive for another. When we think of peace, we often tend to think of war or violent conflict as it's opposite.

Scholars around the world define peace as the existence of peaceful relationships, active association and planned co-operation among persons and groups for achieving greater aims such as justice, security, and constructive transformation of conflicts.

Many people understand peace to be the absence of war. While, this is of course vital, others see it as only first step towards a fuller ideal, using definitions such as: an interweaving of relationships between individuals, groups and institutions that value diversity and foster the full development of human potential.

According to Galtung, peace has two dimensions *negative peace* and *positive peace*. Negative peace can be described as the absence of war or violent conflict [often the agreement between elites] as a static state. Other violence can continue e.g. cultural and structural violence. Positive peace is a dynamic process rather than an end state and implies a condition where conflicts are addressed and solved.

Along the same line, UNICEF, describes positive peace as a situation characterized not only be the absence of war or violent conflict, but also by presence of factors that reduce the likelihood of violent conflicts and promotes a better quality of life for all. These factors include social and economic justice, inter-group understanding, ecological balance, and opportunities for democratic participation in decision-making. Mayor, an another scholar, explains that instead of the absence of war, peace is increasingly seen as a dynamic, participative, long-term process, based on universal values and everyday practice at all levels – the family, the school, the community, as well as the nation.

We define peace as an absence of all types of violence: physical violence, structural violence and cultural violence. According to this understanding, absence of physical violence alone is described as negative peace while absence of all three types of violence is described as positive peace. Physical violence is more visible while structural and cultural violence is less visible.

This understanding of positive peace draws the attention to the fact that it is an ultimate vision that individuals as well as groups and nations should pursue to achieve. It is quite understandable that in today's world the complete elimination of all three types of violence seems impossible. However, through sustained efforts by individuals, groups and institutions it is possible to reduce violence at all levels. Therefore, it is a whole life struggle and all of us must refresh our commitment to work for true peace and justice.

Peace education normally deals with feelings, attitudes, opinions, beliefs, values, and skills as they are held and shared between peoples, individually and in groups. It is about building a human infrastructure of people who are committed to bring about a new culture, a *peace culture,* within the social fabric of communal and inter-communal life.

As a matter of fact, the context in which we are born and brought up sufficiently influences our attitude and behavior. Each of us is born male or female and born into a particular way of life: for example a nomad in a rural area of Asia or Africa and a citizen in Europe have radically different experience of life and things around them.

We each have different sets of values, which guide our thinking and behavior. These values influence us to take certain actions and reject others. This reality of life in fact leads us to a situation where we find people who have different perspective on life and things when we meet them or work with them. In which case, conflict happens when people pursue different perspective and goals that clash.

We find conflicts among ourselves and others in our families and communities; interpersonal conflict, when we find differences or perceived differences among our resources, needs, values, or interests. There is conflict found among the nations of the world, international conflicts, where again there is a difference or perceived difference between resources, needs and values or interests.

Conflict can be defined in a number of ways e.g. controversy, disagreements, disputes, struggle, fight, war and so on. Conflict is positive as well as negative. It is negative in the sense when it becomes destructive due to inability of the people to deal with it effectively. It is positive in the sense when it is used for growth, progress, and positive change. When we tend to define or understand conflict as a struggle between opposing forces or war, the negative connotations of this definition encourage us to avoid conflicts at any cost. However, if we view conflict as an opportunity and motivation for growth and positive change then we accept it as a challenge and try to acquire necessary knowledge and skills and learn how to transform it for growth and development.

Many of us believe that conflict arising from opposing ideas and opinions are to be encouraged. Controversies promote involvement in the group's work, quality and creativity in decision making, and commitment to implement the group's decisions.

To conclude although conflict is not always good, conflict is not always bad either. In fact, conflict exists as a normal part of our everyday lives, and rather trying to make it go away, skills such as conflict analysis, communication, negotiation, and mediation can be learned to deal with the conflicts effectively.

In order to move a conflict habituated system to a peace system, we will need to change the way we think. The preamble of the Charter of the United Nations Educational, Social and Cultural Organization [UNESCO] echoes this sentiment, ***"since war begins in the minds of men, it is in the minds of men that the foundation of peace must be constructed."*** Change in the attitude and behavior can be achieved through formal or informal peace education.

It seems that there is now a growing awareness of the usefulness of peace education not only for children but also for adults. Formal or informal peace education can promote the development of an authentic consciousness that is necessary to change attitude and behavior in order to achieve the greater co-operation and peaceful problem solving. Peace education which involves learning new interpersonal skills and development of broader understanding of different cultures is therefore essential to enable us to strengthen the aspiration of peaceful co-existence and to enable us to function as global citizens and transform the present human conditions for the better.

As a matter of fact the focus of social peace-building or peace education is also on addressing the underlying causes of conflict. This aspect of peace-building in fact plays a vital and complementary role in the whole process of peace. In reality, it constructs a strong foundation for structural and political peace-building processes to flourish, because it tries to involve a large number of people in the process.

One of the dangerous consequences of a lack of opportunity for young people is the potential development of detrimental behaviour. When such a large segment of the population lacks productive channels to direct their energies, a country runs the risk of widespread apathy, discontent, resentfulness, and disillusionment. Faced with few options for legitimate economic advancement, youth fall easy prey to criminal gangs, political groups, warlords, drug-lords, and fundamentalist associations.

For us today, it is essentially important to consider integration of peace education in schools and colleges. We have to develop context-based peace education materials and train teachers in this subject. Experience has shown that through peace education it is possible to promote culture of non-violence and peace among the children, teachers and parents. Peace education ultimately can divert the attention of the people from the mentality of war and violence towards peaceful co-existence, co-operation and mutual respect. Peace education can ensure development of new knowledge, skills, attitudes and values needed to bring about positive behavioral changes.

In our efforts for peace, it is equally important to ensure

the participation of the more vulnerable groups, such as children, disabled persons, elderly and migrants, so we can gain further respect of our diversity and equality. As an example, promoting respect for diversity at an early age can help to reduce future discrimination based on gender. This can have far-reaching impact by helping, more generally, to change stereotyped or perceived gender roles, thereby creating greater and more equal opportunities. It can also help to reduce gender-based violence of which gender inequality is a root cause.

I strongly believe that integration of peace education and training of teacher in peace subject will:

- Enable children and youths to transform conflicts peacefully, and create conditions conducive to peace;
- Reduce violence of any nature [physical, cultural and structural];
- Reduce prejudices and stereotypes;
- Promote culture of peace and peaceful co-existence; and
- Develop new skills and attitude favorable not only to promote respect for diversity but also to pursue the initiatives to appreciate and celebrate diversity.

If we are to promote true peace and peaceful co-existence in our world, we have to come together to advocate very strongly at national and international levels to make peace education subject compulsory in schools and colleges.

At the end, I again want to quote Badshah Khan who says, ***"I offer you peace, I offer you love, I offer you friendship. I see your beauty. I hear your needs. I feel your feelings. My wisdom flows from the Highest Source. I salute that Source in you. Non-violence which is a quality of heart cannot come by an appeal to the brain."***

2. NON-VIOLENCE AND PEACE EDUCATION

Nishad Oza*

Non-violence is often understood as the absence of violence, but the leading proponents of non-violence have always defined it in positive terms. Thus Mahatma Gandhi [1869-1948] spoke of non-violence as *Satyagraha*, literally, holding onto truth. Martin Luther King, Jr. [1929-1968] spoke of it as a commitment to resisting injustice without regarding one's success as a triumph over those who stand for injustice, but as a triumph over injustice itself—a conviction that the universe is on the side of justice, an understanding that violence is not merely physical but psychological and spiritual in nature, and a willingness to suffer harm rather than to perpetrate harm. This last point reflects Jesus' dictum that one should turn the other cheek, and for this reason non-violence is often misunderstood and misconstrued as the path of cowards; of people afraid to fight or stand up for their rights. Gandhi was quite clear about this, however: violence, he said, is always preferable to cowardice, but non-violence is always preferable to both. Non-violence is the determination to suffer rather than perpetrate harm *even when* the ability to inflict harm is an option.

Because non-violence can be understood from so many different aspects, it has never been clearly defined as an academic discipline. To some it is the study of any psychological,

* Dr. Nishad Oza is a senior lecturer at the DIET, IDAR, Sabarkantha [Gujarat], India.

social, or political techniques of social change that do not involve the use of military force; to others it is the study of the spiritual pursuit of a non-violent orientation to the world; to still others it is the study of non-violence as interpreted by particular religions. To most people, it falls somewhere within the area staked out by these three poles.

Extending far back in time, the holy books of various religions speak at least indirectly about non-violence, and commentaries about them often elaborate on those passages. However, explicit writing on non-violence did not emerge until the mid-nineteenth century in the United States and Europe. As a subject of inquiry, the study of non-violence began in the first half of the twentieth century, most notably with Mahatma Gandhi and those who wrote about him. Finally, non-violence became a more or less distinct academic field in the second half of the twentieth century.

Impediments to a Culture of Peace and Non-violence: To be able to live a peaceful and non-violent life, an individual must first have their basic survival needs met. They must have food, shelter and water. Alleviating the poverty of our people in our world is one of the first steps to creating a culture of peace and non-violence. For this to ever happen, it has to be a worldwide effort, however it can start with individuals and on a small scale. The simplest step is sharing your own time and resources to help others. This can be done in our own lives, in our homes, at our workplaces, in classrooms. If everyone contributes a small amount of their time and resources to the cause of alleviating the poverty of others, there would be a drastic change in the number of impoverished people in our world.

Another impediment to peace is intolerance of other

people. Intolerance can be to differences of races, religions, cultures and lifestyles. Through education this can be changed. By educating children about different religions, races, cultures and lifestyles in our world we can help them to understand the similarities among everyone. They will understand how insignificant these differences are, how they are not a reason for discrimination or prejudices. We can promote respect and tolerance of others.

Impact of Media: The media is a very influential source of information and learning. Peace journalism needs to be promoted and people need to question what they see and hear from the media. In North America, during the last several years, the media has begun to have greater impact on people's way of thinking, especially children. This is evident in many areas, such as how children view violence. The media tends to glamorize violence in several different mediums, through music, television, the Internet, movies and also children's toys and games. In the past, when technology was not readily available to children, these topics were not such regular occurrences in children's lives. Now, the most common children's hobbies are playing video games, watching television and movies, listening to music, and surfing the net, all of which often contain themes of violence. The Internet has made it possible for children to access any information they want and without adult supervision they are able to view violent and even pornographic websites. Video games are also contributing widely to depicting violence as fun and exciting. The most popular games among youth include soldiers in war scenes to players as game members and criminals who may even purchase a prostitute for more points in the game. However, it can be thought that these are only cartoon like depictions and therefore children may realize that these ideals should not be extended into reality. Having real life role models who are involved in violent behaviour is particularly detrimental to creating a culture of peace. In music, the most popular songs often contain theses of violence,. gang behaviour, criminal behaviour, and even violence towards women. With children striving to be like their role models that are involved in violent behaviour or just singing about it, how they know that this behaviour is widely unacceptable in our societies? When they are sensitized to conflict and violence, and even view it as exciting or glamorous, how can they understand the impact of violence on real lives?

The Origin of Non-Violent Teachings: Some of the earliest indirect writings on non-violence are found in Buddhist works. The *Dhammapada* in particular describes the effects of developing habits of violence and of non-violence. The *Bhagavad-Gita*, although subject to many different interpretations, provides a philosophical basis for non-violence by pointing to the importance of doing what is right regardless of the consequences to one. Although this can be taken to mean that we are sometimes required to be soldiers, Gandhi understood it to mean that we must not allow fear of bodily harm to keep us from standing up for what is right. Taoism, as expressed Lao Tzu's *Tao Te Ching* also can be interpreted in ways that provide a philosophical basis for non-violence. The Old Testament is also laced with references to what later has become known as non-violence, and rabbinic commentaries over subsequent centuries have only expanded on that. The Gospels, especially the Beatitudes, formed the basis for many Christian attitudes towards non-violence, especially among the Society of Friends and such Anabaptists as the Mennonites and the Brethren. Adin Ballou [1803-90], a nineteenth-century American minister and writer, gave explicit expression to the

Christian call to non-violence, as did Leo Tolstoy, the Russian novelist and Christian anarchist.

Mahatma Gandhi and the Scientific Study of Non-Violence: The scientific study of non-violence probably began with Mahatma Gandhi. However, rather than treating non-violence as an academic pursuit he tested his theories in the world, which he regarded as a laboratory. His study of non-violence [*Ahimsa*] consisted of testing whether his hypotheses were borne out through experience. His term *Satyagraha,* which has been translated as *soul force,* literally means, ***"holding onto*** [*graham*] ***truth*** [*Satya*]**."** The root word of *Satya*, *sat*, means *being,* and Gandhi regarded violence as the destruction of being, of what is; of untruth as the destruction of what is real.

Perhaps one way to understand what Gandhi meant by *Satyagraha* is to picture an episode early in his life, when a stagecoach driver attempted to remove him from the carriage for which he had a legitimate ticket. A few days earlier he had been thrown from a train for insisting upon using his ticket to ride in the first-class coach rather than on top. This time, he was so angered by the injustice of it that he grasped the window frame of the carriage with both his arms as the driver tried to pull him away by his legs. The other passengers eventually intervened and insisted that Gandhi be allowed to ride inside the coach. This image of Gandhi grasping onto the coach window and not letting go, but at the same time not striking out, is one way of understanding what he meant by *Satyagraha*, literally "clinging to truth.

Several people studied and wrote about Gandhi's work while he was alive, most notably Richard Gregg and Joan Bondurant. Both visited Gandhi and interviewed him, Gregg in the 1920s and Bondurant in the 1940s. Both of their writings tended to focus on the dynamics of his non-violent political action, including what he called his constructive programs: his efforts to help people overcome their own powerlessness through self-education, self-employment, and self-sufficiency. After Gandhi's assassination in 1948, more writing emerged. Gene Sharp recognized the politically strategic brilliance of Gandhi's methods, and in 1973 he published a work that has become a classic in the field, *The Politics of Non-Violent Action*. The work did not focus specifically on Gandhi, but offered in the first two chapters a theoretical framework for understanding the power of non-violence; in the next seven chapters an overview of approximately two hundred non-violent tactics, from simple letter-writing to the establishment of alternative governments; and in the remaining chapters an analysis and blueprint of how to create and execute non-violent campaigns strategically as well as tactically.

A little less than a decade later, in 1982 Richard Attenborough's Academy Award-winning film *Gandhi* popularized Gandhi to a much greater extent. In no small way because of the film, Gandhi-based scholarship and discourse on non-violence has become so widespread and deep that theoretical splits within the field are already evident.

Peace Education As:

Conflict resolution training: Peace education programs centered on conflict resolution typically focus on the social-behavioural symptoms of conflict, training individuals to resolve inter-personal disputes through techniques of negotiation and [peer] mediation. Learning to manage anger, *fight fair* and improve communication through skills such as listening, turn-taking, identifying needs, and separating facts from emotions, constitute the main elements of these programs. Participants are also encouraged to take responsibility for their actions and to brainstorm together on compromises.

In general, approaches of this type aim to ***"alter beliefs, attitudes, and behaviours...from negative to positive attitudes toward conflict as a basis for preventing violence."*** [Van Slyck, Stern and Elbedour, 1999, emphasis added] As one peer mediation coordinator put it, ***"Conflict is very natural and normal, but you can't go through your entire life beating everybody up—you have to learn different ways to resolve conflict."***

Democracy education: Peace education programs centered on democracy education typically focus on the political processes associated with conflict, and postulate that with an increase in democratic participation the likelihood of societies resolving conflict through violence and war decreases. At the same time, "***a democratic society needs the commitment of citizens who accept the inevitability of conflict as well as the necessity for tolerance.***" [US Department of State, The Culture of Democracy, emphasis added]. Thus programs of this kind attempt to foster a conflict-positive orientation in the community by training students to view conflict as a platform for creativity and growth.

Approaches of this type train participants in the skills of critical thinking, debate and coalition-building, and promote the values of freedom of speech, individuality, tolerance of diversity, compromise and conscientious objection. Their aim is to produce *responsible citizens* who will hold their governments accountable to the standards of peace, primarily through adversarial processes. Activities are structured to have students, ***"assume the role of the citizen that chooses,***

makes decisions, takes positions, argues positions and respects the opinions of others." Skills, which a multi-party democracy is based upon. Based on the assumption that democracy decreases the likelihood of violence and war, it is assumed that these are the same skills necessary for creating a culture of peace.

Human Rights Education: Peace education programs centered on raising awareness of human rights typically focus at the level of policies that humanity ought to adopt in order to move closer to a peaceful global community. The aim is to engender a commitment among participants to a vision of structural peace in which all individual members of the human race can exercise their personal freedoms and be legally protected from violence, oppression and indignity.

Approaches of this type familiarize participants with the international covenants and declarations of the United Nations system; train students to recognize violations of the Universal Declaration of Human Rights; and promote tolerance, solidarity, autonomy and self-affirmation at the individual and collective levels.

Human rights education ***"faces continual elaboration, a significant theory-practice gap and frequent challenge as to its validity."***

In one practitioner's view:

"Human rights education does not work in communities fraught with conflict unless it is part of a comprehensive approach... In fact, such education can be counterproductive and lead to greater conflict if people become aware of rights which are not realized. In this respect, human rights education can increase the potential for conflict."

To prevent these outcomes, many such programs are now being combined with aspects of conflict resolution and democracy education schools of thought, along with training in non-violent action.

Worldview Transformation: New approaches to peace education are starting from insights gleaned from psychology which recognize the developmental nature of human psychosocial dispositions. Essentially, while conflict-promoting attitudes and behaviours are characteristic of earlier phases of human development, unity-promoting attitudes and behaviours emerge in later phases of healthy development. HB Danesh [2002a, 2002b, 2004, 2005, 2007, 2008a, 2008b] proposes an *Integrative Theory of Peace* in which peace is understood as a psychosocial, political, moral and spiritual reality. Peace education, he says, must focus on the healthy development and maturation of human consciousness through assisting people to examine and transform their worldviews. Worldviews are defined as the subconscious lens [acquired through cultural, family, historical, religious and societal influences] through which people perceive four key issues:

- The nature of reality;
- Human nature;
- The purpose of existence; and
- The principles governing appropriate human relationships.

Surveying a mass of material, Danesh argues that the majority of people and societies in the world hold conflict-based worldviews, which express themselves in conflicted intrapersonal, interpersonal, intergroup, and international relationships. He subdivides conflict-based worldviews into two main categories which he correlates to phases of human development: the Survival-Based Worldview and the Identity-Based Worldview. It is through the acquisition of a more integrative, Unity-Based Worldview that human capacity to mitigate conflict, create unity in the context of diversity, and establishes sustainable cultures of peace, is increased - be it in the home, at school, at work, or in the international community.

Criticism: Toh Swee-Hin [1997] observes that each of the various streams of peace education ***"inevitably have their own dynamics and 'autonomy' in terms of theory and practice."*** Further, Salomon [2002] has described how the challenges, goals, and methods of peace education differ substantially between areas characterized by intractable conflict, interethnic tension, or relative tranquility."

Salomon [2002] raises the problems and its consequences, ***"Imagine that medical practitioners would not distinguish between invasive surgery to remove malignant tumors and surgery to correct one's vision. Imagine also that while surgeries are practiced, no research and no evaluation of their differential effectiveness accompany them. The field would be considered neither very serious nor very trustworthy. Luckily enough, such a state of affairs does not describe the field of medicine, but it comes pretty close to describing the field of peace education. First, too many profoundly different kinds of activities taking place in an exceedingly wide array of contexts are all lumped under the same category label of "peace education" as if they belong together. Second, for whatever reason, the field's scholarship in the form of theorizing, research and program evaluation badly lags behind practice... In the absence of clarity of what peace education really is, or how its different***

varieties relate to each other, it is unclear how experience with one variant of peace education in one region can usefully inform programs in another region."

According to Clarke-Habibi [2005], ***"A general or integrated theory of peace is needed: one that can holistically account for the intrapersonal, inter-personal, inter-group and international dynamics of peace, as well as its main principles and pre-requisites. An essential component of this integrated theory must also be the recognition that a culture of peace can only result from an authentic process of transformation, both individual and collective."***

One major aspect under debate is the issue of conflict itself in peace education theory. Most peace education programs postulate that conflict is an inseparable, indeed beneficial, aspect of human nature and human social relations. Increasingly, this assumption is being questioned.

Non-Violence in the Twenty-First Century: At the outset of the twenty-first century, the academic field of non-violence is divided—not sharply, but divided nonetheless. While many activists and academics have approached non-violence from a spiritual or religious perspective, perhaps most notably those associated with the Fellowship of Reconciliation, others have followed the lead of Gene Sharp, focusing on non-violence as a political strategy that, arguably, can be entirely secular in its orientation. Still others adopt a broader approach.

For over half a century, James Lawson has been a leading voice of those who approach non-violence from a religious or spiritual base. Lawson organized the Nashville lunch counter sit-ins in the early 1960s that led to the desegregation of Nashville. Earlier he had served time in jail for refusing to register for military service. In the late 1960s, it was Lawson who invited Martin Luther King, Jr., to come to Memphis to help with the sanitation worker strikes. After leading a large church in Los Angeles for many years in the latter half of the twentieth century, and serving some of that time as Chair of the Executive Committee of the US Fellowship of Reconciliation, he is presently a distinguished visiting professor at Vanderbilt University, which had expelled him so many years earlier for his efforts at integration.

Gene Sharp's work has attracted a large following, and recently his ideas have enjoyed widespread attention. The production of the PBS series *A Force More Powerful* and a follow-up broadcast *Bringing Down a Dictator* attracted people worldwide to the practical applications of non-violent strategy and tactics in the political and social arenas. The International Center on Non-violent Conflict, an NGO established by Peter Ackerman and headed by Jack DuVall, has helped to disseminate these ideas and develop them further by supporting scholarship, workshops, and conferences around the world. The workshops and conferences have brought together academics and activists from across Asia, Eastern and Western Europe, Latin America, and North America. The result has been a sharing of course materials and scholarship as well as exchanges of ideas among and between those who practice non-violent action and those who study it.

An eclectic approach to non-violence has been championed most notably in the last third of the twentieth century and the early years of the twenty-first century by Michael Nagler of the University of California at Berkeley, Ken Brown of Manchester College, and Robert L Holmes of the University of Rochester. Holmes, Brown, and Nagler draw heavily from the Gandhi's work, emphasizing the spiritual roots of non-violence and acknowledging its manifold applications in everything from personal development and personal relations to institutional practices and international relations. Their scholarship teaching and personal conduct have led to accolades from students across several generations.

Notes/Bibliography:

Ansbro, John J. 1984. *Martin Luther King, Jr.: The Making of a Mind.* Maryknoll, NY: Orbis Books.

Bondurant, Joan V. 1988. *Conquest of Violence: The Gandhian Philosophy of Conflict.* Princeton, NJ: Princeton University Press.

Gandhi, MK. 1993. *Autobiography: The Story of my Experiments with Truth.* Boston: Beacon Press.

Gandhi, MK. 2002. *The Essential Gandhi: An Anthology.* [Edited by Louis Fischer]. New York: Vintage.

Gandhi, MK. 1999. *Vows and Observances.* Berkeley, CA: Berkeley Hills Books.

Gregg, Richard B. 1966. *The Power of Nonviolence.* New York: Schocken Books.

Lynd, Staughton [Ed.]. 1966. *Non-Violence in America: A Documentary History.* Indianapolis: Bobbs-Merrill.

Holmes, Robert L. and Gan, Barry L [Eds.]. 2006. *Non-Violence in Theory and Practice.* Long Grove, Illinois: Waveland.

Nagler, Michael. 2001. *Is There No Other Way: The Search for a Nonviolent Future.* Berkeley, CA: Berkeley Hills Books.

Sharp, Gene. 1973. *The Politics of Non-Violent Action.* Boston: Porter Sargent.

Tolstoy, Leo. 1961. *The Kingdom of God Is Within You.* New York: Noonday Press.

Zunes, Stephen, Kurtz, Lester, and Asher, Sarah Beth [Eds.]. 1999. *Non-Violent Social Movements: A Geographical Perspective.* Oxford: Blackwell.

3. NON-VIOLENCE AND PEACE EDUCATION

Deepti A Raval*

Non-violence is an intrinsic part of the culture of peace in all respects, its definition and UN documents, strategy and tactics, and the various programme areas such as education for a culture of peace and tolerance, solidarity and understanding.

There are two ways to spell the term: non-violence and nonviolence. The former is the usage by the United Nations; the latter is the usage by those who follow the methodology of Mahatma Gandhi. In fact, the United Nations use of the term non-violence is also inspired by Gandhi, so we may consider the two spellings as equivalent.

The most important use of *non-violence* in the UN Declaration and Programme of Action on a Culture of Peace is the title of the Decade: The International Decade for a Culture of Peace and Non-Violence for the Children of the World. This title, which came about as the result of the tireless efforts of Pierre Marchand, has been a breakthrough in the history of the United Nations, for it had never before gone on record for non-violence in such a dramatic fashion. In fact, as this is written at the end of 2005, one still finds very little official documentation other than the Decade when one searches for the words nonviolence or non-violence on the website.

* Ms. Deepti A Raval is a research scholar at the PDPU, Gandhinagar [Gujarat], India.

In addition, Respect for life, ending of violence and promotion and practice of non-violence through education, dialogue and co-operation.

In the strategy of the Global Movement for a Culture of Peace, it should be evident that active non-violence should always be a basic principle. As Gandhi and Martin Luther King insisted, while it is better to be violent than passive, it should always be possible to find a method of active non-violence that is more effective than violence. In particular, education for a culture of peace should be a priority, with an emphasis on education for active non-violence.

As mentioned in the section on tolerance, solidarity and understanding, it is only through the practice of non-violence that one can resolve the apparent contradiction between the necessity of the struggle for justice and the basic principle of a culture of peace that one must have no enemy.

For my own understanding of non-violence, it was also important that I overcome the common idea that non-violence requires that the individual must rid himself of anger. In many Asian cultures and Eastern religions, this idea continues to be taught and to be considered as an important aspect of non-violence. In Western cultures, however, this is not necessarily the case. As Martin Luther King put it, ***"The supreme task is to organize and unite people so that their anger becomes a transforming force."*** Gandhi, despite being heavily influenced by Eastern religion, made similar statements, such as: ***"I have learnt through bitter experience the one supreme lesson to conserve my anger, and as heat conserved is transmuted into energy, even so, our anger controlled can be transmuted into a power which can move the world."*** The conservation and transmutation of anger so that it becomes a *transforming force* requires extensive training and experience, since it is not a skill that one is born with. As King has explained [see section on Understanding, Tolerance and Solidarity] that ***"attack is directed against forces of evil rather than against persons who happen to be doing the evil."*** In tracing the evolution of human anger from its animal origins, I have distinguished the highest level of this evolution as ***"the ability to conceptualize institutions and social systems and to respond to their actions with punishment and anger, just as one might respond to the immoral actions of another individual."*** This highly developed skill needs to be taught as an important component of education for a culture of peace.

Educating not only the children but the whole lot of people not only in India but of the whole world in a culture of peace and non-violence must be the aim of the school. One may ask, has not this education been carried on in the past? Yes. Adi Shankara. Ramanuja, Madhawa, Mahavira, Jesus Christ, Prophet Mohammed, Guru Nanak, Lord Buddha and others like them were great teachers of this school of non-violence. Since ages past, the methodology has changed from time to time. The same old wine in new bottles. That is why the talk of the new millennium in spite of the fact that the sun has never changed its path.

Gandhiji has been a great teacher of this peace education with non-violence as the central focus. Has he taught an abstract subject? No. Day in and day out, in every one of his actions, he experimented and experienced the relevance of non-violence and communicated the results to his fellow humans. His life style becomes a school for anyone to get educated in non-violence and peace.

The 7 Blossoms of Peace Education

1- Community Building: Finding things that unite and bind us together as a group, while at the same time respecting and celebrating our differences. Embracing the interests, experiences, and goals of the community to shape the learning environment and gain ownership of the learning experience. This principle encourages me to incorporate icebreakers and teambuilding exercises into my teaching so that shared experiences rooted in laughter, play, and collaborative problem solving can emerge. It encourages me to integrate large and small group activities and conversations where students can co-create meaning and learn from and about one another. It encourages me to work with learners to establish community agreements that outline what we need from each other as a group in order to accomplish learning goals that we adopt and create together.

2- Enabling Multiple Intelligences: Balancing the learning experience by engaging students in ways that play to their strengths while also challenging them to develop and value other intelligences.

Participants of a nonviolence workshop in Cambodia, fecitated by Daryn Cambridge engaged in group activities

This principle is based primarily in Howard Gardner's work on multiple intelligences in which he identified eight different kinds of intelligences that aid the process of learning, visual/spatial, logical/mathematical, kinesthetic, verbal/linguistic, musical, naturalistic, interpersonal, and intrapersonal. This principle encourages me to be aware of the various ways in which students can learn and explore ideas. It encourages me to be creative and diverse in how I design my lesson plans and workshops so that the learning environment welcomes all learning styles and intelligences. It builds a safe environment where no one learning style is seen as superior as or more important than another.

3- Nurturing Emotional Intelligence: Acknowledging the emotions, feelings, and experiences that each learner brings to the learning environment and helping them find ways to cope with those emotions.

Nurturing compassion and empathy among students in ways that allow them to be sensitive and aware of each other's emotions. This principle is based primarily on the work of psychologists Daniel Goleman and Martin Seligman. This principle encourages me to establish processes where the group can check-in with one another on their feelings and recognize that a learning space does not exist in a vacuum; learners bring emotions into the learning space with them that, when not addressed in a healthy way, can be highly disruptive to the learning process. It encourages me to establish a culture of positive thinking, self-care, and community wellness by incorporating intentional active and reflective listening exercises, yoga and mindfulness practices, and *circle processes*.

4- Exploring Approaches to Peace: Breaking the ideal,

overarching concept of peace into manageable bites and methods of actualization.

This principle is a constant reminder that *peace,* what it looks like as an end goal and the means through which we pursue that goal, are quite diverse and varied. It encourages me to expose learners to the myriad ways individuals, groups, and countries strategize and have worked for peace. It borrows from concepts and frameworks like Ian Harris's 7 strategies for peace, the six principles of Kingian non-violence, The National Peace Academy's five spheres of peace, social action research, and an appreciation for the various foci peace education programs have had throughout history.

5- Reframing History: Challenging the dominance of violence and war in the narratives of cultures, countries, and people. Changing the lens through which we look at major historical shifts, construct heroes, and develop cultural norms.

This principle borrows much from the work of educators like Elise Boulding, Colman McCarthy, James Loewen, Howard Zinn, and Mary King. It helps me be both a critical and hopeful student and teacher of history. It is a recognition that when we bookmark the histories of people, countries, and nations with violent conflict, war, and death, we shape the way we look at how to solve and address conflicts in the future. This principle encourages me to rely on the rich, diverse, and deep histories of non-violence, reconciliation, and community uplift that are found in all cultures.

6- Transforming Conflict Non-violently: Embracing the inevitability of conflict by practicing non-violent ways to wage it, manage it, and resolve it.

This principle is rooted in the fact that conflict is an

inevitable part of life and something that is required for change to occur. It is not the avoidance of conflict that we seek as peace educators, but an understanding of its presence and importance in everyday life and the development of skills to make conflict a constructive force as opposes to a destructive one. It encourages me and learners to be aware of various styles and levels of conflict and to integrate, where appropriate, conflict resolution techniques, restorative justice practices, and other methods like theater of the oppressed to role-play conflicts and experiment with different ways to approach them.

7- Skill Building: All of these pillars are held together and buttressed by the all encompassing goal of building, practicing, and adopting life skills that empower individuals to bring about peace in the world around them, interpersonal skills, intrapersonal skills, analytical skills, conflict resolution skills, organizing skills, and learning skills.

When we teach, educate, and facilitate with intentionality towards peace and non-violence we are ever conscious and mindful about how we teach and why we teach. This determines what is cultivated in our learning environments and influences what blossoms in our classrooms, our communities and the world.

Understanding Life in its Right Perspectives: The Chinese writer Lin Yutang has written a book named, *The Importance of Understanding.* I think most of the violence occurs due to a lack of understanding of men arid matters. If we analyse violence in a family or in an office or for that matter in a nation governed centrally, the violence may be from one person with power who might not have understood this ameobiotic stomach. I would rather put the dictum *War begins in the mind* as against *War beings in the stomachs.* If stomach can condition our brain, our last resort is our heart. Vinobaji used to tell people who get irritated about the social evils that their irritation should not enter into the brain which may lead to disastrous activities but instead enter into the heart which may lead to constructive change.

I will say, all the atrocities carried on in the past or now for example, the killing of the religious saints, the killing of Mahatma Gandhi or the recent killing of the Christian priest Rev. Stains or the injustice done to the nun result due to the disorder in the brain. The same people to whichever religion they may belong to condemn these barbarous acts. Did I say *barbarous*? I should say inhuman acts which any human on this earth should protest against. Natural calamities like the earthquakes, whirlwinds. floods etc. warn the people on the earth that they should as soon as possible break the barriers of their images of different identities, may it be religious, racial, caste and the like, and come together without hatred in the bottom of their hearts for the simple reason that when natural calamities happen they harm everyone irrespective of their identities. I wish to mention here that Gandhi linked the earthquake in Bihar to the sin of unsociability we practiced. Should not one understand life in its fullness, holistically? Here comes the need for the school of non-violence.

In our *Youth for Peace* projects in schools, interaction with the school students reveal that they are merely the revised edition of the school of thought that prevails on that particular day, repeating whatever system of thought is brought out through their parents, newspapers or friends. This type of warping one's own self in a particular school of thought enables clever people to make lobbies for their own products or ideas. The only way to get out of this habit of being influenced is to find out one's own truth.

Thousands of youth are being brain washed into certain ideas like nationalism and patriotism with an interpretation of hating the neighbor countries and think of the thousands also influenced into sacrifice during the freedom movement. Are both the same? No. The former school of thought becomes successful with one's tendency to copy the prominent idea of the moment whereas the latter depends upon one's seeking truth within.

So one has to understand one's own body, psyche, relationship between the body and mind, the functioning of life's system and the role one has to play in bringing peace and harmony in life. That is what. I would call the school of non-violence.

Secondly, the aspect of appreciation; it need not be dealt with separately, because wherever there is real understanding, there is appreciation. But I would give great emphasis to this aspect of appreciation because when people fail to form the right understanding, they are fooled even without an awareness of their being fools, they go on appreciating the follies. So if they fail in the first step, let them be stopped at least in the second step. With that aim let me elaborate what I mean by appreciation.

Life is full of diversities. They cannot be understood in their full from unless you have the sense of appreciating them. Wonder becomes a wonder only if appreciated at least within oneself.

I will elaborate it with an example. Do our children appreciate the present education system? Or do our teachers or at least the vice chancellors? None appreciate it. I heard in one meeting a vice chancellor confessing to the audience that he has been instrumental in producing thousands of *mentally retarded* students from the educational institutions under his control: But where to stop?

A few days back we conducted the *Youth for Peace* programme for the VIth std. students. They were sitting in chairs in a hall. I made a suggestion that they could sit together on the floor. Immediately they pushed away the chairs and sat on the floor. I wanted to ask them whether they can remove their shoes. Certainly they would welcome it. I did not want to disturb the school routine very much. But we should realize that the students are always under certain pressure either from the school authority or from their parents. Under pressure one cannot have tile freedom to be educated i.e. to learn to observe, wonder, share and be joyful.

And is there a motive for education? Of course, one has to face life's challenges in the right way. A boy of twenty came to our office seeking a job. His hair was not combed. He was not neat and tidy. I gave him oil soap and comb and asked him to freshen himself. He did. After half an hour of work, he said he had stomach pain and returned home. Two days later he came again, with uncombed hair. Again he was helped for combing, washing etc. He seemed not to have eaten. When enquired it was found to be correct. I gave money and asked him to eat in the nearest hotel. He left in the evening and came back after two days, of course with his hair uncombed. I lost my patience but before I started shouting at him he started telling the painful incidents that happened in his house. Father quarreled, beat his mother and mother became unconscious. He did first aid and reached the office. His sister studying in the X1 std. stopped going to school from that day. And he told that this quarrel was going on since many years as far back as his memory goes. His father is a government employee earning a handsome salary.

A few years ago, I was watching TV with my son. In the news, the parliamentary session was being shown. Our politicians were throwing mikes and chairs on one another. After seeing the behaviour of the aged people in our parliament, my son with a sad face asked me 'why papa, is our country like this?' I did not answer him but his sad face ever since haunts me.

The houses as well as the nation are in the same condition. Challenges like the above have to be met with in the right way by our youth. Does our present education help them in this regard? Lessons taught are completely unrelated to the present but promise future prosperity, the system of inculcating skills is unconnected to gaining wisdom, trying to convert humans into robots...finally ends in a business transaction of mutual exploitation. Just for show, one or two classes for value education or moral education or leadership training etc. are taken. We are cheating ourselves.

The one and only aim of education must be to enable them to appreciate - appreciate one's own qualities and at the same time appreciate the qualities in others, if the Chief Ministers of all the states were taught to appreciate the beauty of the rivers, the beauty of the rice and wheat crops, they will spontaneously realize the importance of linking the rivers and provide water for the needy states. I see people becoming crazy by taking up minor issues like a quarrel in a village being politicized and taken to the notice of the President of India by a petition or telegram! Appreciation starts with people revering life in its totality.

Finally, the third point. I would call it action-reaction factor. Nowadays there is no action at all but only *reaction*. As science and technology develops, everyone tries to lead a life not on one's own but as a response to the development around.

One of my friends is conducting a driving school. He does not need a cell phone. But he has one. When asked, he replied, ***"When the cell-phone is in the market how can I live without it?"*** His *minimum needs* include a cell phone. I hope I am making myself clear by saying that we are all *reactionaries* or in the words of J Krishnamurti, we are all second-hand human beings. We are all victims of the consumerist pattern of life and already we are in chains. Will a second freedom movement free us? Even the revolutions for the upliftment of the poor are planned as a reaction, comparing the life-styles of haves and have-nots.

All such experiments end up in violence. Any comparison, competition results in reaction that would obviously end up in violence.

So can there be action? Is there an action which emerges from one's heart spontaneously, not out of any response to the previous experience or as notes of comparison and without any sense of possession? It is very difficult because from childhood one is being taught to live in reaction. Let me explain with another incident.

I happened to be in my native village when the incident occurred. That day dawned with one of the youth in the village committing suicide. The reason? On Christmas Eve, a few youths drank and danced on the roadside where the local political party flag poles were planted. In a drunken state they pushed each other on the poles and so one of the pole's broke. In the morning the respective 'disciples' of the political party caught hold of the youths, garlanded them with chappals, beat them and like dogs drove them throughout the streets of the village compelling them to shout a slogan pleading for pardon. Shameful! That night one of the punished youth's committed suicide. This is what I learnt from the villagers.

What was the result? Youths belonging to other parties, other castes and religions joined hands and carried the body and put it across tile main road, blocking traffic. Since that is the only road connecting the towns which are twenty-five km apart, traffic stopped completely. Those vehicles which tried to pass through were destroyed by the youths.

It went on for hours. Around mid-day RDO came and tried to pacify the crowd on behalf of the collector. It did not help. At last the collector of that district came and assured proper action would be taken against the culprits. A part of the crowd did not yield and demanded immediate action. But the collector did not yield and there was a lathi charge. The crowd at last melted. Are the acts of the youth and the police, actions or reactions?

Another experience, in one of our sessions in a school, during a three hour programme for the VI Std. children, we were completely exhausted by the naughty behaviour of the children. Most of them did not allow us to say what we wanted to say. Yelling, jumping, and quarreling with each other. But we were patient telling them stories, mono acting etc. Suddenly there was pin drop silence when a lady teacher entered the class room with a stick in her hand.

Is the teacher's act action or reaction? I would call them as reactions in both cases. Reactions always lead to violence and destruction.

So what is action? I would explain it with the Satyagraha launched by Gandhiji. He said that *Satyagraha* is conceived from his inner voice. The inner voice coming out of his relative truth. Of course it is also a reaction in response to an action already happened but out of one's own realization of *truth within,* which makes it a complete action leading to peace and harmony. So the purpose of the school of non-violence should enable one to act but not trot to react.

The best example can be given from Gandhiji's *Satyagraha* movement. *Satyagraha* when interpreted might have taken different implications. But according to Gandhiji, *Satyagraha* means, ***"sticking stubbornly to one's own truth of the moment."*** Whatever one realises as truth for the moment must be put into action, even risking one's life. This can only be possible with the former two steps i.e., understanding and appreciation of the situation.

To educate people in these three aspects necessary for *action* Gandhiji gave very relevant programmes which can even now be followed by everyone. For getting the right understanding, Gandhiji evolved eleven *vratas* [vows] for every individual and for appreciation, he gave the concept of constructive work for the people to work out and to consummate the above two aspects he demonstrated that *Satyagraha* is interrelated and inter-dependent. Without practicing one, the other is not possible. All put together, it leads to a holistic view of life making the man into a Mahatma. Now, one would ask is there no system for the school of non-violence at all? There cannot be a system for system brings violence. But, any one with great care and attention may evolve a system which is time and context oriented in an appropriate way. It depends upon one's vision of the above three aspects.

4. NON-VIOLENCE AND PEACE EDUCATION

Ved Prakash Chaudhari* and Rakesh Kumar Verma**

We are living in a critical juncture in human history. We have built up massive misunderstanding and engaged in bloody wars and conflict. We now posses the means to fully destroy the humanity. The terrorist attack of September 11-2001, December 13, 2001, Iraq war, shocked the world and forced us to a great awakening and transformed our consciousness and education.

What has brought the human kind to hate each other so much that killings are needed to resolve conflicts? As educators what have we failed to do and what should we do to build peaceful world? Peace education provides a forum for students to explore issues of global peace and educational measures in promoting peace. The peace education firstly emphasizes the development of an understanding on urgent peace issues facing the humanity. Then the class would study and reflect on the roots of violence, critically analyzing inequality and injustices in the world based on racism, classism sexism and other factors. We explore ways for quelling violence and building peace. Broadly, the goal of peace education is to nurture awareness and enhance competencies for the building of long lasting global peace, through discussions to discover

* Dr. Ved Prakash Chaudhari and Dr. Rakesh Kumar Verma are assistant professors at the GNCE, Greater Noida [UP], India.

our inner self, and foster a holistic understanding of the interconnected impact of family, school and society on our perspective on peace. We aim to foster compassion for the whole humanity and nurture a form of all encompassing love that transcend hatred and heal wounds. Globalization or global village type of market economy what type of violence does this market economy lead to? What challenges does it pose for peace educators? Do we look at the increased communication between people from different culture though travels in the air , on land or in cyber space ? What does this communication mean in term of problems, challenges and possibilities for peace educators? Peace education is term often used for a variety of programs, studies and initiatives; the field of peace education is one that includes a diverse array of scholarly prospective, programmatic considerations and underlying value.

Globalization: It is the system of interaction among countries of the world in the order of global economy. The internet and other communication technologies also have made it easy for people to buy and sell product to people around the world.

Network World: In other words globalization is the way by which local or national way of doing things become global that is done together around the world. It is about economics or trade, technology, politics and culture, many authors claim that the world has become a global village. Economies are inter connected, computer and fax machines connect people across ocean. Millions of people all over the world have become *netizens,* a new word coined to denote the inhabitants of internet. We surf internet and though most of us do not have the time, our kids have hang out online a lot, we communicate daily and swiftly around the global, send each other articles and whole manuscripts within seconds.

Bradshaw and Wallace [1996] find that the most striking feature of the global village may be summed up in one word: disparity.

Ulf Hannertz [1996] argues against the idea of *global village,* which to him suggests interconnectedness, together near and homogenization of culture. In his argument, using a transnational perspective, he emphasizes creative interpretation, which results in creolization rather than homogenization, also called Mc Donaldization. The transnational perspective shows that individuals may live with multiple cultural and linguistic contexts without losing their identity rather than they develop transnational identities.

Ballard [1994] argues that just as individuals can be multilingual, they can also be ***"skilled cultural navigators"*** who are multicultural with the competence to behave appropriately in a number of different areas.

There is small group of people who enjoy the benefits of a shrinking world. They are the transnationalists, the cultural commuters *die ortspolygame menschen* they have responsibility not only enjoying the benefits but also analyzing what is happening to the majority of population.

They have responsibility of working against a policy leading to greater disparities.

Adopting talcott parsons, well elaborated social system theory where a social system is known to have four sub systems, namely the economic, political, social and culture.

Piertse [1995] has summarized the manner in which each academic discipline, through focusing on certain sets of these multi dimensional processes defines globalization. In economics, globalization is being equated with economic internationalization and the spread of capitalistic market relations in international relations the focus is on the increasing density of interstate relation, new role of the state and the development of global politics.

In sociology the concern is with the increasing world-wide densities and the emergence of *world society.* In cultural standardization as a cocacolaniization, McDonaldization or post colonial culture. [Piertse 1995]

Peace Education: Peace education is a term often used for a variety of programs, studies, and initiatives the field of peace education is one that includes a diverse array of scholarly perspectives programmatic consideration and underlying value. The world conference on human right in Vienna in June 1993 looked at human right education as, ***"Human Right education should inclued peace, democracy development and social justice as set forth in international and regional human rights instruments in order to achieve common understanding and awareness with a view to strengthening universal commitment to human right—the proclamation of united nations decade for human rights education in order to promote, encourage and focus these educational activities should be considered"***

Betty Reardon defines the purpose of peace education this way that ***"the general purpose of peace education, as I understand it is to promote the development of authentic planetary consciousness that will enable is to function as global citizens and to transform the present human condition by changing social structure and the patterns of thought that have created it.***

"I have elsewhere defined peace education this way: that by peace education I mean the social process through

which peace, as I have defined it is achieved. This includes the practicing of equality of right and equal power sharing for every member of a given community, it further includes the learning of skills of non-violent conflict resolution it also includes respect for human right." [Brock Utne 1985]

Education for Peace: When we try to analyze more closely the difference between the more cognitive fact- oriented and formal approach to peace education found in the term education about peace and the broader approach found in term education for peace, we discover that not only do the two preposition differ in the two juxtapositions, but so does the seemingly same word *education* depending upon preposition education mean the more limited formal learning of subject matter acquisition of knowledge [education about] or the broader in formal learning of attitudes value and behaviour [education for affective aspect].

Peace Educating in Globalized World: When we deal with the cognitive realm of peace education, the education about peace, we need both to look at the possibilities for word wide communication that are the uniting people across continents in an unprecedented way at the effects of a globalized world economy.

Links for Peace Education: For those who have the possibility to access the internet there is a wealth of information that can be used in peace education. Swift communication through e-mail has led to the formation of many electronic bulletin boards within the field of peace studies. With the availability of communication in cyber-space it is also possible to form group consisting of individual from all parts of the globe who are interested in peace education.

Peace Education in Globalized World: The task of the

educator had been much easier had there been a clear correlation between the knowledge one is exposed to and the attitudes that develop. Such correlation is often a prerequisite for an attitude change. The UNESCO Institute of education located in Hamburg Germany some year ago made a study of the attitudes towards certain social questions and knowledge about the same question among elementary and secondary school students in several of the member states of the UNESCO. In a Swedish report from the project the conclusion is drawn that there was no clear correlation between the knowledge level of students and their attitudes. [Samhallssyn 1976] Normally the following six main type of explanation for the less racist attitudes of highly educated people have been put forward:

- Tolerance and conception of rights are among the norms that the educators try to impart. The longer the education, the greater the change of the students internalizing these norm;
- Education will confer knowledge and thus break down stereotype belief about immigrants;
- Long-time education will increase the cognitive competence and so make people more resistant to hostile propaganda about immigrants and more able to understand the situations of conflicts;
- High education will lead to job with nigh social status, protected from direct competition with immigrants on job and housing markets;
- High education will strengthen the general ability of mastering, reducing the danger situation creating conflicts and aggression; and
- High education will create both motivation and ability to act opportunistically in this conflict laden matter. Highly

educated people know that they are expected to demonstrate tolerance and open mind and their knowledge and verbal aptitude will make it easy to disguise eventual hostility.

The Goal of Peace Education: a goal for peace education is the creation of critical and analytical mind. Another goal would be the development of a co-operative way of working in order to be able to solve life- threatening and global problems. We need to develop an ability to co-operate, but what does normal formal schooling do? People can solve problem constructively only if they have confidence in themselves and a feeling of self security and self worth.

It is not easy to work for these goals in the normal competitive school system. Even though the goal are also the proclaimed goals of formal schooling, the structure built up around individual for further goals enhancing co-operation and self worth, it is difficult to teach peace in a setting where children are taught to compete against each other. It is difficult to teach about equality between state large and small when there is so little equality between teacher and pupils, to teach about the equality of the sexes when the boys in the class are allowed to dominate the girls in a discussion of this the class are allowed to elsewhere raised the question : is it at all possible to teach democracy in an authoritarian school or university.

Conclusion: global peace education has four inter related components: knowledge, analysis, skill and action [KASA] first there is the knowledge of world current events, economics and international relations second is the capacity to critically analyze media, religious message, dogma, superstition hate literature extremism, and fundamentalism, third it involves political skills, such as persuasion negotiation lobbying, demonstrating, fourth are disposition for joint action, which these day include networking through communication technology, starting website or joining international forums of young people working for peace these all essentials ingredients for a solid global active world citizen who understand the causes and effect of conflict, who do not join radical groups, who vote out politician who go to war, who do not support religions leaders, who preach hate and who join other to make their voice for peace more potent.

References:

Beck,Ulrich, 1997. Was Ist globalisieung? Frank fart am main suhrkamp.

Brecher, Jeremy and Costelli, Tim .1994. *Global Village: Economic Re-Construction from the Bottom Up- or Global Collage* Boston: South End Press.

Bradshaw, York and Wallace, Inichqel. 1995. *Global Inequalities.* Thousand Oaks: Pine Forge Press.

Bajaj, MI. 2004. *Human Right Education and Student's Self-Conception in the Dominican Republic* in the Journal of Peace Education [1: 21-36].

OXFAM. 1997. *A Curriculum for Global Citizenship.* Oxford: OXFAM.

5. NON-VIOLENCE AND PEACE EDUCATION IN INDIA

G Andrews*

While we turn the pages of the Indian History, we come to know that India is a holy land, the paradise of Gods and Goddesses. She is the fountain of spiritual knowledge and the home of all world ancient religions. Indian Civilization is the only oldest and continuous civilization in the world. The world's

* Capt. G Andrews is an associate professor at the St. Johns College of Palayamkottai [Tamilnadu], India.

first university was established in Takshila around 700 BC. More than 10, 500 students from all over the world studied more than sixty subjects there. The navigator Christopher Columbus was attracted by the natural beauty of India and was looking for a route to India when he discovered America by an accident.

Today, India is much affected by violence and terrorism externally and internally. The ungrateful and selfish neighboring countries like Pakistan and China are the cause for the external violence and terrorism. The Fundamentalist, the Communalist, the narrow minded religious organizations and the Naxalite Maoist insurgency are the seed for the internal violence and terrorism. The government of India has identified sixty five terrorist groups active in the country. The minister of state for home RPN Singh said available intelligence inputs show that militant organizations active in India are often supported and funded by their parent outfits based abroad, particularly in Pakistan in terms of shelter, training, weapons and finance. The regions with long drawn terrorist and violence activities today are Jammu and Kashmir, Mumbai, Central parts of India and the seven sister states. As on 2006, at least 232 districts were affected at different intensities by various insurgent and terrorist movements. In 2008, the National Security adviser MK Narayan has said that there were as many as 800 terrorist cells operating in the country. In August 2013, the minister RPN Singh said Jammu and Kashmir had five terrorist organizations including Lashkar-e-Taiba, Hizbul-Mujahideen, Jaish-e-Mohammad, Harkat-ul-Mujahideen and Al-Badr. Northeast Assam has eleven, Meghalaya four, Tripura two, Nagaland four, Mizoram two and Manipur thirty four. Babbar Khalsa International, Khalistan Zindabad Force, Kalistan Commando Force are the three militant groups active in Punjab.

Moreover, various terrorist groups like Let, IM, HM, Huji, Al-Badr are active in the hinterland of the country, especially in Uttar Pradesh, Maharashtra, Gujarat, Karnataka, Kerala, Rajasthan, Andhra Pradesh and Delhi. There were 285 incidents of Naxal violence in the country in just three months from May to July 2013, in which 117 people lost their lives. Of the deceased, 47 were in killed in Chattisgarh, 37 were killed in Jharkhand and 15 in Bihar.

A number of Intelligence, Military and Police organizations with in the Indian government contribute to counter terrorism. The state run police force, the special security force, the Para military forces patrol the borders and assist the army when necessary. The Research and Analysis Wing [RAW] is the external intelligence agency, the Intelligence Bureau [IB], a division of the home affairs ministry monitor intensively the terrorist activities.

The Government of India has banned 36 outfits and nine organizations in the country. As regards the initiatives taken in the left wing Extremism [LWE] affected regions, the Indian government has a two pronged approach in the left wing extremism states.

Firstly, the government is to deal with LWE in a holistic manner in terms of security, development, good governance and public perception management.

Secondly the government of India has banned the communist party of India [Marxist-Leninist], the people's war, all its formations and front organizations, the Maoist Communist Centre, all its formations and front organizations in the left wing extremism hit areas. Some states are also doing extremely well in tackling Naxalism, some states are doing moderately well and some are lagging behind. This is a serious matter of concern.

Anyhow, at the present context, with regard to socio-cultural life of man, the violence and terrorism are perhaps one of the most challenging problems. For some of us, the effect of violence and terrorism may have not hit personally. Yes! Having not yet suffered in the hands of terrorist, it might just be a matter of time, it will. Can one say for sure that we are absolutely safe? The unfortunate reality is that terrorism and violence has gone global. Every world citizen is equally susceptible and vulnerable.

To bring back the ancient culture of peace and harmony, we need peace education today. It is a series of teaching encounters that draw from peoples' desire for peace, non-violent alternatives for managing conflict and skill for critical analysis of structural arrangements that produce legislatimize injustice and in-equality. Peace education is the panacea for all kinds of violence and terrorist activities.

Peace is a state of harmony characterized by the lack of violence, conflict behaviors and freedom from the fear of violence. According to Mother Teresa, ***"Peace begins with a smile."*** Mahatma Gandhiji pointed out that ***"Peace is its own reward."*** Nelson Mandela directs us that ***'if you want to make peace with your enemy, you have to work with your enemy, then he becomes your partner."***

Love is the fundamental concept of non-violence. The ultimate goal of non-violence is not to defeat the enemy but to win him through tolerance, understanding and love. The principle of non-violence is a code of conduct for the *Hindus*. In the Sermon on the Mount, Jesus urges his followers 'Love your enemies'. The principle of *Ahimsa* or Non-Violence towards any being is shared by both Buddhism and Jainism. Notable Humanists Leo Tolstoy, Mohandas Karamchand Gandhi, Martin Luther King were influenced by the principle of non-violence. They believed that individual resistance to the civil government is nothing but a moral opposition to an unjust state. Martin Luther King said that ***"non-violence means avoiding not only external physical violence, but also internal violence of spirit, you not only refuse to shoot a man, but you refuse to hate him."***

Since 1945, the United Nations Organizations has sent her peace keeping forces to the countries by affected Terrorism and Violence. Nearly fifty five peace missions have been completed in Africa, America, Asia, Europe and Middle East. At present, sixteen peace missions are deployed in the above mentioned areas for peace. At the beck and call of the United Nations about thousand young men and women from ten countries took part in the seventh International peace festival at Chandigarh last year. They declared October 2, as the *International day of Non-Violence and Peace*.

For the same noble cause, Dr. SN Subba Rao, the living spirit of Gandhi, the founder of National Youth Project of India inspired and lifted up the spirit of youth in the world for building a new society based on love, peace, harmony and social justice. He founded Mahatma Gandhi Sewa Ashram in the Chambal Valley at Joura, Morena district, Madhya Pradesh. His constructive education programme for the youth led to the historic surrender of the notorious dacoits like Mohan Singh, Madho Singh and others on April 14, 1972. These effects also gave a green signal to the mass surrender of dacoits at Bateshwar in Uttar Pradesh and Talebshahi in Rajasthan.

In addition to this, Dr. SN Subba Rao organized a special International peace and Harmony youth camp from April 22 to April 28, 2013 in Kota, Rajasthan. About 280 foreign youth participated, where he gave a call to the youth that they must get away from bad habits including the use of drugs, liquor and the use of energy for constructive work. The life and contribution of Dr. Subba Rao is a role model for Peace education in India.

The reality of peace education reached the minds through the principle of tolerance for in sight the Australian Missionary Dr. Graham Stuart Stains and his two sons Philip and Timothy were killed by a gang led by Darasingh, the Bajrangdal activist Mohoharpur village in Keonjhar district, Odisha on January 22, 1999. This was a great shock to the entire minority Community in India. But after five years, the widow Gladys Stains stated that, ***"It is my desire and hope that they would repent and would be reformed."*** This is the confident and the firm belief of the widow over the Indian terrorist.

Now-a-days, the principle of non-violence has obtained a level of institutional recognition and endorsement at the global level. Thus, we too have a positive hope that India will be free from violence very soon; let us stand for unity and good will.

References:

1. Fischer, Loius, The life of Mahatma Gandhi, New York, Harperk row publishers, 1950.
2. Gandhi, M.K. "My religion" Nayajivan Trust, Ahmedabad, India, 1955.
3. Gandhi M.K., 1961, The power of Non Violence Resistance, New Delhi, Schoker.
4. Jennifer, E. Turpin, Encyclopedia of violence, peace and conflict, p-557, 1999.
5. John Dear, S.J. Collection of essays answers fundamental questions of non-violence in Christianity National Catholic Reporter, 115 E, Armour Blvd, Kansas city, mo (64111-1203)
6. Merton .T, 1980, The violence Alternative, New York, Farrar, Straus and Giroux.

7. Nojeim, Michael J. Gandhi and King. The power of Non Violent Resistance, Greenwood publishing, group . p. 179, 2004.
8. Report of – Dr. S.N. Subba Rao, National Youth Project, Deen Dayal upadhayamerg, New Delhi.
9. Sharp, G., 1971, A syudy of the meaning of Non violence in Ramachandran and T.K. Mahadesan Gandhi, His relevance for our times, Berkeley, World without war, pp. 21-66.
10. Stanley M. Brustein and Richard Shek, "World History Ancient Civilizations". page 154, 2005
11. The Economic Times, New Delhi, 28 May 2013
12. The Hindu, New Delhi, August 27, 2013
13. The Times of India, "66 terror groups active in India: Govt", 27 August, 2013.
14. Tolstoy, L. 1967, Tolstoy on civil disobedience and non violence, New York: Signet.
15. Tolstoy, Leo, Tolstoy's letters, vol. 2 (1880-1910) E.d. and trams by R.F. Christian, New York, Charles Scribne's sons, 1978.
16. Weber, T. 1990, Conflict resolution and Gandhian Ethics, New Delhi, Gandhi Peace Foundation.
17. Z News, Nayals succeed due to forces failure to adhese sops, August 07, 2013

6. PEACE EDUCATION AS A TOOL FOR PREVENTING VIOLENCE

AK Kulshrestha*, Rati Verma and Pravendra Singh Birla*****

"Peace is not the absence of conflict, but the presence of justice." *-Martin Luther King Jr.*

* Dr. AK Kulshrestha is an assistant professor, **Ms. Rati Verma is a research scholar and ***Mr. Pravendra Singh Birla is a M.Phil student at the DEI, Agra [UP], India.

As technology brings the world closer together, it also changes the way we communicate and socialize. A breakdown of a sense of community belonging has led to greater isolation, especially for vulnerable groups like the elderly who may feel left behind. Youth can also be affected by a loss of community support systems. This can reinforce vulnerabilities and foster the appearance of different forms of communities such as gangs, particularly in urban settings.

There is a growing level of intolerance in many countries, especially between local and immigrant populations. A lack of cultural awareness can channel this intolerance into violent clashes that oppose segments of the population along lines of cultural or religious belonging and lead to exclusion. Violence, discrimination and exclusion affect people in every corner of the globe, endangering health, lives and livelihoods and limiting human potential. While their effect is most severe on the vulnerable, no one is immune.

Changing a culture of violence into a culture of peace requires a transformation of problems to creative and constructive solutions that answer the needs of those involved. **What is Violence?** Violence is ***"the intentional use of physical force or power, threatened or actual, against oneself, another person, or against a group or community, which either results in or has a high likelihood of resulting in injury, death, psychological harm, mal-development, or deprivation."*** Violence, however, is preventable. Evidence shows strong relationships between levels of violence and potentially modifiable factors such as concentrated poverty, income and gender inequality, the harmful use of alcohol on one hand and the absence of safe, stable, and nurturing relationships between children and parents on the other hand.

Types of Violence: Self-directed violence refers to violence by an individual against oneself. It is subdivided into suicidal behaviour and self-abuse. Suicidal behavior includes suicidal thoughts, attempted suicides and completed suicides. Self-abuse covers self-mutilation and substance abuse or misuse. Interpersonal violence is violence that occurs between individuals. It can occur in homes, schools, workplaces and institutions. Examples include child abuse, bullying and harassment, family violence and abuse of the elderly.

Community violence is a type of interpersonal violence that takes place at the community level [e.g. in urban settings] between people who may or may not know one another. [Ibid] Common forms of community violence include gang violence, violence by supporters of sports teams, mob attacks and sporadic crime.

Collective violence that is committed to advance a particular social agenda includes, for example, crimes of hate committed by organized groups, terrorist acts and mob violence. Political violence includes war and related violent conflicts, state violence and similar acts carried out by larger groups. Economic violence includes attacks by larger groups motivated by economic gain, such as attacks carried out with the purpose of disrupting economic activity, denying access to essential services, or creating economic division and fragmentation. Clearly, acts committed by larger groups can have multiple motives.

Non-physical violence includes those acts that result from a power relationship, including threats and intimidation, neglect or acts of omission, in addition to more obvious violent acts. Violence has a broad range of outcomes –including psychological harm, deprivation and mal-development. Violence that does not necessarily result in injury or death, but nonetheless poses a substantial burden on individuals, families, communities and health care systems worldwide. Many forms of violence against women, children and the elderly, for instance, can result in physical, psychological and social problems that do not necessarily lead to injury, disability or death.

What is Non-Violence? Non-violence is the practice of being harmless to self and others under every condition. It comes from the belief that hurting people, animals or the environment is unnecessary to achieve an outcome and refers to a general philosophy of abstention from violence based on moral, religious or spiritual principles. Non-violence had always been the founding principle of Gandhian spirituality, and bedrock of his political philosophy. Gandhi's distrust of violence as a mode to assume political power and as a tool of revolution was ingrained in his world-view from the very early days of his political career. Gandhi's political goals were ultimately specific correlatives of higher commitments to humanity and world peace.

In modern times, non-violent methods of action have been a powerful tool for social protest and revolutionary social and political change.

Non-Violent Actions: It consists of acts of protest and persuasion, non-cooperation and non-violent intervention designed to undermine the sources of power of the opponent in order to bring about change.

Non-violent protest and persuasion is a class of methods which are *mainly symbolic acts of peaceful opposition or of attempted persuasion, extending beyond verbal expressions*. These methods include marches, vigils, pickets, and the use of posters, street theatre, painting and protest meetings.

Non-cooperation the most common form of non-violent action involves the deliberate withdrawal of co-operation with the person, activity, institution or regime with which the activists have become engaged in conflict. These methods include the provision of sanctuary [social]; strikes, boycotts and war tax resistance [economic] and boycotts of legislative bodies and elections [political]. Political non-cooperation also includes acts of civil disobedience –the *deliberate, open and peaceful violation of particular laws, decrees, regulations ... and the like which are believed to be illegitimate for some reason.*

Non-violent intervention is a class of methods involving the disruption or destruction of established behaviour patterns, policies, relationships or institutions which are considered objectionable, or the creation of new behaviour patterns, policies, relationships or institutions which are preferred. The *disruption* class of methods includes non-violent occupations or blockades, fasting, seeking imprisonment and overloading facilities [such as courts and prisons]. The *creation* class of methods includes establishing alternative political, economic and social institutions such as non-hierarchical co-operatives, markets, ethical investment groups, alternative schools, energy exchange co-operatives as well as parallel media, communications and transport networks. This last class of methods is what the Gandhian literature refers to as the constructive programme.

Concept of Peace Education: Peace education is more effective and meaningful when it is adopted according to the social and cultural context and the needs of a country. It should be enriched by its cultural and spiritual values together with the universal human values. It should also be globally relevant. Peace education could be defined in many ways. There is no universally accepted definition as such.

Peace education in the UNICEF refers to the process of promoting the knowledge, skills, attitudes and values needed to bring about behavior changes that will enable skills, such as being able to:

- Solve problems and conflicts in positive ways including through negotiation and mediation;
- Communicate feelings and perspectives and transform anger;
- Understand others' feelings and perspectives;
- Co-operate with others;
- Think independently and critically; and
- Take part responsibly in decision making.

Further, attitudes, such as having:

- Concern for others and the environment;
- A desire to help and be of service;
- Honesty, trustworthiness and fairness;
- Respect other cultures, religions and lifestyles; and
- Tolerance [rangimarie], generosity [manaakitanga] and compassion [aroha].

Moreover, knowledge of:

- How problems and conflicts can be solved;
- The values of oneself and others;
- Human rights and responsibilities;
- The roles and effectiveness of local, national and international organizations that promote peace and help solve conflicts;
- Developing peace at home and internationally.

Peace Education as a Tool for Preventing Violence: Values and skills-based education instills humanitarian values, like respect for diversity, compassion, care and friendship, mutual understanding, co-operation, equality and peace. In addition, it enables the development of interpersonal skills to live peacefully and interact harmoniously together, such as empathy, active listening, non-violent communication and peaceful resolution of tensions. This type of education is participatory and stimulates critical thinking and independence. It puts those involved at a level of equality, where both learners and 'transmitters' learn from each other and value this as part of a lifelong learning process.

An integral part of values and skills-based education is a non-cognitive methodology, as an entry point for learning. Values are ***"core beliefs that guide and motivate attitudes and actions."*** Therefore, starting values and skill-based education as early as possible is essential. This can be done in a variety of settings such as family, preschool and school, sport clubs and social activities.

The culture of peace and non-violence is a commitment to peace-building, mediation, conflict prevention and resolution, peace education, education for non-violence, tolerance, acceptance, mutual respect, intercultural and interfaith dialogue and reconciliation. It is a conceptual as well as a normative framework envisaged to inspire thoughts and actions of everyone. Therefore, it requires cognitive as well as the emotional abilities to grapple with our own situation in a rapidly changing world as well as with the emerging world society. This aim entails not just more factual knowledge, but also the broadening of our consciousness and the willingness to develop a new awareness, a new way of being in this world, a new *mental mapping*.

The culture of peace continuously brings new challenges prompting us to reconsider the fundamental principles of humanity by highlighting what binds cultures and societies to each other and from within. Since what unites us is deeper than what separates us, there is a true ethic of living together that is taking shape in the culture of peace and non-violence process.

Peace Education in Different Context: Each different form of violence requires a unique form of peace education to address strategies that could resolve its conflicts. Peace education in intense conflicts attempts to demystify enemy images and urges combatants to withdraw from warlike behavior. Peace education in regions of interethnic tension relies upon multiculturalism and awareness about the sufferings of various groups involved in the conflict to promote empathy for the suffering of others and to reduce hostilities. Peace educators in areas free from collective physical violence teach about the causes of domestic and civil violence and try to develop an interest in global issues, the problems of poverty, environmental sustainability, and the power of non-violence. Peace educators concerned about the problems of underdevelopment, starvation, poverty, illiteracy, and the lack of human rights seek an understanding of the crises that exist in poorer countries and solutions for the problems of underdevelopment. Peace educators use development studies to provide insights into the various aspects of structural violence, focusing on social institutions with their hierarchies and propensities for dominance and oppression. Such study highlights the problems of structural violence and emphasizes peace-building strategies to improve human communities.

Peace Education Imparting as:

Conflict Resolution Training: Peace education programmes centered on conflict resolution typically focus on the social-behavioural symptoms of conflict, training individuals to resolve inter-personal disputes through techniques of negotiation and [peer] mediation. Learning to manage anger, *fight fair* and improve communication through skills such as listening, turn-taking, identifying needs, and separating facts from emotions, constitute the main elements of these programs. Participants are also encouraged to take responsibility for their actions and to brainstorm together on compromises.

In general, approaches of this type aim to ***"alter beliefs, attitudes, and behaviours...from negative to positive attitudes toward conflict as a basis for preventing violence."*** [Van Slyck, Stern and Elbedour, 1999, emphasis added]

Education for Democracy: Peace education programs centered on democracy education typically focus on the political processes associated with conflict, and postulate that with an increase in democratic participation the likelihood of societies resolving conflict through violence and war decreases. At the same time, ***"a democratic society needs the commitment of citizens who accept the inevitability of conflict as well as the necessity for tolerance."*** [US Department of State, The Culture of Democracy, and emphasis added] Thus, programs of this kind attempt to foster a conflict-positive orientation in the community by training students to view conflict as a platform for creativity and growth.

Approaches of this type train participants in the skills of critical thinking, debate and coalition-building, and promote the values of freedom of speech, individuality, tolerance of diversity, compromise and conscientious objection. Their aim is to produce *responsible citizens,* who will hold their governments accountable to the standards of peace, primarily through adversarial processes.

Human Rights Education: Peace education programs centered on raising awareness of human rights typically focus at the level of policies that humanity ought to adopt in order to move closer to a peaceful global community. The aim is to engender a commitment among participants to a vision of structural peace in which all individual members of the human race can exercise their personal freedoms and be legally protected from violence, oppression and indignity.

Approaches of this type familiarize participants with the international covenants and declarations of the United Nations system; train students to recognize violations of the Universal Declaration of Human Rights; and promote tolerance, solidarity, autonomy and self-affirmation at the individual and collective levels.

Worldview Transformation: New approaches to peace education are starting from insights gleaned from psychology which recognize the developmental nature of human psychosocial dispositions. Essentially, while conflict-promoting attitudes and behaviours are characteristic of earlier phases of human development, unity-promoting attitudes and behaviours emerge in later phases of healthy development. HB Danesh [2002a, 2002b, 2004, 2005, 2007, 2008a, 2008b] proposes an *Integrative Theory of Peace* in which peace is understood as a psychosocial, political, moral and spiritual reality.

Initiatives for Peace Education: Can be mentioned as:

Global Campaign for Peace Education [GCPE]: Founded in 1999 at The Hague Appeal for Peace Conference in the Netherlands, the Global Campaign for Peace Education

[GCPE] is an international organized network that promotes peace education around the world. In seeking to foster a culture of peace in communities around the world the Global Campaign has two goals:

To build public awareness and political support for the introduction of peace education into all spheres of education, including non-formal education, in all schools throughout the world; and 2-To promote the education of all teachers to teach for peace.

The GCPE publishes a monthly newsletter featuring articles and news as to how and where peace education is active and growing. It includes reports from the field chronicling successes and challenges; profiles of peace educators; listing of events, conferences, and trainings in peace education from around the world; new publications in the field; and job postings.

International Institute on Peace Education [IIPE]: Founded in 1982, the IIPE is an annual week-long residential learning experience in peace-education.

The IIPE is not a traditional conference but rather a *learning community* in which the organizers and participants work together to nurture an inclusive, highly interactive learning environment. It is an intensive multicultural and cooperative learning opportunity in which participants learn from and with each other about substantive peace issues and interactive teaching approaches. The IIPE is also an opportunity for networking and community building among those who educate and work for a culture of peace in the host region and around the world.

Community-Based Institutes on Peace Education [CIPE]: A Community-based Institute on Peace Education [CIPE] is a sustainable and recurring learning opportunity that enables formal and non-formal educators in local communities to learn with and from each other about ***"the role and possibilities for education in the prevention of deadly conflict; the rethinking of global security; preparing individuals for engaged, democratic citizenship; and the realization of human rights, social justice and ecological balance."***

Further, CIPEs are informed by six strategic goals:

1. To provide local support for peace educators;
2. To provide opportunities for educators to learn from each other about best practices;
3. To address current and relevant local content and issues;
4. To support school and community based peace education initiatives;
5. To increase the possibility for affecting policy locally, nationally, and globally; and
6. Increase potential for research and new developments in the field of peace education.

Conclusion: Peace is certainly the greatest collective challenge that mankind has ever faced. Conflict is unavoidable, but violence is not. Peoples need to be taught of alternatives in resolving conflict, that violence is not necessary means to achieve their goals. Peace education is means to achieve this ends. Peace education raises the awareness of the roots and causes of conflict, and it provides people with the necessary skills and knowledge on how to respond conflict.

In spite of tremendous growth of peace education in twentieth century, peace education has not really taken hold in school systems around the world. A few countries have used United Nations mandates to stimulate formal school-based peace education activities. Most countries have ignored them. Local groups throughout the world, horrified by violence in their communities, attempt to convince their fellow citizens to oppose the violent policies of militaristic governments. This is by far the most widespread use of peace education at the beginning of the new millennium.

It is only recently that peace educators are starting to unify around a common curriculum for peace education that would include its historic roots in international education as well as modern conventions for human rights, the feminist orientation on violence in interpersonal relations, a concern for the problems of structural violence, an emphasis upon building a culture of peace, and an urgency to address environmental issues—insights that were provided during the previous *bloodiest century.* [Harris and Morrison, 2003]

7. PEACE EDUCATION IN THE ERA OF GLOBALIZATION: RELEVANCE AND SCOPE

Shiny Bhardwaj*

Today when we stand in the Twenty-First Century and look back at the transformations since barely three decades back, it would be an understatement to say that one may feel overwhelmed and taken aback by the progress that has taken place. The electronic media alone has drastically reframed the

* Ms. Shiny Bhardwaj is a research scholar at the Central Institute of Education in the University of Delhi [India].

world panorama. It has made possible activities that were unthinkable a few decades ago. The growing communication has led to what is termed as *globalization*. Put in simple terms, globalization refers to processes that increase worldwide exchanges of national and cultural resources. Advances in telecommunications and transportation infrastructure are some of the major factors that have contributed to the growth of relations between nations across the globe and have thereby enabled globalization. It is worth noting that globalization and modernization have played an important role in aiding faster growth of countries and has brought stability in their economies. It has opened job avenues for people, thereby enabling a better standard of living for many. Yet there exist huge insecurities and poverty that have emerged as a result of globalization itself. In such a scenario there must be a value system to sustain the mental and emotional structures of people so that they don't break down and peace is maintained within their lives. This paper would attempt to decipher ways in which an interface can be built up between the contours of globalization and education for peace, with emphasis on children's well being- since they are the forbearers of the world's future.

Globalization, Meaning and Impacts: Globalization is not a single concept that can be defined and encompassed within a set time frame, nor is it a process that can be defined clearly with a beginning and an end. Furthermore, it cannot be expounded upon with certainty and be applicable to all people and in all situations. Globalization involves economic integration; the transfer of policies across borders; the transmission of knowledge; cultural stability; the reproduction, relations, and discourses of power; it is a global process, a concept, a revolution, and ***"an establishment of the global market free***

from socio-political control." [Nikitin and Elliot, 2000] Globalization encompasses all of these things. It is a concept that has been defined variously over the years, with some connotations referring to progress, development and stability, integration and cooperation, and others referring to regression, colonialism, and destabilization. Despite these challenges, this term brings with it a multitude of hidden agendas. An individual's political ideology, geographic location, social status, cultural background, and ethnic and religious affiliation provide the background that determines how globalization is interpreted. Globalization is a term in heavy current usage but one whose meaning remains obscure, often even among those who invoke it. Indeed, Jan Aart Scholte states that ***"globalization stands out for quite a large public spread across the world as one of the defining terms of late twentieth century social consciousness."*** The term is often distinguished more by what it is not, rather than what it is. James Rosenau recognizes such a tendency when he states that ***"Globalization is not the same as globalism, which points to aspirations for an end state of affairs wherein values are shared by or pertinent to all the world's five billion people, their environment, their roles as citizens, consumers or producers with an interest in collective action designed to solve common problems. Nor is it universalism—values which embrace all humanity, hypothetically or actually."*** Al-Rodhan [2006] proposes the following definition of globalization keeping in mind the holistic effects and intricacies of the phenomenon:

"Globalization is a process that encompasses the causes, course, and consequences of transnational and transcultural integration of human and non-human activities."

Globalization, according to him, is a process, a current that has been impacting communities, cultures, and economies for hundreds of years. It is a result of the transnational and transcultural integrations that have occurred globally throughout human history. It encompasses the causes, the course, and the consequences of these integrations. This intermingling has transpired through activities that are both human and non-human in nature. Human activities encompass the linguistic, cultural, economic, and political aspects of human life [along with many others] that are a part of the human and social sphere. It is also important to include non-human activities, which incorporate, but are not limited to, the spread of bacteria and non-human diseases such as bird flu, as well as natural disasters such as tornadoes, tsunamis, earthquakes, and hurricanes. It is important to recognize that globalization is not a force that needs to be stopped; rather, it is a process that influences each of us in a number of ways, both to our benefit and also to our detriment.

India opened up the economy in the early nineties following a major crisis led by a foreign exchange crunch that dragged the economy close to defaulting on loans. The response was a slew of domestic and external sector policy measures partly prompted by the immediate needs and partly by the demand of the multilateral organizations. The new policy regime radically pushed forward in favor of a more open and market oriented economy. Major measures initiated as a part of the liberalization and globalization strategy in the early nineties included scrapping of the industrial licensing regime, reduction in the number of areas reserved for the public sector, amendment of the monopolies and the restrictive trade practices act, start of the privatization programme, reduction in tariff rates and change over to market determined exchange rates.

Over the years there has been a steady liberalization of the current account transactions, more and more sectors opened up for foreign direct investments and portfolio investments facilitating entry of foreign investors in telecom, roads, ports, airports, insurance and other major sectors.

Rising per capita income, higher purchasing power, a better standard of living and more job opportunities. These are some of the things which have visibly increased due to globalization. The Indian economy, which is predominantly agricultural based, has seen a revolution in the fields of manufacturing, IT, medicine, business etc ever since the liberal policies were adopted by the Government. Globalization has certainly made trade, import-export and business an integral and pivotal part of the economy and has provided opportunities to prosper to the people. But despite the advantages, there is a darker side of globalization which needs to be taken care of. We may sum them up precisely as follows:

Globalization has certainly improved trade and business opportunities. However, majority of these opportunities are limited to the people who already lead a respectable life. Educated and wealthy people from the urban areas have made the most of opportunities to study, start businesses, get employment in MNC's etc., which has further enhanced their standard of living. But the population in the rural areas, which forms the majority of the citizens of the country, is deprived of even the basic needs of living. In India, even today, the people in the rural areas struggle for basic amenities like drinking water, hygienic food, medical facilities, electricity, roads etc. The benefits of globalization are mainly limited to the rich class in the urban areas and haven't percolated to the people living in the semi-urban and rural areas.

Globalization has affected the poor people severely. Big international companies have entered in the untapped Indian market, and they use the agricultural land for setting up industries, offices etc. Even here, there is tremendous partiality shown against the farmer, which further neglects the agricultural sector. This causes a socio-economic divide amongst the people of the country which causes an increase in crime, migration to cities, drug-dealers, human trafficking etc. All these factors have been on the rise due to the huge gap that globalization has created amongst the haves and the have-nots.

Another ill effect of globalization is the excessive use of technology. If the technology is used for developmental purposes it becomes a great tool for prosperity. But the same technology in the wrong hands becomes a curse. Growth in terrorism and crime has also been fueled by the growing parity between the rich and the poor. Terrorists often use the normal mobile technology, which was primarily created to help people connect, to spread terror.

Also, due to globalization, developed countries as well as emerging economies have their economies interlinked. This is the reason why if there is an economic depression or financial fluctuation in one country, it creates a huge panic globally. The markets in all the countries go for a toss creating an economic instability in the world of business.

Children in the Prevailing Era: It is no hidden fact that the children are directly affected by any change in the familial atmosphere. The aspects that have been discussed above are bound to have a significant impact on the well-being of any bread winner in a family. With the risk of the extreme always hanging around, there must be a stabilizing technique that must be embedded in the socializing process of the young minds.

Childhood is often referred to as a time when the child's mind is a 'tabula rasa'- implying that it is devoid of any knowledge or experience. It is for this reason that the experiences are credited as being crucial and formative towards building the personality of the child for the future. Childhood comes with certain basic needs that are essential for a healthy and balanced development till later on in life. These are by nature largely physical and emotional needs. Any laxity in the provision of either of them is bound to jeopardize the child's all-round growth till a long time. The fast and dynamic world we inhabit poses major challenges and circumstances that render children vulnerable to facing unpleasant situations that prove to be detrimental in ensuring their well-being. It is here that peace education gains all the more importance in our society.

Since schooling is one of the most impacting institutions in a child's life, therefore schooling must provide the child with competencies that enable her to deal with most of the challenges when they grow up and face the real world of work. Therefore it is school education that must foster peace education.

Meaning and Relevance of Peace Education: Peace, as an integrative perspective for the school curriculum, is an idea whose time has come. Education for peace, as distinguished from peace education, acknowledges the goal of promoting a culture of peace as the purpose shaping the enterprise of education. If implemented with vigor and vision, education for peace can make learning a joyful and meaningful experience. Peace and Education for Peace are then defined, and the need to introduce education for peace in the school curriculum is viewed, albeit very briefly, from the global and national perspective. Education for Peace requires a reduction in curriculum load. Peace offers a contextually appropriate and pedagogically gainful point of coherence for all values. The complementarity of peace and justice is underlined. In the event of a conflict of interests, the claims of justice must take precedence over the dynamics of peace in the interests of peace in the long run, lest peace becomes a repressive or retrograde ideology.

While designing a curriculum for peace education for children, following points must be kept in mind about the developmental stages of the children:

The primary school years could focus on laying the value foundations for personality formation and the development of the social skills necessary to live together in harmony. Focus could then shift gradually to a perspective on peace, especially to enable students to understand the value-foundations of peace. The area of special emphasis here is the need to promote skills for the peaceful resolution of conflicts.

In the upper primary years, students could be enabled to view the culture of peace from the perspective of Indian history, philosophy, and culture.

Thereafter, education for peace could focus more on citizenship education. A brief introduction to the basic features and ethos of the Constitution is what is envisaged here. The emphasis may shift, thereafter, to *peace as a lifestyle movement*. Students can be made aware of the need to for lifestyles conducive to the integrity of creation and stability of society. The various challenges to national unity can be the focus thereafter. The main emphasis here must be on promoting an attitude of respect for diversity and difference. Students also need to be made aware of the various hindrances to unity. At the plus two level, the foci of education for peace could be:

* Understanding the logic, modes and expressions of violence;
* Skills for an objective understanding of issues; and
* Developing a global perspective on peace.

In all of this, what stands out is the crucial role that the teacher plays in an approach to education that promotes a culture of peace. The fact that learning has to necessarily be pupil-oriented does not contradict this. Learning can be pupil-oriented only if the teacher facilitates it. It would be naïve to understand the pupil-oriented approach in a way that devalues the role that the teacher plays in the learning process. For education for peace, a great deal depends on the peace-motivation of teachers, especially in the integrated approach. The teacher has to be alert to peace opportunities and creative in appropriating them in respect of the curriculum as a whole. Teachers who are either aggressive or indifferent to the culture of peace, and hence see teaching only as the warehousing of information, may remain blind to the exciting scope that every lesson and every experience in the school offers to promote the cause of peace. The teacher is the best judge when and where to use them.

Conclusion: Schools are potential nurseries for peace: School education involves the formative years in a person's life. The mansion of life is built on the foundation laid at this stage. To educate is to orient. We can orient children either to peace or to its opposite. Not to orient children to peace is to allow them be oriented to violence: subtle or gross. In different parts of the world there is a growing awareness today that propagating a culture of peace through education needs to be deemed a non-negotiable goal of education.

8. PEACE EDUCATION IN MULTI-CULTURAL AND MULTI-ETHNIC SOCIETY

Rashmi Sharma*

"Last night I had the strongest dream; I had ever dreamt; I dreamed the world had all agreed; To put an end to war!" [From an American folk song by Ed Mc Curdy] Today every citizen of the world is having the same dream, but reality is far away from it. In reality each and every nation is building the latest machine so as to make it powerful so that it can maintain peace. But has anyone ever thought that how this war machine can bring peace? They can only endanger the peace.

What we observe today is that the world is divided basically into two groups. These groups are of haves and have-nots, may it be at national or international level. There is a threat to peace, because some countries have nuclear power and some do not have. Those who do not have this power are living in the danger of attack from those powerful nations. How can peace prevail in such conditions? Inside a nation also there are two groups; one who has all the economic power and socially accepted status and the other who does not have any economic stability and social acceptance. This often becomes a threat to internal peace. So the idea comes that economic and social equality is pivotal in bringing about

* Ms. Rashmi Sharma is a HOD at the Gautama Buddha Degree College of Lucknow [UP], India.

peace inside the country. When any group or individual is deprived of their fundamental need or requirement, they become a threat for the society. For example hunger in any form is dangerous for the society, because it shakes the very foundation of our survival. The economic scarcity and social negligence also result in the same.

Conditions for Emergence of Peace: This includes:

- Meeting the basic human needs, such as primary health care and elimination of poverty and unemployment in the society;
- Creating conditions for guaranteeing and enforcing basic rights and freedoms in countries;
- Creating awareness for existing unjust economic relations in the world and to support UN efforts for a new economic social order. [VK Rao and RS Reddy, 2008, P131];
- Creating an understanding of, and respect for the diversity of customs and cultures on both the national and international level; and
- Having respect for other religions in case of multiethnic society.

Unless and until we are able to create basic environment, where our basic demands meet, there will always be threat to peace. Let us take a simple example: if we overlook any small infection or ailment in our body, it results in severe disease, which sometimes becomes a threat to our life. In terms of a country, if we ignore any group or community unattended or do not give the due attention, they are asking for, they can become violent and a threat to peace. The Naxalites in Bihar and the Bodos in Assam of the formation of Telangana are examples of the same theory.

Actually our first problem is to survive. It is not a

question of the survival of the fittest: either we survive together or we perish together. Survival requires that the world must learn to live together in peace. *Learn* is the operative word. [Montreal Declaration, 1960] Now the question arises how we can learn to make peace in the society? What could be the contribution of education? As we all know education since time immemorial has been instrumental in bringing about any change in society at large. In our country there is a long tradition of peaceful co-existence with various communities and ethnic groups. Our culture has always taught us tolerance, respect for other cultures and brotherhood among various communities. It seems that due to the westernization these values subsided and we were deviated from our roots which were strong enough to keep us intact. Today what the whole world realizing is the basic human values, if these values being nurtured through our education system can bring about a positive change in our attitudes and thinking and can lead us to a peaceful co-existence. These basic values can be inculcated through education in the following ways:

Education for Environment: Deeper understanding of the laws of nature and harmonious ways of living with our natural world are part of our structure of peace. As we have seen recently [occurrence of Himalayan tsunami in Uttrakhand] that disturbing the balance of nature can result in natural calamity.

Education for Human Rights: Understanding the three aspect of human rights are very important in this regard: 1-political and civil rights, that were emphasized by western nations, 2- economic and social rights which have been stressed by socialist countries and 3- social justice and development rights which the third world countries have stressed. [VK Rao and RS Reddy, 2008, Page 31]

Education for Disarmament: In this education, facts, role and need for reducing and eliminating arms are explained as a means for conflict resolution. It is to be further explained that damage caused by these weapons and cost of making these weapons can be used for the betterment of the society.

Education for Cultural Understanding: This is educational work directed at the understanding of different cultures of people in our own country and in other countries. The fear, suspicion and distrust among them must be replaced by positive concepts and information.

Education for Equality: Peace begins at home. Gender inequality starts from home. It should be started immediately. The loving, tender, and understanding nature of women must be learnt by all of us.

Education for Feeling and Culture of Peace: Effective education is based on feeling and emotion. Music, poetry, literature, painting, sculpture and all the arts have important role to play. Creating music together or writing songs together can reinforce us at an emotional level. Concepts which are difficult to understand simply through reading or discussion can be easily explained by music and art.

The definition of peace education given by Helena Kekkonen is worth appreciating in this regard. She says that ***"peace education is a process, which gives possibility for people to grow in consciousness of the world's problems, as citizens who work actively on behalf of world-wide positive peace."***

Our goal as peace educators should be to contribute to the creation of culture of peace. We need to construct vision of world without armed struggles. We must engender a reverence for life, a love for life. (VK Rao and RS Reddy, 2008]

Curriculum for Peace Education: The curriculum for peace education must include:

- Cultural programme showing unity in diversity;
- Inter-state college trips;
- Conducting debates on topics of world peace, disarmament, gender-sensitization etc.;
- Imparting education of human right;
- Creating awareness for preservation of natural environment;
- Practice of yoga, meditation etc.; and
- Teaching music and art etc.

In this way we can contribute in the development of the culture of peace in our school system and even beyond it.

Bibliography:

- Rao, VK and Reddy, RS. 1960. *Contemporary conceptions of Education.* New Delhi: Commonwealth Publishers.
- UNESCO. 1960. Montreal Declaration.

9. PEACE AND NON-VIOLENCE: THE MOST POWERFUL WELFARE WEAPON

Aparna Shukla*

The first priority of human being is to establish an

* Dr. Aparna Shukla is an associate professor at the Avadh Girls Degree College of Lucknow [UP], India.

effective system of world law that will assure peace and justice among the citizens of the world. Peace is not just the absence of violence but the manifestation of human compassion. Mankind must put an end to war or war will put an end to mankind. Since war begins in the minds of men, it is in the minds of men that defenses of peace must be constructed.

Unity in Diversity: Fear, suspicion and hatred are fuel which disturbs the peace. Lasting harmony between heterogeneous communities can only come through recognition of the oneness of mankind, a realization that differences which divide us along ethnic and religious lines have no foundation. Just as there are no boundaries drawn on the earth to separate nations, distinction of social, economic, ethnic and religious identities imposed by people are artificial, they have only benefited those with vested interest. On the other hand naturally occurring diverse regions of the planet, or the country such as mountains and plains, each have unique benefits. The diversity created by God has infinite value while distinctions imposed by man have no substance. Within people of each ethnic group or culture lies an important piece of human experience. Each has something to contribute to the larger society.

Consider the flower in a garden: Though differing in kind, color, form and shape, yet this diversity increase their charm, and add to their beauty. A house divided against it cannot stand.

Peace: The Greatest Glory: According to Chinese Philosopher Lao-Tse, ***"If there is to be peace in world, there must be peace in nations, If there is to be peace in the nations, there must be peace in the cities, If there is to be peace in the cities, there must be peace in the***

neighbours, If there is peace between the neighbors, there must be peace in the home, If there is to be peace in the home, there must be peace in the heart."

We all know that peaceful life offers the greatest opportunity for happiness and prosperity. Today there is no greater glory for man than that of service in the cause of Peace. Today we are face with the preeminent fact that if civilization is to survive, we must cultivate the science of human relationships –ability of all people, of all kinds, to live together and to work in the same world, at peace. One is the happiest whether royal or peasant, when one finds peace at home.

Someone has said, ***"Lights of peace become Circles of peace, Circles of peace become Communities of peace, Communities of peace become a peaceful world."*** Faith is greater than any bomb. Faith is the most potent weapon ever devised. We should not lose faith in mankind and in the purposes of the Creator. Our defense is not in armaments, nor in science, nor in going underground. Our defense is in law and order. Science of non-violence alone can lead to pure democracy. The best way to destroy enemy is to make him a friend. At the center of non-violence stands the principal of Love.

Gandhiji's Philosophy of Life: What is the secret of Gandhiji's worldwide fame and unquestioned influence? For one thing his culture has all the traits of what is called the culture of character. He thought closely and seriously, he insisted on seeking fact or truth for one self boldly and clearly and not merely echo it as hear say, he cherished not fashion or expedients of thinking, but true convictions with a strength of feeling which neither the coaxing of friends nor the thrust of opponents could weaken. Throughout his career in whatever continent or country he lived, whether in South Africa, Sabarmati, or elsewhere, he worked with unquestionable conviction, that he would be trusted. It was because he inspired such trust that he proved a determining force in the formation of public opinion. He was essentially a man of action, not of sweet words. He had further, what many others lacked, a constructive faculty. He would not merely denounce other men and other measures; he would show them a way and method better than theirs.

Gandhiji had a philosophy of his own and a way of life steeped in *Sanatana Dharma*, and neither that philosophy nor that way of life to which it lead one, was such as may be dismissed. No wonder so many leaders in Europe and America have been profoundly struck and influenced by his ideas of plain living and high thinking, non-violence even in the face of extreme provocation and a life of service to all.

Gandhiji's Views on Education: According to Mahatma Gandhiji goodness must be clubbed with knowledge. If we are going to bring about peace in the world, we have to begin with the children. Gandhiji's emphasis was not so much on making education a tool for raising the standard of material living, but emphasizing on the life which is rich in human qualities. He said always help others that is never hurt anyone. Surely one can pursue modern education, but along with it, one must learn ancient wisdom. There must be harmonious blend of these two.

According to Gandhiji, ***"A student is one who is acquiring education and one who conducts himself with humility, obedience and discipline."*** Students should keep a watch on their words, actions, thoughts, character and heart.

There must be calm and serene atmosphere in campuses where a number of students pursue their education.

Education should become a stirring call for self awakening, self learning, self motivation and self acceleration at attaining perfection in various endeavors of life. It should bring problem solving and intercultural skills and strategies, for dealing with diverse settings and rapid Change.

Gandhiji said that education given through social activities represent a person's relationship to the world which surrounds them and accumulated human experience. Education should be created collaboratively in work teams, in scientific research laboratories, and through community development. Education should serve ever as a catalyst for activating a democratic culture, promoting national integration, reinforcing social justice, nurturing in students the social skills and outlook to look together in harmony. Student should be taught in such a way that they are able to teach others and guide as team leaders, as community workers, as officials in voluntary organizations. Students should be open to diversity and change. Students should be taught to learn in more than one way, to think in more than one way, to be intelligent in more than one way, so that their intelligence becomes communicative, technical and process oriented. It may be factual, theoretical, applied, emotional, analytical, creative or critical.

Gandhiji emphasized that students should be able to learn and work productively alongside, as well as learn from and with people, whose ways of thinking, being and learning that are different from their own. The students should be able to take many different kinds of raw material in the world [culturally and local specific information], and workout that different interpretative frame work, with in which that information fits, that is, different world views, theories, belief systems-professional cultural, technical and utilize these understandings to do something that works in the world of transfer of understandings.

The concept of transfer of understanding is very important which helps us to strengthen the bond of human relationship. The more powerful is this bond, the more are the chances of unity in diversity and reflection of brotherhood in every individual from home to home, land to land, nation to nation and planet to planet.

Synthesis of Spirituality and Science to Foster Peace: Religion is the greatest of all means for the establishment of order in the world and for a peaceful contentment of all that dwell there in. In this present age, religion must again support all efforts to solve the problems in the most challenging area of human growth. The laws of faith, its scriptures, prayers and meditation all pivot to the basic principal of the oneness of mankind. All the religions have common belief to serve all and to love all.

Science V/S Religion: A Perfect Blending for Human Happiness: Science is the sum totals of some basic principles their theories and derivations, experiences and their applications in various forms. Both Science and Religion aims at the investigation of the truth for promotion of human happiness. Their investigation is one and the same but their scope, approach and methods are different. Einstein has said science without religion is lame and religion without science is blind. The *Bhagavad-Gita* describes three paths to salvation: the path of devotion, the path of work and path of knowledge.

Scientific discoveries are exactly the conclusions of the Vedantic philosophy expressed in the *Upnishads,* the *Puranas* and the *Vedas*. The *Vedantic* truth shows the unification of science and religion. The uncertainty principle, conservation of energy, nature of space, time and matter are the common basis of Science and the *Vedas*.

Modern physics has reached a new height and now cannot be separated from religion. It is connected with metaphysics. According to principle of gravitation bodies attract each other in a particular manner and their centre of gravity is relative. In a similar way, the bodies of universe are held together by a Single force, we may call it the Universal Centre of Gravity, or we can say there is a cosmic centre everywhere with its circumference nowhere. We may call this the *God of Universe*.

Hence, we can says that cosmic laws supports the fact that united we stand and divided we fall, i.e. whole cosmos is attracted to each other with one binding force, so how we as a human can ever think of getting separated from each other and live independently. When the bodies of universe have such a strong cohesion force and this cosmic planet is supporting human life, so how can we think of disturbing the total ecological and cosmic balance by creating any kind of disturbance in human chain i.e. all human are same and we should follow the simple principle of *live and let live.*

Religion uncontrolled by science is likely to lead us into ignorance and superstition. Science unrelieved by Religion is likely to make us rude. In our uphill journey of life, we require a harmonious co-existence of both science and religion. Both science and religion have the same role of helping man to grow and lead a better life and a better entity.

Role of ICT in Non-Violence: In general, information and communication technologies can be used in peace-making efforts in different ways i.e. to provide information, to help people process information, to improve decision making, to reduce scarcity, to support relationships and to help people understand each other. The internet encourages chances of information sharing; mobile technologies such as cell phones can dramatically increase the flow of information. Email discussion and forums can connect communities and encourage ongoing discussion over the internet. With skill facilitator and communication guidelines the internet relay chat can be very effective method to allow groups to anonymously conduct negotiation or discuss sensitive issues.

ICT can be of tremendous help to those who are trying to maintain or form new relationship. The ability to communicate through written words, photos, sound clips and web cameras can keep people connected regardless how apart they are geographically. ICT can help people understand each other and even people of different cultural background can go a long way in reducing conflicts.

While it is true that media and technologies cannot create peace, they can nevertheless contribute to an environment where people can more easily communicate, understand current situations, visualize the implication of their actions and understand each other's point of view. Thus communication can help in peace building efforts.

Conclusion: So let us think of education as the means of developing our greatest abilities, because in each of us there is a hope and dream which when fulfilled can be translated into benefit for everyone and strength for world nation. But peace does not rest in charter and covenants. It lies in the hearts and minds of all people. So let us not rest all our hopes on parchment and on paper, let us strive to build peace, desire for peace, and kindle willingness to work for peace in the hearts and minds of all our people.

Bibliography:

- Aruna, V and Mohanta Priya P. 2011. *Education in the Emerging Indian Society*. Delhi: Manglam Publishers and Distributors.
- htpp: // desicritics.org.
- http: // sivanandaonline.org
- aroj Saxena NR. 2008. *Philosophical and Sociological Foundation of Education.* Meerut: R Lall Book Depot.ignca.nic.in
- Satija, BR. 2003. *Trends in Education.* New Delhi: Anmol Publication Pvt. Ltd.
- sathya.sai.o.tripod.com
- Vil'anilam, JV. 2007. *The Challenges before Higher Education in the Twenty-First Century.* New Delhi:BR Publishing Corporation.
- www.indiatimes.com.
- www.mltanesus.net.
- www.swachid.com.
- www.swaraj.or.
- www.vedanta-atlanta.org/articles/religion.html.

*****

C: Case Studies

1. SOME PEACE EDUCATION INITIATIVES IN DENMARK

John Scales Avery*

The Danish Peace Academy and its enormous website are interesting because they were founded and developed almost single-handedly by one person: Holger Terp, who has for many years been nearly blind as a result of a stroke. A few years ago he also suffered a severe heart attack which required a 5-fold bypass operation. Despite these seemingly insurmountable health problems, Holger works from early morning to late at night in the cause of world peace and international understanding.

Holger Terp completed his education as a librarian in 1992. In 1996, he participated in a course on *Internet and Presentation Technique* at the Academy of Fine Arts in Copenhagen. However, in 1999 he suffered a stroke, which

* Professor John Scales Avery is an internationally known peace activist; he is currently in the Danish Peace Academy, Denmark.

made him blind in one eye and almost blind in the other. The stroke also affected Holger's speech, so that it was difficult to understand him when he talked. Instead of giving up, as many people would have done, Holger resolved to devote the remainder his life to the cause of world peace. Despite his severe handicap, he has achieved almost incredible results, a full account of which can be found on the link: www.fredsakademiet.dk/ht.htm.

Holger's greatest achievement has been to found the Danish Peace Academy and to single-handedly create its enormous website. The website contains more than 79,000 images and files related to peace, in Danish, English and German, and it is currently visited by between 2,000 and 4,000 different people each day. Many of the visitors are from schools and universities in various parts of the world, who use the information on the website as a part of their studies.

In creating his website, Holger has used both his training as a librarian and the knowledge that he gained from the 1996 course at Copenhagen's Academy of Fine Arts. As a result, many parts of the website have great visual beauty because of the liberal use of images. For example, one can enjoy Holger's *Greenham Common Songbook,* which is an account of the successful efforts of the woman's peace movement in England to prevent common land at Greenham from being used as a base for nuclear weapons. The songbook is a piece of history, illustrated not only by the songs, which the visitor to the website can hear performed by such artists as Peggy Seeger, but also by countless beautiful posters and photos from the era. Other special features of the website are numerous books, articles, poetry and song collections, a peace-related encyclopedia, and a timeline showing the history of the peace movement, from the middle ages up to the present.

Holger himself is the author or editor of numerous books, and he has translated Gandhi's autobiography into Danish. The example of Gandhi's life has always been a guide for Holger, and perhaps Holger's life can be a guide for our own efforts, as we strive to work for peace. If he could achieve so much with such a severe handicap, then the rest of us ought to be able to do something too.

Other activities of the Danish Peace Academy include organizing symposia, publication of books, radio programs, and organizing exhibitions, but its main activity continues to be the website.

The Danish National Group of Pugwash Conferences on Science and World Affairs: In March, 1954, the US tested a hydrogen bomb at the Bikini Atoll in the Pacific Ocean. It was 1000 times more powerful than the Hiroshima bomb. The Japanese fishing boat, Lucky Dragon, was 130 kilometers from the Bikini explosion, but radioactive fallout from the test killed one crew member and made all the others seriously ill. Concerned about the effects of a large-scale war fought with such bombs, or even larger ones, Albert Einstein and Bertrand Russell published a manifesto containing the words, ***"Here then is the problem that we present to you, stark and dreadful and inescapable: Shall we put an end to the human race, or shall mankind renounce war? There lies before us, if we choose continual progress in happiness, knowledge and wisdom. Shall we, instead, choose death because we cannot forget our quarrels? We appeal as human beings to human beings: Remember your humanity, and forget the rest. If you can do so, the way lies open to a new Paradise; if you cannot, there lies before you the risk of universal death."***

The Russell-Einstein Manifesto called for a meeting of scientists from both sides of the Cold War to try to minimize the danger of a thermonuclear conflict. The first meeting took place in 1957 at the summer home of the Canadian philanthropist Cyrus Eaton at the small village of Pugwash, Nova Scotia. From this small beginning, a series of conferences developed, in which scientists, especially physicists, attempted to work for peace, and tried to address urgent problems related to science. These conferences were called Pugwash Conferences on Science and World Affairs, taking their name from the small village in Nova Scotia where the first meeting was held. From the start, the main aim of the meetings was to reduce the danger that civilization would be destroyed in a thermonuclear war.

Many countries have local Pugwash groups, and the Danish National Pugwash Group is one of these. Our activities include conferences at the Danish Parliament, aimed at influencing decision-makers, but other activities are aimed influencing public opinion. Peace education activities include the award of student peace prizes on United Nations Day.

United Nations Day Student Peace Prizes: In collaboration with the Danish Peace Academy, and with the help of the Hermod Lannung Foundation the Danish National Group of Pugwash Conferences on Science and World Affairs has offered prizes each year to students at 10 Danish gymnasiums for projects related to global problems and their solutions and to the United Nations.

These projects were essays, dramatic sketches, videos, websites, posters, etc., and they were judged on the UN Day, before large audiences of students. The background for this project is as follows: In 2007, in collaboration with the Danish

Pugwash Group several other NGO's, we arranged a visit to Copenhagen by Dr. Tadatoshi Akiba, the Mayor of Hiroshima. In connection with his visit, we arranged a Peace Education Conference at the University of Copenhagen.

In connection with Dr. Akiba's visit, we also arranged a day of peace education at Copenhagen's Open Gymnasium. About 15 people from various branches of Denmark's peace movement arrived at the gymnasium at 7.00 a.m., and between 8.00 and 10.00 they talked to 15 groups of about 25-50 students about topics related to peace. At 10.30, all 500 students assembled in a large hall, where Dr. Akiba gave an address on abolition of nuclear weapons. A chorus from the gymnasium sang, and finally there was a panel discussion.

The students were extremely enthusiastic about the whole program. The success of our 2007 effort made us want to do something similar in 2008, and perhaps to broaden the scope. Therefore we wrote to the Minister of Education, and proposed that October 24, United Nations Day, should be a theme day in all Danish schools and gymnasiums, a day devoted to the discussion of global problems and their solutions. We received the very kind reply. The Minister said that he thought our idea was a good one, but that he did not have the power to dictate the curricula to schools. We needed to contact the individual schools, gymnasiums and municipalities.

In the autumn of 2008 we arranged a United Nations Day program on October 24 at Sankt Annæ Gymnasium with the co-operation of Nørre Gymnasium. We offered prizes to drama students at the two gymnasiums for the best peace-related dramatic sketch, a condition being that the sketches should be performed and judged before a large audience. Our judges were the famous actress Mia Luhne, Johan Olsen, the lead singer of a popular rock group, and the dramatist Steen Haakon Hansen. The students' sketches and the judges' speeches about the meaning of peace were very strong and moving. Everyone was very enthusiastic about the day. The judges have said that they would be willing to work with us again on peace-related cultural events.

Our successes in 2007 and 2008 have made us wish to continue and possibly expand the idea of making United Nations Day a theme day in Danish schools and gymnasiums - a day for the discussion of global problems and their solutions, with special emphasis on the role of the United Nations. The Hermod Lannung Foundation supported our project for extending this idea to 10 Danish gymnasiums in 2010, 2011 and 2012.

The Hermod Lannung Foundation has generously awarded us funds to continue the project in 2013. The Danish United Nations Association worked with us on this project in 2011, and we hope that they will help us to expand it in the future, with additional funding from the Ministry of Education.

The Gruntvigian Peoples' Colleges: A unique feature of the Danish educational system is the adult education that is available at about a hundred Folkehøjskole [Peoples' High Schools]. This tradition of adult education dates back to the Danish poet-bishop NFS Grundtvig [1783-1872]. Besides writing more than half of the hymns presently used in Danish churches, Grundtvig also introduced farmers' co-operatives into Denmark and founded a system of adult education.

At the time when Grundtvig lived, the Industrial Revolution had already transformed England into a country that exported manufactured goods but was unable to feed itself because of its large population. In this situation, Denmark began a prosperous trade, exporting high quality agricultural produce to England [for example dairy products, bacon, and so on]. Grundtvig realized that that it would be to the advantage of small-scale Danish farmers to process and export these products themselves, thus avoiding losing a part of their profits to large land-owners or other middlemen who might do the processing and exporting for them. He organized the small farmers into co-operatives, and in order to give the farmers enough knowledge and confidence to run the co-operatives, Grundtvig created a system of adult education: the Peoples' Colleges. The co-operatives and the adult education system contributed strongly to making Denmark a prosperous and democratic country.

Of the hundred or so Grundtvigian Peoples' Colleges exiting today, about forty offer peace education as a subject. An example of such a peace education course was the two-week summer school *Towards a Non-violent Society,* held at the International College in Elsinore during the summer of 1985. Since it was supported not only by the students' fees but also by a government subsidy, the summer school was able to pay the travel and living expenses for lecturers who came from many parts of the world.

Among the stars of the summer school were former US Governor Harold Stassen, the only living person who had signed the UN Charter; the famous Cambridge University Ethnologist, Professor Robert Hinde, Professor Suman Khanna from India, an expert on non-violence and Gandhi; Sister George, a Catholic nun from Jerusalem, who spoke 12 languages during the course of her daily work and who was an expert on the conflicts of the Middle East; and Meta Ditzel, a member of the Danish Parliament who advocated legislation to make excessively violent videos less easily available to children. Other lectures were given by representatives of Amnesty International and the Center for Rehabilitation of Torture Victims.

Since the summer school took place outside the regular term, all of the rooms at the International College were available, and students came not only from Denmark, but also from other parts of Scandinavia and Europe. Part of the summer tradition of the Grundvigian High Schools is that students of all ages pay the modest fees in order to have an intellectually stimulating vacation, during the course of which they will form new friendships. Thus the summer school had a social function as well as a pedagogical one. Accordingly, Suman Khanna taught a yoga class as well as a class on the Gandhian tradition of non-violence.

In order to illustrate how horrible excessively violent videos can be, the Danish Parliamentarian Meta Ditzel was scheduled to show one of the worst videos of this type to the group. She went to a video shop and asked for the worst one available, saying that it was needed as part of her campaign to make violent videos illegal. The owner of the shop, realizing that his livelihood was being threatened, gave her the most innocent film that he could find, and the horrible example later that evening turned out to be less than horrifying. [Meta Ditzel had not previewed it]

Ethics for Science and Engineering Students: The summer school *Towards a Non-violent Society,* which I helped to plan, had an interesting consequence, which affected my activities in the peace movement: One of the other people involved in organizing the summer school urged me to enter an essay contest sponsored by the Nuclear Age Peace Foundation. The contest called for essays on how to give scientists and engineers a sense of social responsibility. Following my friend's suggestion, I wrote an essay saying that universities ought to offer courses on the history and social impact of science. As the course reached modern times, it would be natural to introduce a discussion of the ethical, social and political problems created by the extremely rapid development of science and technology.

My essay did not win the contest, but the friend who asked me to write it was so pleased with what I had written that he translated it into Danish and submitted it to *Politiken,* one of the major Danish newspapers. When it was published, students from the University of Copenhagen, where I was teaching, came to me and said, ***"Well, if you really believe what you have written, you have to make such a course!"*** As the result of their urging I planned a course entitled, *Science, Ethics and Politics,* but I had great difficulties in getting the studies committee to accept it as part of the curriculum. They apparently thought that science, ethics and politics were three entirely separate things, which ought not to have anything to do with each other.

Finally the course was accepted under the condition that neither I nor any of the students who attended the course should get any credit for it. However, it was a great success. Later, the name was changed to *Science and Society,* and the students were finally given credit for attending the course. Meanwhile, the President of the University of Copenhagen heard about the course, and he kept sending me encouraging notes. One day he called me on the telephone, and said that since he knew that I was interested in global problems related to the rapid development of science and technology, he wondered whether I would like to be the Contact Person for Denmark for the Pugwash Conferences on Science and World

Affairs. They had asked him to do this job, but he was too busy with his work as President. Since he was my boss, I had to say yes.

I continued to give the *Science and Society* course until my retirement in 2003. Meanwhile, at the Niels Bohr Institute and at the Royal Agricultural College, similar courses were started. Finally, all of us who were involved in these courses wrote to the Minister of Education and proposed that such courses ought to be compulsory for all science and engineering students in Denmark. The Minister called together the Heads of the Danish Institutions of Higher Education and put the question to them. They accepted the idea, but it could not be put into practice immediately because there were not enough people qualified to give the courses.

A programme was started by Professor Claus Emmeche of the Niels Bohr Institute to train people to teach the new courses. Finally, everything was ready, and starting in the autumn of 2004, all Danish science and engineering students at the university level have been required to take a course on the philosophy of science and its ethical aspects. The curriculum covers the history of science and technology, emphasizing cases where technology has produced socially harmful results as well as cases where the results have been beneficial. Global problems related to science are also being a part of the curriculum.

Peace Education in Danish Elementary Schools: A book entitled *Et barn har brug for fred!* [A Child Needs Peace!] by Nils Hartmann of the Danish UNICEF Committee provides a good example of peace education at the elementary level. Here are rough translations of a few of the paragraphs of Nils Hartmann's book, ***"Peace and solidarity: A more just division***

of the resources of the world requires that we, in our part of the world, feel more solidarity with people in the less developed countries. In other words we must feel that we have much in common with them. People who feel solidarity with each other don't fight. They are friends. Solidarity means more than just making sacrifices for each other. If we only give others things we have too much of, something is missing. True solidarity also means that we must have respect for each other - respect for each other's culture, actions, religions and life. When we respect each other, we are also open towards each other. We need each other and learn from each other.

"Peace and fundamental needs: When people's fundamental needs are satisfied, they are able to feel secure, and the reasons for war and conflicts disappear. But it is important that every person satisfies this fundamental need in a way that doesn't harm or exploit others.

"1. If I buy a weapon in order to feel safer, there will be others who feel threatened;

"2. If I exploit others in order to satisfy my own needs, there will be dissatisfaction and conflicts.

"3. If I use more food than I need, others will go hungry.

"4. If I dig a well and claim all the water for myself, others will go thirsty.

"5. If I buy unnecessary things, others will go without necessities."

Further, *"Education for Peace: What can we get for the money that is wasted on armaments? In 1985 the world used about 8,000 billion (8,000,000,000,000) kroner4 for military purposes. In other words, half a billion kroner*

are being wasted while this lesson is going on. Here are a few examples of things we could have bought for a fraction of that amount of money:

"Health: Almost everywhere in the world there is a lack of doctors, nurses and hospitals. This is especially true in the poorest country districts and slums of developing countries. A large number of children in these countries need to be vaccinated against some of the illnesses that are already eliminated from our part of the world. Measels, whooping cough, diphtheria, polio, tuberculosis and lockjaw cost the lives of millions of children each year. Also, many children need to come to a health clinic to get medicine and vitamins. Building up even a very basic health system would do wonders. The cost of a basic health system for the whole world is estimated to be 17 billion kroner per year.

"Safe drinking water: More than 2 billion people have no way of getting safe water. Impure water and lack of water lead to many diseases. Today, diarrhea is the most common cause of death for small children in the developing countries. The United Nations has declared the period 1981-1990 to be the International Water Decade. The United Nations has calculated that by using a total of 50 billion kroner, it would be possible to give pure drinking water to all the people of the world.

"Education: In developing countries, less than half of the adults have more than a year of schooling. Education is the best investment that we can make if we want to modernize a society and to create positive development. Building schools for all of the developing countries, educating teachers, and producing teaching materials

would cost 55 billion kroner. [Eight Danish kroner = one US dollar]"

These paragraphs from Nils Hartmann's book are illustrated with photographs of children from the developing countries. The paragraphs are written in simple language, and the examples used are related to the needs of children.

Denmark has for many years had an educational policy that aims at teaching children co-operative attitudes and habits rather than purely competitive ones. This system makes use of projects in which several children co-operate rather than individual projects. The use of co-operative projects in the Danish educational system can be thought of as an indirect form of peace education. Even at the university level, the Danish educational system makes much more use of co-operative projects than is the case in most other countries.

Alternative media in Denmark: Modern power holders are acutely aware of the importance of propaganda. Thus the media are a battleground where reformers struggle for attention, but are defeated with great regularity by the wealth and power of the establishment. This is a tragedy because today there is an urgent need to make public opinion aware of the serious problems facing civilization, and the steps that are needed to solve these problems. The mass media could potentially be a great force for public education, but in general their role is not only unhelpful - it is often negative. War and conflict are blatantly approved of by television and newspapers.

Today we are faced with the task of creating a new global ethic in which loyalty to family, religion and nation will be supplemented by a higher loyalty to humanity as a whole. In case of conflicts, loyalty to humanity as a whole must take precedence. In addition, our present culture of violence must be replaced by a culture of peace.

How do the media fulfill this life-or-death responsibility? Do they give us insight? No, they give us pop music. Do they give us an understanding of the sweep of evolution and history? No, they give us sport. Do they give us an understanding of need for strengthening the United Nations, and the ways that it could be strengthened? No, they give us soap operas. Do they give us unbiased news? No, they give us news that has been edited to conform with the interests of the military-industrial complex and other powerful lobbies. Do they present us with the need for a just system of international law that acts on individuals? On the whole, the subject is neglected. Do they tell of the essentially genocidal nature of nuclear weapons, and the need for their complete abolition? No, they give us programs about gardening and making food.

In general, the mass media behave as though their role is to prevent the peoples of the world from joining hands and working to change the world and to save it from thermonuclear and environmental catastrophes. The television viewer sits slumped in a chair, passive, isolated, disempowered and stupefied. The future of the world hangs in the balance, the fate of children and grandchildren hang in the balance, but the television viewer feels no impulse to work actively to change the world or to save it. The Roman emperors gave their people bread and circuses to numb them into political inactivity. The modern mass media seem to be playing a similar role.

Since today's power holders completely control the mass media, workers for peace must create alternative media. In Denmark, several people have been active in this field. Holger Terp's Danish Peace Academy website can be thought of as an important alternative medium for peace education Holger has also produced a series of radio programs devoted to the history of peace songs.

Another important worker for peace education via alternative radio programs is Arne Hansen. He also maintains a website, where recordings of his radio programs can be accessed. In addition, Arne has an Internet newsletter with a large readership, which calls attention to his radio broadcasts, and to other matters of interest to the peace movement.

Troels Peter Schmidt and his wife Nina Larsen produce an extremely valuable alternative television station called *TV Gaderummet* [TV Streetspace]. Although they are only able to broadcast their programs at times when not many viewers can see them, the broadcasts have a large impact because they are available on YouTube. Troels uses his Internet mailing list to call his programs to the attention of people who might be interested in them.

These are a few examples of peace education initiatives in Denmark. It is my great hope that some of the techniques described above will be useful for peace education in other countries also.

Suggestions for Further Reading:

- Aldridge, R and J. Aldridge, 1989. *Children and Nonviolence.* Pasadena, CA : Hope Publishing House.
- American Friends Service Committee. 1999. *Trading Books for Soldiers: The True Cost of JROTC, AFSC National Youth and Militarism Program.* AFSC: Philadelphia PA.
- Amnesty International. 1999. *In the Firing Line: War and Children's Rights.* London, UK: AI.
- Barash, DP. 1999. *Approaches to Peace: A Reader in Peace Studies.* New York: Oxford University Press.

- Barash, DP. 1991. *Introduction to Peace Studies*. Belmont, CA: Wadsworth Publications.
- Benoit E and Boulding, KE. 1978. *Disarmament and the Economy*. Westport CT: Greenwood Press.
- Education for Peace
- Bischak, GA. 1991. *Towards a Peace Economy in the United States: Essays on Military Industry, Disarmament and Economic Conversion*. New York: St. Martin's Press.
- Bisch, PM. 1995. *Culture of Democracy: A Challenge for Schools*. Geneva: UNESCO-IBE.
- Boulding, E [Ed.]. 1992. *New Agendas for Peace Research: Conflict and Security Reexamined*. Boulder, CO : Lynne Rienner Pubs.
- Boulding, E. 2000. *Cultures of Peace: The Hidden Side of History*. NY: Syracuse University Press.
- Boulding, K. 1972. *Economics of Peace*. Salem, NH: Ayer Co. Pubs.
- Boulding, K. 1975. *Peace and the War Industry*. New Brunswick, NJ: Transaction Books.
- Bridgeman, DL [Ed.]. 1983. *The Nature of Prosocial Behavior*. New York: Academic Press.
- British Atlantic Committee. 1983. *Peace and Conflict Studies: A Syllabus in Peace Studies*. London: BAC.
- Brock-Utne, B. 1985. *Educating for Peace: A Feminist Perspective*. New York: Teachers College Press.
- Brock-Utne, B. Feminist. 1989. *Perspectives on Peace and Peace Education*. New York: Elsevier.
- Chandy, AKK. 1992. *Peace Culture Amidst Power Conflicts*. Kerala, India: FOR.
- Connell, JO and Curle, A. 1987. *Peace with Work to Do: The Academic Study of Peace*. New York: St. Martin's Press.
- Dasgupta, S. 1984. *Philosophical Assumptions for Training in Non-Violence*. Ahmedabad: Gujarat Vidyapith.
- Ehrlich, R [Ed.]. 1987. *Perspectives on Nuclear War and Peace Education*. Westport, CT: Greenwood Press.
- Esenberg, N [Ed.]. 1982. *The Development of Pro-Social Behaviour*. New York: Academic Press.
- *Essays in Peace Studies*. 1987. Brookfield, VT: Dartmouth Pub.
- Fairbairnes, Z. 1974. *Study War No More: Military Involvement in British Universities and Colleges, Campaign for Nuclear Disarmament*. London.

- Fedoseyev, PN. 1987. *Peace and Disarmament: Academic Studies.* Chicago, IL: Imported Pubs.
- Feller, G et al [Eds.]. 1981. *Peace and World Order Studies: A Curriculum Guide.* New York: World Policy.
- Ford, BR. 1997. *Educating for Peace: Curriculum with a Global Perspective: Pre-Kindergarten, Kindergarten, and Early Elementary Grade.* Grand Rapids, MI: Inst. for Global Education.
- Five College Program in Peace and World Security Studies. 1997. *A Guide to Careers, Internships and Graduate Education in Peace Studies*, Amherst, MA: PAWSS, Hampshire College.
- Gordon, H and Grob, L [Eds.]. 1987. *Education for Peace: Testimonies from the World's Religions.*, Maryknoll, NY: Orbis Books.
- Goodenough, WH. 1963. *Cooperation and Change: An Anthropological Approach to Community Development.* New York: Russell Sage Foundation.
- Hartmann, N. 1986. *Et barn har brug for fred!* Denmark: Danish UNICEF Committee.
- Haavelsrud, M. 1976. *Education for Peace, Science and Technology Press.* GB: Guilford, Surrey.
- Harris, IM. 1994. *Peace Education.* Jefferson, NC: McFarland and Co.
- Harle, 31. V. Harle, Essays in Peace Studies, Dartmouth Pub., Brookfield, VT, (1987).
- Heater, D. 1984. *Peace Through Education: The Contribution of the Council for Education in World Citizenship.* PA, Philadelphia: Taylor and Francis.
- Hicks, D. 1988. *Education for Peace: What Does It Mean*? Lancaster, England: Centre for Peace Studies.
- Hicks, D [Ed.]. 1988. *Education for Peace: Issues, Principles and Practices in the Classroom.* Routledge, Boston: MA.
- Hinde, RA and Parry, DA [Eds.]. 1989. *Education for Peace.* Philadelphia, PA: Spokesman Books.
- Hovey MW and Gordon, GC. 1989. *ROTC and Catholic Higher Education.* Charlestown, MA: The Center on Conscience and War.
- Jacobs IT and DeBoer JJ [Eds.]. 1940. *Educating for Peace: A Report of the Committee on International Relations of the National Council of Teachers of English.* New York: D. Appleton-Century Co.
- Jampolsky, GG et al [Eds.]. 1982. *Children as Teachers of Peace* .Milbrae, CA: Celestial Arts Pub.

- Janke RA and Petersen, JP. 1995. *Peacemakers ABC's for Young Children: A Guide for Teaching Conflict Resolution with a Peace Table*. C St. Croix, MN: Growing Committee for Peace.
- Keefe, T and Roberts, RE. 1991. *Realizing Peace. An Introduction to Peace Studies*. Ames, IA: Iowa State Univ. Press.
- Klare, MT [Ed.]. 1994. *Peace and World Security Studies: A Curriculum Guide*. Boulder, CO; Lynne Rienner Pub.
- Kreidler, WJ and L. Furlong. 1995. *Adventures in Peacemaking: A Conflict Resolution Guide for School-Age Programs*. Cambridge, MA: Educators for Social Responsibility.
- Kreidler, WJ. 1994. *Conflict Resolution in the Middle School, Educators for Social Responsibility*. MA: Cambridge, MA.
- Kreidler, WJ. 1990. *Teaching Concepts of Peace and Conflict, Educators for Social Responsibility*, in the Elementary Perspectives No. 1. MA: Cambridge.
- Kreidler, WJ. 1994. *Teaching Conflict Resolution through Children's' Literature*. New York: Scholastic Press.
- Kung, H. 1992. *Global Responsibility: In Search of a New World Ethic*. New York: Coninuum Press.
- Larsen, ON [Ed.]. 1968. *Violence and the Mass Media*, UK: Harper and Row.
- Lasley, TJ. 1994. *Teaching Peace: Toward Cultural Selflessness*. Westport, CT: Birgim and Garvey Pub.
- Lawler, PA. 1995. *Question of Values*. Boulder CO: Johan Galtung's Peace Research, Lynne Rienner.
- Levin, DV. 1994. *Teaching Young Children in Violent Times: Building a Peaceable Classroom*. Cambridge, MA: Educators for Social Responsibility.
- Liebert RM et al. 1982. *The Early Window: The Effects of Television on Children and Youth*. Elmsford, NY: Pergamon.
- Lopez, GA. 1989. *Peace Studies: Past and Future*. Beverly Hills, CA: Sage Pubs.
- Macauley JR and Berkowitz, L. 1970. *Altruism and Helping Behavior*. New York: Academic Press.
- Maddava, KA. 1994. *Peace Studies: Towards a Transformative Process*. Dekalb, IL: LEPS Press.
- Manniche, P. 1939. *Living Democracy in Denmark*. Copenhagen: Gad.
- McGinnis, J et al. 1985. *A Manuel for Teachers* [3 Volumes]. St. Louis, MO: Inst. for Peace and Justice.

- McGinnis, J. et al.. 1985. *Educating for Peace and Justice* [3 Volumes]. St. Louis, MO: Inst. For Peace and Justice.
- Møller JC and K. 1944. *Watson, Education in Democracy: The Folk High Schools of Denmark.* London: Faber.
- National Council of Women of Great Britain. 1983. *Educating People for Peace*. London: NCWGB.
- Noble, G. 1975. *Children in Front of the Small Screen*. London: Constable.
- Reardon, B. 1988. *Comprehensive Peace Education: Educating for Social Responsibility*. New York: Teachers College Press.
- Reardon, B [Ed.]. 1987. *Educating for Global Responsibility. Teacher Designed Curricula for Peace Education*. New York: Teachers College Press.
- Reardon B and Nordland, EN [Eds.]. 1994. *Learning Peace: The Promise of Ecological and Cooperative Education*. Albany, New York: SUNY Press..
- Rorodam, T. 1965. *The Danish Folk High Schools*. Copenhagen: Det Danske Selskab.
- Reys, BF. 1977. *Education for World Peace*. Amer., Ojai, CA: World Univ.
- Schramm, W [Ed.]. 1973. *Grundfragen der Kommunikationsforschung*. Munich: PNK.
- Schneider, SJ Das. 1980. *Gesch ft mit dem Verbrechen. Massenmedien und a Kriminalit t, Kinddler*. Munich:NPNA.
- Singer JL and Singer DG. 1981. *Television, Imagination and Aggression: A Study of Preschoolers*. Hillsdale: Erlbaum.
- Skornia, HJ. 1965. *Television and Society*. New York: McGraw-Hill.
- Smoker P et al [Eds.]. 1990. *A Reader in Peace Studies*. New York: Pergamon Press.
- Stomfay-Stitz, A. 1993. *Peace Education in America, 1828-1990: Sourcebook or Education and Research*. Lexington, MA: Scarecrow Press.
- UNESCO-IBE. 1995. *International Conference on Education, 44th Session* [in Geneva, 3-8 October, 1994]. UNESCO-IBE, Geneva: Final Report.
- UNESCO-IBE. 1994. *Situation of Education for International Understanding* [in the International Conference on Education, 44th Session, Geneva, 3-8 October, 1994]. Geneva: UNESCO-IBE.
- UNESCO. 1978. *Peace Research Trend Report and World Directory*. Paris: UNESCO.

- UNESCO. 1990. *Yearbook on Peace and Conflict Studies*. Westport, CT: Greenwood Press.
- UNESCO. 1988. *World Directory of Peace Research and Training Institutions*. Herndon, VA: Berg Pubs.
- Universitetsforlaget. 1964-20-13. *Journal of Peace Research, periodical*. Oslo, Norway: Universitetsforlaget.
- University Conversion Project. 1991-2013. *Study War No More, Periodical*. Cambridge, MA: UCP/War Research Information Service.
- Wallensteen, P [Ed.]. 1988. *Peace Research: Achievements and Challenges*. Boulder, CO: Westview.
- Wein, B [Ed.]. 1985. *Peace and World Order Studies: A Curriculum Guide*. New York: World Policy, United Nations.
- White, AG. 1989. *Educating for Peace: A Selected Bibliography*. Monticello, IL: Vance Bibliographies.
- Wichert, S. 1989. *Keeping the Peace: Practicing Cooperation and Conflict Resolution with Preschoolers*. Philadelphia, PA: New Society Pubs.

2. HEALING OUR WOUNDED HUMANITY THROUGH EDUCATION FOR PEACE AND NON-VIOLENCE: THE AFRICAN EXPERIENCE

Jude Thaddeus Langeh Basebang*

In Gandhi's time, India and many African nations were stuck under the yoke of a, thieving, enslaving and despicable

---

* Fr. Jude Thaddeus Langeh Basebang is the secretary of the CM in Cameroon, Africa.

racist colonialism; a pathetically preposterous aberration of human nature that the Mahatma decided to bring to an end. Looking at the world in general, it is still clear that it is still in the hands of its same Colonial Powers now referring to them as the *International Community of Nations,* or until recently that paragon of virtue *–The Free World.* These so-called *Great World Powers* claiming to be examples of democracy for the rest of us, practiced their democracy during the bestial colonisation of the ancient cultures of mankind's heritage, remain the perpetrators of thousands of crimes against humanity in a world investors have made into commodities to buy, sell or destroy. Our humanity thus is in a vicious circle of wounds seeking healing.

On the one hand therefore we can identify violence coming from others being inflicted on other nations. But on the other hand there is violence from within as shown in the situation of so many African countries. From within Africa, there are also many problems. Africa is spoken of in our contemporary era only in pessimistic terms as a land of misfortunes, wars, despotisms, corruption, etc. These problems are not only peculiar to Africa. I am sure too that the problems in India like the recent cases of gang rape, murder and kidnapping do not come from outside. These are internal problems.

Today more than ever, around the world, the bright future depends on peace education as a panacea to embrace total non-violence as Gandhi did. On this note, some proposals will be given on how his theories have been successful in bringing peace and how this peace can come through education. It is our aim therefore to heal a wounded humanity through education for peace and non-violence.

Africa in the spiral of violence[1]**:** When looking at the modern world, one still sees flood of blood. We are in a modernity where ***"murder, massacre, extermination, world wars, the unimaginable absurdity of the Shoah, the Genocide of the Tutsis in Rwanda give the measure of the world's inhumanity"***[2]. Ela Gandhi in a keynote address opined that, ***"Violence is a spiral...Non-violence provides lasting solutions...If you tackle the same issues on a non-violent basis, you stop the violence"***[3]. Seeing the almost unending concatenation of violent events and stories in the African continent, one tends to agree with Ela. Africa has a tragic history of suffering in many ramifications.

Africa is not only in a spiral of violence, but in a descending spiral as Martin Luther King Jr would have it:

"The ultimate weakness of violence is that it is a descending spiral, begetting the very thing it seeks to destroy. Instead of diminishing evil, it multiplies it. Through violence you may murder the liar, but you cannot murder the lie, nor establish the truth. Through violence you may murder the hater, but you do not murder hate. In fact, violence merely increases hate. So it goes. Returning violence for violence multiplies violence, adding deeper darkness to a night already devoid of stars. Darkness cannot drive out darkness; only light can do that. Hate cannot drive out hate: only love can do that"[4]

This view of MLK goes a long way to make one reflect on some concrete situations of in Africa as shown below.

A. The Savagery of Political Instability: The political instability caused by poor regime performance in many African countries engenders the widespread of war and violence. It is no longer new to hear that in the post-colonial landscape in Africa, political instability has been an enduring feature. Violence reveals itself in the form of wars [like in Congo DR, Angola, Burundi, Rwanda, Sierra Leone, Liberia, Sudan, Cote d'Ivoire, Mali, Egypt, just to mention a few], ritual killings, injustices, rigging of elections etc. Such violence in Africa seems to come in most cases from rulers who terrorise their citizens. Such leaders terrorise their people with arbitrary laws.... Those who succeeded them have invariably had to resolve to the case of force.[5] It is easier to project the above litany of woes to the so-called *Great World Powers* as the cause of the spiral violence. While not totally against this assertion, it is worthwhile noting that most of our violence comes from within Africa as is the case of ritual killing.

B. The Saga of Ritual Killing: Many African nations are facing what we can call the *Paradox of Twenty-First Century Savagery.* There is a widespread venom of kidnapping and ritual killing currently going on in many African Nations like Nigeria, Cameroon and Ghana[6]. The last two nations will serve as example.

The International Television Network, Al-Jazeera, broadcasted to the global audience a video footage of ritual killings of disabled Ghanaian children accused of being possessed by evil spirits. These killings were uncovered mid last year by Anas Aremeyaw Anas, a Ghanaian journalist. The latter revealed this to the Daily Guide Newspaper in Ghana that ***"Thousands of such children have been killed in Ghana because the communities they were born into believe they are evil spirits and many more continue to get killed on the quiet and the fact that I have gone undercover to cause the arrest of a handful of such killers does not mean the practice has ceased."***[7] Thank God those local leaders in northern Ghana have announced the abolition of the ritual killing of babies born with physical disabilities, who were believed to have been possessed by evil spirits.[8]

The events in Yaoundé the capital of Cameroon at the end of the year 2012 and the beginning of the year 2013 spread fear among the citizens. The men of the underworld wrecked the city with series of rape, sodomy and worst still weird killings. These took the form of ritual killings because the cadavers were discovered with vital organs missing. These are not new happenings in Yaoundé but it has taken a very high tenor that one can no longer ignore. Many corpses were recently discovered on the streets of a quarter known as Mimbomanand the bodies are mutilated before they are dumped on the street. This phenomenon is noticeable at night because most people are afraid of going out of the house after 6pm. The case of Rwanda in the African Continent tickles our fancy in a very special way.

C. Genocide of Rwanda: Violence in its Barbaric and Inhuman Summit: In Rwanda, violence reached its peak point in 1994 when two social groups of brothers – Hutu and Tutsi ethnic groups were strongly convinced that they could not share the same terrain. In the approximately 100 days that followed[9], an estimated 500,000 to 1 million Rwandans, mainly Tutsi, were killed. God was relegated from their conscience and they stopped being real brothers. As a result, one of the greatest genocides of our time occurred. This country has attracted the regards of the whole world because violence reached its barbaric and inhuman summit. This genocide was ***"Conceived, thought, pacified, orchestrated and methodologically realised by a part of the population that decided to have recourse to ethnical extermination as a final solution to solve the global contradictions and antagonisms of a society."***[10]

This violence therefore is *of the first order* because it was thought of, constructed and executed by those who thought their culture was superior to that of others. ***"This cultural superiority was founded on an ideological system weaved by stories which attached the Tutsi to the divine sphere and confined the Hutu to a sub-human level."***[11] Jay Janson, would not mince words to blame the US and the international community[12] for their passivity:

Although the Clinton Administration and the international community were aware of the genocide taking place in Rwanda, no action was undertaken. By the end of July, nearly two million of Hutus fled the country for safety, spawning the growth of refugee camps in neighboring countries. As thousands of people died of disease and starvation in these refugee camps, Clinton ordered airdrops of food and supplies for the Hutu refugees, including known genocidaires. In July, he sent 200 non-combatant troops to the Rwanda capital of Kigali to manage the airport and distribute relief supplies. These troops were subsequently withdrawn by October 1994. Clinton and the United Nations faced criticism for their non-response to the genocide. When Clinton traveled to Africa in 1998, he said that the international community, presumably including the US, must accept responsibility for the failure to respond to the massacres. When speaking about the Rwanda Crisis, Clinton called it his worst failure, admitting ***"I blew it."***[13]

There is no gainsaying the fact that the barbaric genocide fuelled by the tribal tendencies of the Tutsis and the Hutus and partly supported by the so-called world powers have left unhealed scars. Efforts are being made to rebuild the country through peace education[14]. Let us pray for Rwanda especially during this period of the reconstruction of the country.

Many citizens in African countries have started

appreciating the philosophy of non-violence. It is not by chance but by conscious choice that non-violence, peace and education are being preferred to violence. On this note thus, education to peace and non-violence remain the greatest panacea.

2. The Urgency of Peace Education as a Panacea: Jill Strauss[15] will insist that ***"if we want people to behave less violently, we have to teach the knowledge, skills and attitudes of non-violence."***[16]

The Fourteenth Dalai Lama, Tenzin Gyatso in the same vein will opine that ***"Peace must first be developed [through education] within an individual. And I believe that love, compassion and altruism are the fundamental basis for peace. Once these qualities are developed within and individual, he or she is then able to create an atmosphere of peace and harmony. This atmosphere can be expanded and extended from the individual to his family, from the family to the community and eventually to the whole world.***[17]

Peace education must be understood as a dynamic all round concept. Bella Das would see it as education that is directed to the full development of human personality and to the strengthening of respect for human rights and the fundamental freedoms. It promotes understanding, tolerance and friendship among all nations, racial or religious groups.[18] It is in this light that Gandhi comes in as a great catalyst.

A. Gandhi, A great Catalyst for Peace and Non-violent Education: Education for Gandhi does not mean *de-indianising* oneself or moving one away from one's culture. The school for him must be the extension of the home while local languages must be preferred to other foreign languages. Studying in these foreign languages is as good as the betrayal of our duty towards our mothers. The harm done by this alien type of education does not stop here; it goes much further.

It has produced a gulf between the educated classes and the masses. Gandhi insists, ***"All these are for me – signs of our slavery and degradation...The sooner, therefore, educated India shakes itself free from the hypnotic spell of the foreign medium, the better it would be for them and the people."***[19] I can imagine how many Indians and Africans feel higher than others because they speak foreign languages, while looking down on those who speak the national languages.His concept of Education is based on an all-round development of human personality that includes physical development, intellectual development and spiritual development.[20] A closer look on the concept of education expounds Gandhi's thoughts better.

Ravindra Kumar beautifully moves from the etymology[21] of education and of peace to identify a very important concept in Socrates and Plato which Gandhi will latter on put into practice: Education as drawing out. ***"By education,"*** Gandhi says ***"I mean an all-round drawing out of the best in child and man."***[22] Gandhi therefore ***"presents challenging insightful formulations of basic and new education with regard to character building as the goal of education, the centrality of word and productive manual labour, the focus on real needs and simple living, the development of non-violent relations, and a holistic approach that involves the integrated training of body, mind, and spirit."***[23]

For him the western education did not meet up to these standards. Our rich cultures and languages have it all. Gandhi thus serves as a valuable catalyst in any discussion on education to peace. With the declaration of October 2 as the international Day for Non-violence, there is thus a renewed interest on Mahatma Gandhi and on his clarion call for peace.

Despite the above fact, one still hears of violent

crackdown of peaceful protests by governments, assaults, rape, brutality terrorism, murder, war, tribal wars, sexism, racism, lack of education and health services. There is thus urgent need to advocate for peace which is not only the absence of personal and institutional violence, but the presence of wellbeing, social justice, gender equity and human rights. The aim here is not only to encourage education about peace as propagated by Mahatma Gandhi, but education for peace which intends to use the Gandhian way to nurture knowledge, values, behaviours and capacities to confront violence in all facets of life.

b. Gandhi's Copernican Revolution in Peace Education: Gandhi's special touch on Peace Education can be seen as a great breakthrough in the field of Education. He sees education as liberation. Allen Douglas tactically draws this from his thought when insisting on the fact that ***"Gandhi offers many valuable insights on education. Educators can benefit greatly by studying his formulations of the true goal of education as liberation: providing a means for service to meet the needs of others, for liberation from all forms of servitude and domination, and for one's ethical and spiritual liberation.***"[24]

Still reflecting with Douglas, one can identify what I will term ***"Gandhian Copernican Revolution in Education. In most cases we feel our successful students and professors who are equipped with doctorates and credited with numerous publications are the most intelligent and are to be endowed with wealth and power. Gandhi identifies that in most cases they are morally and spiritually underdeveloped. In effect they are uneducated human being slacking deep moral character and not motivated to live according to the ideals of truth and non-violence.***"[25]

Without mincing words, one can call them Gandhian who *failed experiments in truth,* since the status quo educational system precludes or deemphasises any sense of Gandhi's ideal of Truth, which shapes his view of the human potential for the moral and spiritual development of truly educated human beings[26]. Gandhi thus emphasises on character building and moral and spiritual development.

But how has Gandhi's view on Education to non-violence been used all through? How is it propagated and how is it affecting the world today?

3. Concrete usage of Peace Education: This conference is already a number one classical way of spreading Peace Education. We must therefore commend the efforts of the organisers and especially the great Professor Ravindra Kumar [World Peace Movement Trust], who has spent time, energy and financial resources to spread the necessity for peace education. In addition to this, Marshall Rosenberg proposes non-violent communication, Jay Janson uses the media to condemn war and create awareness on the necessity of peace education, while Jill Strauss will propose the school as the required medium to teach and disseminate peace education.

A. Non-Violent Communication: A Breakthrough in Education for Peace: One of the greatest modern breakthroughs in peace education can be seen in the Non-violent Communication as propagated by Marshall Rosenberg[27], a communication process that helps people to exchange the information necessary to resolve conflicts and differences peacefully. At times due to improper communication skills one turns to be so violent.[28]

Language plays a very preponderant part in communication. Slightly rewording Wittgenstein we can say:

"Whereof one has nothing to say, thereof one should be silent." While studying the factors that affect our **ability to stay compassionate**, we are surprised by the crucial **role of language** and our use of words. We can cultivate in ourselves a specific approach to communicating—speaking and listening—that leads us to give from the heart, connecting us with ourselves and with each other in a way that allows our natural compassion to flourish. It is at the backdrop of this truism that one must learn proper communication skills based on the virtues of peace and non-violence.

As NVC replaces our old patterns of defending, withdrawing, or attacking in the face of judgment and criticism, we come to perceive ourselves and others, as well as our intentions and relationships, in a new light. Resistance, defensiveness, and violent reactions are minimized. Through its emphasis on deep listening—to ourselves as well as others—NVC fosters respect, attentiveness, and empathy, and engenders a mutual desire to give from the heart. NVC brings to light another breakthrough: rather than look to others [parents, teachers, peers] for the answers, people begin to look within themselves and trust their feelings and ideas. There will be a new understanding of how an individual's behaviour can positively or negatively influence an interaction or situation. Knowing how to non-violently decrease conflict in a situation is empowering and essential of peace-making. The ability to *think out of the box* requires imagination, problem-solving skills, and a willingness to collaborate with others toward a common goal.

This is achieved through what we call the four components of the NVC model.

First we must observe what is actually happening in a

situation: What we are observing others saying without introducing any judgement or evaluation.

Next we state how we feel when we observe this action: are we hurt, scared, joyful, amused, irritated, etc?

Thirdly, we say what needs of ours are connected to the feelings we have identified.

Lastly, a very specific request: this implies addressing what we are wanting from the other person that would enrich our lives or make life more wonderful for us.[29]

When we focus on clarifying what is being observed, felt, and needed rather than on diagnosing and judging, we discover the depth of our own compassion.

B. Learning to Create Awareness: We must join the fight of people like Jay Jansen[30] who cries at the top of his voice, "***When shall the arrival of new men like Mahatma Gandhi or a Martin Luther King Jr. herald in an era of popular prosecution in the street of crimes against humanity of a wealthy made powerful through violent thievery from the commonweal***?" Now-a-days the internet is identified as one of the greatest media to disseminate information and create awareness.Education for peace is all about creating this awareness! The founders of the King Condemned US Wars International Awareness Campaign led and managed by Jay Jason, act as sentry to tell the world of the frightening level of destruction and violence perpetrated and financed by the US and the so called *World Powers.*

I commend once again this international conference which acts as a means of creating awareness. But, I would love to cry high and create more awareness on the corruption, the poverty, the violence that pervades the land. I read this information on the internet. ***"India's rising rape rate [one every 22 minutes, according to the National Crime Records Bureau] is a proof of what is wrong within certain sects of that society."*** I would love to cry high that the innocent bloods that are being shed in Libya, in Egypt and in many countries are to a great extent fuelled by the so called *world powers* and I ask them to stop all this. It is the time to create awareness of the so many dictatorial regimes that are in the world. This can be done at the level of schools and colleges too.

C. Putting Peace Education in the Curriculum of Schools: There is dire need to include non-violence education in the curriculum of schools in order to teach this great value. The target groups will be on the one hand the teachers and on the other one the students. With these, we can boast of a non-violent society. Gandhi said, ***"We must be the change we wish to see in the world."*** Non-violence thus is about personal as well as societal transformation. Through non-violence and peace training, people come to appreciate that although so many of the problems in society seem overwhelming; each one of us has the power to take action to create change. Teachers worldwide should promote non-violent values, in the classroom by raising these issues, in schools by establishing procedures of mediation and reconciliation, in the community by upholding the right to a non-violent education and education in non-violence.

Jill Strauss goes a long way to give concrete example of how peace education has been successful in schools. All round the world there are conflict-zones in which teachers educate the young in almost impossible conditions. In Afghanistan women teachers are continuing covertly to teach girls, though the fundamentalist ruling regime forbids it. In

Burundi, the Peace School brought together children from all backgrounds, encouraged them to imagine a word without war ['What if...?]'), and in he process stimulated local moves towards reconciliation in which the children took part. There have been other kinds of heroism: in Nazi-occupied Norway teachers, pacifists and non-pacifists alike, refused to obey orders to teach the Nazi party line, and consequently hundreds were imprisoned in harsh conditions [while others continued teaching secretly in their pupils' homes].[31]

We can be inspired from what is done by the UNESCO and also the GOIPEACE foundation in Japan. Yearly essays are organised in for youths and Children. With Education for non-violence among youths, there will be a greater awareness of the dangers of stereotyping and prejudging, the importance of asking questions and seeking to understand. This annual essay contest is organised in an effort to harness the energy, imagination and initiative of the world's youth in promoting a culture of peace and sustainable development. It also aims to inspire society to learn from the young minds and to think about how each of us can make a different in the world. They will equally learn to speak up and be heard both as an advocate for others and for themselves. ***"Educating the children regarding peace, non-violence and most importantly mutual respect towards each other is very important."***[32]

Peace Education is an on-going process which if well stratified, organised and implemented can change situations.

Conclusion: The above presentation makes us understand that our humanity lives in wounds with examples from India and to a greater extent Africa. The aim has not been to shift blames on the colonial powers. That is why we identified concrete situations from within. There is need for healing. It is a time of true reconciliation and true reconstruction through peace education, being the change we want in others, adopting non-violent communication in our day to day lives, striving to create more awareness using all possible means at our disposal and above all teaching youths and children the pathway to non-violence and peace.

Our aim all through this essay has been to proof the fact that there is urgency for the African continent in particular and for the world in general to look up to Gandhi to have the basic tenets for any successful peace education. Even Gandhi sees his life as a story of Experiments with the truth. From the above exposition, it becomes clear that there is URGENCY[33] to adopt peace education and in thinking of the leadership of Africa in terms of the welfare of the people. There is urgency in putting in place political, economic and cultural institutions capable of heightening our capacities to invent and organise themselves. There is urgent need to build a sound political systems. Since there is urgency, we must hasten to organise our countries so that we will succeed. We need to clear the path even if it means carving roads through solid rocks. In effect the time has come to make our countries shine with the light of the new independence. There is urgency to adopt peace education. There is urgency in thinking of the new independence of Africa in terms of grandeur, liberty and creative power. There is urgency to reconstruct the future of Africa.

To sum I am announcing that enrolments are currently going on into the school of non-violence. The main teacher is Gandhi and we are all students and teachers of this school. S Kulandhaisamy encourages us to all enrol into this *School of Non-violence*. It aims at educating not only the children but the whole lot of people not only in India but of the whole world in a culture of peace and non-violence will be the aim of the school Gandhi has been a great teacher of this peace education with non-violence as the central focus. For getting the right understanding, Gandhiji evolved eleven *vratas* [vows] for every individual and for appreciation; he gave the concept of constructive work. He gave *Satyagraha* as a reaction in response to an action already happened but out of one's own realisation of truth within which makes a complete action leading to peace and harmony. Admissions have begun into this school of Gandhi; let us all together join hands to make the world a better place[34]. This school will teach us to avoid and to destroy violence which is defined as ***"the world the way it is, the way it has been till now and the way we don't want it to be"***[35].

Footnotes:

1 We borrow his term fromHelderCamara. Spiral of Violence for him is a symbol for the central problem of today's world: the violence of poverty which keeps over two - thirds of the world's people in a sub - human condition, the violence of revolt when peaceful demands have no effect and the violence of repression with which the powerful try to crush the demands of the poor. His book *Spiral of Violence* was published in 1971. http://www.alastairmcintosh.com/general/spiral-of-violence.htm

2 Mgr Jean-Bosco Ntep, *Preface*, in *Pour la voie africaine de la nonviolence,* Yaoundé, Cle, 2009, p. 12, translation is mine)

3 Ela Gandhi, "The Crises of the 21st Century – Some Gandhian Solutions" Keynote address delivered at a Student Union in October 4, 2007 to mark the start of Asian American Heritage Observance month. Quoted by KalaKachmar - October 15, 2007, http://advance.uconn.edu/2007/071015/07101503.htm

4 Source: MARTIN LUTHER KING, JR., Where Do We Go from Here: Chaos or Community?, pp. 62-63

5 cf. I. M. ONYEOCHA, Idealism, Politics and Nation Building: The Nigerian Experience, Washington DC, the Council for Research and Value, 1994, p. 55. In Africa, most countries practicing democracy do not meet up to the standards required. Presidents in Democratic regimes remain on seat for many decades. African countries have been

turned into political states where those who cry for justice are arrested, detained, tortured, imprisoned and even killed, but yet claim that these countries are oases of freedom. Even in countries where there seem to be apparent peace [e.g. Cameroon] one can still identify nations bleeding in silence.

6 Information Published on January 22, 2013 by AllAfrica.com explained such happenings in Imo State, Owerri and in Kogi state. In the latter state, someone was busy scooping the brains out of his four-month-old son whom he had just murdered.

7 http://www.dailyguideghana.com/?p=7214

8 http://www.bbc.co.uk/news/world-africa-22335634

9 The airplane carrying Rwandan president Juvénal Habyarimana and Burundian president Cyprien Ntaryamira was shot down as it prepared to land in Kigali, Rwanda. This assassination which took place on on the evening of 6 April 1994 went through mid-July of the same year. This was the catalyst for the Rwandan Genocide.

10 EkottoNdome et al, «Pour une éthique africaine de la nonviolence», in «*Pour la voie africaine de la Nonviolence*», p.75-76. (Translation is mine).

11 *Ibidem,* page 76

12 Most of the world stood on the sidelines during the Rwandan genocide... The colonialism of Belgium played a role in the beginning of the genocide. It was Belgium who decided on the separation of the Tutsi and Hutu. Belgians introduced ID cards and distributed them between the two tribes. When the Belgian rule had ended most of the land and power were in the minority hands of the Tutsi, where Hutu was in the positions of forced labor.... On August 5, 2008, an independent Rwandan commission said France was aware of preparations for the 1994 Rwanda genocide and helped train the ethnic Hutu militia perpetrators. It accuses France of training Hutu militias responsible for the slaughter, helping plan the genocide, and participating in the killings. http://en.wikipedia.org/wiki/Role_of_the_international_community_in_the_Rwandan_Genocide

13 Jay Janson, A Brief Country by Country History of US Crimes Against Humanity, US Crimes from 1945 Through 2012 http://prosecuteuscrimesagainsthumanitynow.blogspot.it/ I am interested in knowing the place India played in this! I understand we are looking for place in the UN. Also cf. William Ferroggiaro, The US and the Genocide in Rwanda 1994", Evidence of Inaction, August 20, 2001, http://www2.gwu.edu/~nsarchiv/NSAEBB/NSAEBB53/

14 Shalom Educating for Peace [SEP] is a non-governmental, non-profit organization working for building and sustaining positive peace through education. The organisation is based in Rwanda and is establishing a branch in Burundi. SEP pursues the following objectives: [i] educating for peace, [ii] researching for peace and [iii] cultivating the culture of non-violence.

15 Nonviolence Education Coordinator at The Temple of Understanding, a global interfaith NGO. Strauss writes on peace education curricula and has been actively involved in Middle East coexistence and interfaith/interethnic relations.

16 Jill Strauss, *Non-violence Education for Youth*, in *SGI Quaterly,* April 2005, http://www.sgiquarterly.org/feature2005Apr-9.html An education for peace is an education for co-operation, for caring and sharing, for the use of nonviolence in conflict-solving, but an education that fosters competition, conquest, aggression and violence is an education for war.'

17 Quoted by Ravindra Kumar, *Education For Peace* in *Global Peace*, vol 12, num. 2, Dec 2012, p. 4.

18 Cf. Bella Das, *Conflict Resolution through Peace Education: A Gandhian Perspective*, in *Resolving Conflicts the Gandhian Way,* Meerut, World Peace Movement Trust, 2011, p. 33-34. Bella Das got the inspiration from Art 26 of the Universal Declaration of Human Rights.

19 cf. The selected works of Gandhi, vol. 5, The voice of Truth, www.mkgandhi.org/edugandhi/education.htm

20 Cf. KumariManju and RaghuvanishSujata, *Locating Education for Peace in Gandhian Thought*, www.mkgandhi.org/articles/peace_education.htm

21 Kumar Ravindra, *Education Meaning and Purpose*, in *Global Peace,* special issue-2, August 2012, p. 4.

22 Kumar Ravindra, *Education for Peace*, in *Global Peace,* vol. 12, No. 2, December 2012, p. 4.

23 Douglas Allen, *Mahatma Gandhi on Violence and Peace Education*, in *Philosophy East and West,* Vol. 57, No. 3, Jul., 2007, p. 294.

24 Douglas Allen, *Art. Cit.*, page 294

25 *Ibidem.*

26 *Ibidem.*

27 Marshall Rosenberg [born October 6, 1934] is an American psychologist and the creator of Nonviolent Communication. He is the founder and former Director of Educational Services for the Center

for Nonviolent Communication, an international non-profit organization. The abbreviation *NVC* is used to refer to Nonviolent or Compassionate Communication. The approach of NVC presented in the course is mostly from the contributions of Marshall Rosenberg. [visit: http://www.cnvc.org]

28 Even before using bombs and machines, the tongue is one of the most destructive elements if not well used. Just as you get hurt from the aggressive communication of others, your own mode of communication may cause pain to those who live with you. Often it is the mode of communication that causes more hurt than the core issue of conflicts.

29 Rosenberg Marshall, *The Nonviolent Communication Training Course,* Sounds True, 2006, pp. 2-3

30 Jay Janson [alias MajoríaHumanidad] is an archival research peoples historian activist, musician and writer; has lived and worked on all continents [67 counties]; He has many articles in many renowned journals and websites. Above all, he is coordinator of the Martin Luther King Jr. Condemned US Wars International Awareness Campaign: [King Condemned US Wars] http://kingcondemneduswars.blogspot.com/ and website historian of Prosecute US Crimes against Humanity Now Campaign http://prosecuteuscrimesagainsthuma nitynow.blogspot.com/ featuring a country by country history of US crimes and laws pertaining.

31 Jill Strauss, *Nonviolence Education for Youth,* http://www.sgiquarterly.org/feature2005Apr-9.html

32 cf. Kumari Manju and Raghuvanish Sujata, *Locating Education for peace in Gandhian Thought*, www.mkgandhi.org/articles/peace_education.htm

33 Cf. KA MANA, *Il y a urgence pour une nouvelle Independence de l'Afrique et de notre pays,* Kinshasa, Editions Universitaires Africaines, 2010, p. 175-176. We can read more on the way forward for Africa in KA MANA, *L'Afrique, notreprojet,* Yaoundé, Editions Terroirs, 2009

34 S. Kulandhaisamy, Peace Education for the Millenium [www.mkgandhi.org/nonviolence/Kulandhaisamy.htm]

35 Ka Mana « La nonviolence un tournant de civilisation » in *Pour la voie africaine de la nonviolence,* page 19

*****

D: Role and Contribution of Teachers

1. NON-VIOLENCE AND PEACE EDUCATION: ROLE OF TEACHERS AND TEACHER-EDUCATION

Mala Tandon*

Peace is the basic principle of living for mankind as well as nature. Disequilibrium and disturbances arising in nature, within human beings, in society and our surroundings ultimately end and tranquility and a state of equilibrium is restored. Peace and the desire to live peacefully is inherent in us. Our lives are affected by certain disturbances created around us due to misunderstandings among individuals, ignorance on the part of some human beings and also due to intentionally mollifying the surrounding atmosphere of peace and tranquility due to sadistic tendencies and vested interests.

---

* Dr. Mala Tandon is a director of the DMC Saxena College of Education at Lucknow [UP], India.

Non-violence means abstaining from the use of physical force to achieve an aim. It is a philosophy, a principle, and a practice. It upholds the view that moral behaviour excludes the use of violence; it maintains that violence is self-perpetuating and can never provide a means to a securely peaceful end. It supports the pacifist position that war and killing are never justifiable. It has been used by pacifists and non-pacifists alike to achieve social change and express resistance to oppression. There's no doubt that non-violence requires courage. Much of this courage goes unnoticed, being part of private actions in private lives.

To be able to live a peaceful and non-violent life, an individual must first have their basic needs for survival fulfilled. They must have water, food and shelter. Alleviating the people from poverty is one of the first step to creating a culture of peace and non-violence. Another impediment to peace is intolerance of other people. Intolerance can be to differences of races, religions, cultures and lifestyles. Through education this can be changed. By educating children about different religions, races, cultures and lifestyles in our world we can help them to understand the similarities amongst all and understand how insignificant the differences are. They would realize that these should not be a reason for discrimination or prejudice.

Pandit Jawaharlal Nehru says, ***"Peace cannot suddenly be deserved from the heavens. It can only come when the root cause of troubles are removed."***

Changing a culture of violence into a culture of peace requires a transformation of problems to creative and constructive solutions that answer the needs of those involved. When we think about violence, discrimination and exclusion, the challenges may seem insurmountable. However, these challenges are fundamentally connected. Ignorance, misunderstandings, assumptions based on a lack of communication and mistrust give rise to discrimination and violence. All influence and reinforce one another. Vulnerability to violence, discrimination and exclusion can also be linked to a number of common social determinants, such as alcohol and drug misuse or abuse, poverty, inequalities of income, gender or power and misuse of power. Seeing these connections, it becomes clear that it is essential to systematically address common root causes. Just as there can be common roots of violence, discrimination and exclusion, there can be common solutions. Successfully addressing these three humanitarian challenges require a change of mindsets, attitudes and behaviors. We need a global mind and behavior shift from the way we currently think and interact: from being locked into differences.

Peacemaking, peacekeeping, and peace-building are complex and important responses to the proliferation of violent conflict. The root of these approaches lies in the basic knowledge and commitment to the practice of non-violence and critical thinking. When we eliminate violence as an option for resolving conflicts, we make room for creative alternatives. Co-operation, critical thinking, communication and problem-solving become essential tools. Conflict itself can be viewed as an opportunity for growth and expanded communication rather than a precursor to violence and a threat to dignity, security and life. Peace educators are developing tools to help transform the current *culture of violence* in which hurt and harm are advocated and glorified to a *culture of peace* in which the preservation of life and human dignity are the central guiding principles for living together in a secure world.

Global Responses to Peace and Non-Violence: Non-violence, as an effective way of dealing with conflict, needs thought, resourcefulness, vision, planning, patience and commitment. There are organizations which provide training in non-violent techniques, and group of experts in non-violent conflict resolution who go into troubled areas, much as relief workers do, acting as mediators and passing on their non-violence skills. In a world where the currently prevailing systems are caught in the arm lock of violence, non-violence cannot offer instant remedies or results. However, it is catching on. Most people reject violence and killing.

Over the years the United Nations, particularly the UNESCO, have developed a number of standard-setting instruments, declarations and action plans; which are widely accepted by the international communities and which provided basic framework for promoting the concept of education for a culture of peace worldwide.

Peace education began as a response to violence and war. As stated in the preamble of the Constitution of the UNESCO [the United Nations Educational, Scientific and Cultural Organization], ***"Since wars began in the minds of men, it is in the minds of men [and women] that the defenses of peace must be constructed."*** The knowledge, skills and attitudes needed to prevent violence and promote the non-violent resolution of conflict are central to the process of educating for a culture of peace. As summarized by one organization:

"A culture of peace will be achieved when citizens of the world understand global problems, have the skills to resolve conflicts and struggle for justice non-violently, live by international standards of human rights and equity,

appreciate cultural diversity, and respect the Earth and each other."

On November 10, 1998, the United Nations General Assembly unanimously voted to proclaim the first decade of the twenty-first century, an *International Decade for Promotion of a Culture of Peace and Non-violence for the Children of the World.* [2001-10] The UN made this declaration specifically for children because they are the most vulnerable individuals and most likely victims of violence of all kinds. Gandhiji aptly stated that, ***"If we are going to bring about peace in the world, we have to begin with the children."*** Article 29 of the Convention on the Rights of the Child [1989] states, ***"...the education of the child shall be directed to...the preparation of the child for responsible life in a free society, in the spirit of understanding, peace, tolerance, equality of sexes, and friendship among all peoples..."*** The 1990 World Declaration on Education for All says that: ***"Every person, child, youth and adult – shall be able to benefit from educational opportunities designed to meet their basic learning needs. These needs comprise both essential learning tools [such as literacy, oral expression, numeracy, and problem solving) and the basic learning content [such as knowledge, skills, values, and attitudes] required by human beings to be able to survive, to develop their full capacities, to live and work in dignity, to participate fully in development, to improve the quality of their lives, to make informed decisions, and to continue learning ...The satisfaction of these needs empowers individuals in any society and confers upon them a responsibility to ... further the cause of social justice, ... to be tolerant towards social political and religious systems which differ from their own, ensuring that commonly***

accepted humanistic values and human rights are upheld, and to work for international peace and solidarity in an interdependent world."

"...Both the content and the process of education should promote peace, social justice, respect for human rights and the acceptance of responsibility. Children need to learn skills of negotiation, problem solving, critical thinking and communication that will enable them to resolve conflicts without resorting to violence."

The *Anti-War Agenda* of the UNICEF set out in *The State of the World's Children 1996*, which declares, ***"...Disputes may be inevitable, but violence is not. To prevent continued cycles of conflict, education must seek to promote peace and tolerance, not fuel hatred and suspicion."*** The focus on behavioural change in the UNICEF definition of peace education reflects the fact that behaviour does not occur in a vacuum; it is nested within the context of the family, peer group, the community and the larger society. Behaviour development is intrinsically linked to and interdependent with the values and norms of those groups. Existing values and norms can either contribute to or hinder behaviour that promotes peace. Peace education in the UNICEF promotes the development of values as the basis for behavioural change, and views behaviour as an indicator of an individual's or group's values. The effectiveness of peace education is increased when strategies are used that address the values of the entire community.

Education as a Means for Developing Peace: Peace is a discipline which should be practiced by all. Education helps us to realize our ultimate goal in life – i.e. To live peacefully and harmoniously as a well adjusted individual in our surrounding.

According to Dean Gooderham Acheson, ***"Peace is positive and it has to be waged with all our thought, energy and courage."*** Education for peace is essentially required for our future citizens i.e. our children, in order to develop the right attitude towards life.

Albert Einstein stated, ***"Peace cannot be kept by force. It can only be achieved by understanding of and feelings for values. We must acquire a vivid sense of the beautiful and of the normally good. The school should always have as its aim, that the young man learns it as a harmonious personality."***

Dr. S Radhakrishnana stated that ***"Education for peace should encourage the exercise of these qualities, adventure in the world of spirit, the tradition of tolerance, the instinct of live and let live, these are deeply ingrained in us. Men are born for love and friendship and not for hatred and war....It is the task of education, to create in us, love for the new world of peace and fellowship."***

The Most Needed Education of The Day: The first responsibility of an educator or any other enlightened citizen of India is to provide scope for developing the excellences that each child has within and which can be lighted up by giving him appropriate environment. Swami Vivekananda says, ***"Education is the manifestation of the perfection already in man."The best in every individual is to be drawn out, cultivated and cultured by the society for meeting the real educational needs of the country. National or international peace can come through education for citizenship. It is much more than acquiring skills. An educated person has the regional, national and international standing, through which he brings social and super social goods. He can***

criticize all problems sanely and squarely and act accordingly."

Peace is the basic principle of living for mankind. Education helps us to realize our ultimate goal in life, i.e., to live peacefully and harmoniously as a well adjusted individual in our surrounding. Education for peace is essentially required for our future citizens i.e. our children, in order to develop the right attitude towards life. We need a global mind and behavior shift from the way we currently think and interact. Non-violence as an effective way of dealing with conflict needs thought, resourcefulness, vision, planning, patience and commitment. We know that human beings are inhabited with five great enemies of peace, i.e., avarice, ambition, envy, anger and pride. Where these reside peace can never be. The knowledge, skills and attitudes needed to prevent violence and promote the non-violent resolution of conflict are central to the process of educating for a culture of peace. There are many impediments to a culture of peace and non-violence it will take great efforts to achieve the same. It can be achieved through collaborative efforts among families, colleagues, neighbors, classmates, governments and all other people in our world. Everyone can be involved in creating a culture of peace; even if in a minor way, there can be major impact. If peace is achieved in all of our families there would be positive consequence.

Role of Teachers in Encouraging a Non-Violent and Peaceful Atmosphere: As educators of children, we all have a role in teaching children about peaceful behavior. We need to be positive role models for children by showing those peaceful ways of thinking and behaving. It can be achieved through collaborative efforts among families, colleagues, neighbors, classmates, governments and all other people in our world. Everyone can be involved in creating a culture of peace.

The global process of learning peaceful behavior can be achieved in classrooms through Learning Activities utilizing the valuable tools of active listening, critical thinking, and imagining creative, non-violent responses to conflict, which can be used with all ages and levels of student, though most suited for youth over the age of twelve, by giving rewards of working cooperatively to achieve a goal.

"An education for peace is an education for co-operation, for caring and sharing, for the use of non-violence in conflict-solving", says a peace education expert: but an education that fosters competition, conquest, aggression and violence is an education for war. Teachers world-wide are reported to be promoting non-violent values, in the classroom by raising these issues, in the school by establishing procedures of mediation and reconciliation, in the community by upholding the right to a non-violent education and education in non-violence. Teachers have been practicing non-violent resistance to aggression. All round the world there are conflict-zones in which teachers educate the young in almost impossible conditions. In Afghanistan, women teachers are continuing covertly to teach girls, though the fundamentalist ruling regime forbids it. In Burundi, the Peace School brought together children from all backgrounds, encouraged them to imagine a world without war and in the process stimulated local moves towards reconciliation in which the children took part. There have been other kinds of heroism: in Nazi-occupied Norway teachers, pacifists and non-pacifists alike, refused to obey orders to teach the Nazi party line, and consequently hundreds were imprisoned in harsh conditions [while others continued teaching secretly in their pupils' homes]. Many of the teachers were interned in a concentration camp together, and so were able to support each other's resolve; significantly, they also made it clear to each other that anyone who wished to give in would also receive support and sympathy without judgment. The recent is the effort of Malalah Yusafzay, a Pakistani school pupil and education activist from the town of Mingora in the Swat district of Pakistan's northwestern Khyber Pakhtunkhwa province. She is known for her education and women's rights activism in the Swat Valley, where the Taliban had at times banned girls from attending school. Malala said she will never want to seek revenge from the Talib who tried to assassinate her, even if she had a gun in her hand. She cried, ***"This is what my soul is telling me: Be peaceful and love everyone... This is the philosophy of non-violence that I have learned from Gandhi, Badshah Khan and Mother Teresa."***

Violence is one of the many possible responses to conflict. Non- violent conflict–resolution skills could be nurtured and applied constructively to disputes between the individuals, groups and nations. Education for peace seeks to nurture ethical development, including the values, attitudes, and skills required for living in harmony with oneself and with others, including nature.

Role of Teacher in fulfilling the Objectives of Non-Violence and Peace Education: The teacher needs to coordinate all efforts to fulfill the objectives of education for peace and non violence in class:

- Promote non-violence and develop attitudes and values like autonomy, responsibility, co-operation, creativity and solidarity;
- Respect the differences and similarities amongst fellow beings;

- Learn to live together;
- Develop co-operative learning based on dialogue and intercultural understanding;
- Adopt non-violence solutions to conflicts through mediations and conflict-resolving strategies;
- Focusing on children and young people, particularly in the school educational process to integrate peace and non-violence in theory and practice; and
- Integrating peace and non-violence in every aspect of teaching and learning processes, including curriculum development activities, teacher training and management of the educational institutions.

Peace Education in Practice: While educating children, the teachers should take care that *Schooling* and other *educational experiences* to promote peace education should ensure that:

- Schools function as 'zones of peace', where children are safe from conflict in the community;
- Children's basic rights as enumerated in the CRC are upheld;
- An appropriate climate is developed within the school or other learning environment, that models peaceful and rights-respectful behaviour in the relationships among all members of the school community: teachers, administrators, other staff, parents, and children;
- Principles of equality and non-discrimination in administrative policies and practices are demonstrated;
- Knowledge of peace-building that already exists in the community, including means of dealing with conflict that are effective, non-violent, and rooted in the local culture, are well utilized;

- Conflicts—whether between children, or between children and adults—are handled in a non-violent manner that respects the rights and dignity of all involved;
- An understanding of peace, human rights, social justice and global issues is integrated throughout the curriculum whenever possible;
- A forum for the explicit discussion of values of peace and social justice is provided;
- Teaching and learning methods that promote participation, co-operation, problem-solving and respect for differences are used;
- Opportunities are allowed for children to put peace-making into practice, both in the educational setting and in the wider community;
- Opportunities are provided for continuous reflection and professional development of all educators in relation to issues of peace, justice and rights;
- This vision of peace education, consistent with the UNICEF concept of rights based; and
- Child-friendly learning environments [UNICEF 1999, E/ICEF/1999/14], includes elements such as the realization of the rights of every child, gender sensitivity and responsiveness to diversity, the promotion of quality learning outcomes such as life skills and successful problem solving, and the enhancement of teacher capacity.

In the class room, peace education aims to develop skills, attitudes, and knowledge with co-operative and participatory learning methods and an environment of tolerance, care, and respect. Through dialogue and exploration, teachers and students are nurtured and empowered to take responsibility for their own growth and achievement while teachers care for the wellbeing of all students. The *school's timetable* should have enough planned activities and provision of incorporating value of peace in life, so that students are adequately exposed for peace making behavior. Enough opportunities will lead students to engage in a journey of shared learning. *School* should try to develop a suitable teaching-learning environment, so that the students can develop the traits of leadership for tomorrow. With the help of peace making activities, their minds become the fertile grounds for conceiving ideas based on peace and harmony.

Encouragement for participation in scout and guide, cub and bulbul, sports, National Cadet Core, National Social Service, cultural programme, several healthy contests conducted by various approved agencies; motivation towards becoming the members of local peace organizations, visits to the riot-affected areas, are some of the pedagogy through which teachers in schools can develop the culture by spreading peace education practiced in the form of social service rendered to need people and society in and around the school.

Conception of peace education recognizes that the requirements of peace education must be: transmitted, include training in skills of interpretation; employ the development of reflective and participatory capacities; and focus on applied knowledge for overcoming real life problems.

The teacher must make efforts to incorporate all these in school curriculum and classroom activities through associations and comparisons using effective examples and good explanations of curricular content related to the different subjects studied by the children.

The role of teachers towards a child's education is to create a caring environment in the classroom. Teachers who listen to what the students have to say and develop a curriculum that is meaningful to the children have the most successful students. Teachers are the builders of the nation. They prepare persons and create manpower for every sector of human activity. The quality of people and their level of thinking largely depend on the contribution made by the teachers.

Teacher can play an important role in imparting the peace education as they:

- Value and model lifelong learning;
- Know the curriculum and communicate expectations to students and parents;
- Are approachable and have a positive relationship with students, colleagues, parents and community members;
- Provide a safe, supportive and inclusive environment in their classroom and school;
- Design and implement effective and meaningful instructional and assessment strategies;
- Challenge students to reach their potential and foster independent learning;
- Are firm, fair and consistent with discipline; and
- Assist their students in recognizing and understanding their role in a local and global community.

Role of Teacher Education in Promotion of Peace and Non-Violence: Teachers and their trainer's, i.e., teacher educators play an important role in promotion of peace and non-violence. Teachers directly handle curricular and co-curricular activities in classrooms and are in direct contact with children. They are role models and can foster healthy feelings promoting peace and non-violence through a variety of learning activities.

Teacher Educators indirectly influence class situations and directly interact with pupil teachers, preparing them to handle peace education issues and promote non-violence and peace education amongst pupil teachers and further amongst the students being taught by the pupil teachers.

Teacher education content can thus be highly beneficial in training these future teachers in such a manner so as to emphasize on and promote peace and non-violence. Through Teacher education, the new generation of nation builders can inculcate skills, knowledge, attitudes, values and qualities that equip them to prevent conflict and violence and develop; tolerance, respect for others, healthy relationships amongst people in homes and society. Provide opportunities for continuous reflection and professional development of all educators in relation to issues of peace, justice and rights. Peace education is an essential component of quality base education. Peace education is most effective when the skills of peace and conflict resolution are learned actively and are modeled by the school environment in which they are taught. Teacher Education should take care of this aspect by providing training where teachers can be role models for their students. New technologies provide children and youth around the world with the opportunity to discuss issues of common concern the school and trained teachers have to play a positive and constructive role to strengthen the innate human potentials natural one's true self. The role of school in peace education is mostly dependent upon the school's organizational climate. The emphasis of Teacher Education and Teacher Educators are to meet standards of academic excellence and to develop valuable life skills of good character. Understanding the relationship between school discipline and student achievement, they should strive to provide a world class holistic education in which all pupil teachers and the students taught by them find success academically, socially, emotionally and physically.

Conclusion: Based on experiences and psychological need of present generation, some useful strategies are discussed and included in teacher education course content, these may help in reducing misconduct among students, e.g., ***"Start the day with full faith in them."*** We should know the calibers of the students. Teaching children values such as honesty, respect, compassion and responsibility can start at a young age. Parents and teachers alike have the ability to convey messages to children every day regarding appropriate behaviors and how to live ethically. Including children in daily activities, routines and specific lessons pertaining to ethical living can increase the overall morality of their upbringing. Teachers and Teacher Education content used to train these teachers need to be carefully selected so that the desired outcome of peace and non-violence in the whole society be obtained.

It is high time that the teachers and their trainers realize that any negligence on their parts will result in great damage for the future citizens and the society at large. If education for peace and non-violence is not given to the young generation then it would lead to disaster and the entire human race may have to suffer the brunt.

2. ROLE OF LANGUAGE IN PEACE-EDUCATION

Ruksana Khan*

Peace is a broad concept with practical and spiritual

* Ms. Ruksana Khan is a research scholar at the Jai Narain Vyas University of Jodhpur [Rajasthan], India.

connotations. It can imply a state of inner calm or end of conflict. Peace education is the process of acquiring the values, the knowledge and developing the attitude, skill and behaviors to live in harmony with oneself, with others and with natural environment.

Achieving peace is not just the responsibility of diplomats and politicians. It is the task of all educators. Peace education promotes an understanding of peace and social justice issues. They range from the interpersonal to the international, and include efforts to prevent bullying in schools, stop civil wars, unmask prejudice and prevent genocide. At its core, peace education represents the philosophy, language and practice of non – violence.

Definition: Webster defines peace as ***"A state of quiet or tranquility, freedom from disturbance or agitation, calm repose."*** From this definitions, it can be agreed that in the absence of elements such as tolerance, understanding, empathy, co-operation and respect for the difference in others there cannot be peace.

Peace Education and Language Teaching: Peace education offer language teachers an exciting chance to rethink their language teaching goals, content and methods. This new fields invite us to reconsider the mission of our teaching profession and our roles as educators. They are empowering in that they show us how our language teaching can contribute to making a better world and to promote attitudes of social responsibility and international understanding.

As Maria Montessori has said, ***"Establishing lasting peace is the work of education: all politics can do is keeping us out of war."***

Language teachers already face the complex task of

developing educational theories and processes sensitive to cultural diversity and individual needs. They are primarily concerned with the process of language acquisition. They apply, adapt, and develop topics and activities as they attempt to facilitate language learning, a dynamic process which involves interpretation and reflection. For precisely these reasons, the language teachers are well suited to promote thinking about peace.

Peace education and language teaching share a number of common techniques, dialogues, debates and conversation, for example, are important ways to practice language and are also a means of connecting the person or individual to the cultural or multiculture. Written and verbal exchanges of ideas give meaning to language and, at the same time, promote the understanding of differences. Active listening is part of the language of non-violence and is also a vital skill in the acquisition of language. Peace education is also concerned with co-operative interactive learning, a necessary prerequisite for good language learning.

Need for Peace Education: To mention:

* To make learners aware of the basis of conflict in their daily lives;
* To prepare students to become good citizens with skills to promote peace and human dignity at all levels of interaction;
* To build public awareness and political support for introduction of peace education into all spheres of education including non–formal education;
* To promote the education of all teachers, leaders and people to teach and advocate for peace;

* To promote respect for oneself and respect for others on individual level as a pre-requisite for the prevention of violence and conflict at society level; and
* To promote international understanding between the people of different worlds.

Conclusion: Peace education is an attempt to respond to an appeal enshrined in the UNESCO Constitution, ***"Since wars begin in the minds of men, it is in the minds of men that the defenses of peace must be constructed."*** A Narrow view of peace education limits the field of issue of war, disarmament and conflict resolution. However, when mentioning the term *peace education* most expert are referring to *comprehensive peace education* [Reardon, 1988] –a broad field covers human rights, the environment and development issues such as world poverty. As Gandhiji quote, ***"Poverty is the worst kind of Violence."***

Suggestion: If language students are really to become socially responsible world citizens, then, peace education concepts and the global education goals of knowledge, skills, concern and action must appear explicitly in the curriculum.

Language teachers can also integrate peace and global awareness themes into such areas as Grammar. Starkey [Pike and Selby 1988, page 239] describes how teaching the past and future tenses becomes much more meaningful when students study the historical background of world problems and do future oriented activities concerned with solving them. Similarly, comparatives can be practiced through comparing human rights in various countries or inequalities of First World wealth and Third World poverty.

One of the most significant attempts to deal with language teaching and peace is UNESCO's *LINGUAPAX seminar series.* LINGUAPAX I, was held in Kiev, USSP in 1987. The resulting *Kiev Declaration* made four specific reconditions to language teachers:

- To be aware of their responsibility in furthering international understanding through their teaching;
- To increase language teaching effectiveness so as to enhance mutual respect, peaceful co-existence and co-operation among nations;
- To exploit extra – curricular activities to develop international understanding; and
- To lay the basis for international co-operation through classroom co-operation using language teaching approaches responsive to students' interests and needs.

3. PROMOTING PEACE EDUCATION THROUGH LANGUAGE TEXT BOOKS: PROSPECTS AND POSSIBILITIES

Rekha Rani Kapoor*

According to RD Laing [1978], ***"Peace education is an attempt to respond to problems of conflict and violence on scales ranging from the global and national to the local and personal. It is about exploring ways of creating more***

* MS. Rekha Rani Kapoor is a research scholar at the Central Institute of Education in th University of Delhi [India].

just and sustainable future." In contemporary scenario, where violence is emerging in an unprecedented manner in human society, significance of peace education cannot be undermined. It becomes essential to understand what role can schools play in promoting a culture of peace? Are schools encouraging young minds to inculcate habits promoting non-violence, universal brotherhood, co-operation, unity and synergy? In the words of Federico Mayer, ***"Peace is possible for life at all stages and it is up to man to choose his destiny or to suffer from the horror of war. Today mankind is at the crossroad where one has to choose with courage, determination and imagination."*** Against this backdrop, the present paper explores prospects and possibilities with regard to text books in promoting peace education.

Promoting Peace Education through Text Books: Vision and Practice: Although there are diverse views on the necessity of peace education in curriculum and there are arguments with regard to introducing it as a separate paper or the emerging need to include in text books, yet there is a consensus on the significance of peace education and the point that whole education should be geared towards peace education. One major aspect under debate is the issue of conflict itself in peace education theory. Increasingly, this assumption is being questioned. Peace education is a wider term which would include education for social justice, equality, elimination of oppression, providing equal opportunities to marginalized sections, ensuring safe and clean environment, absence of negative feelings enhancing mutual understanding and universal brotherhood and imbibing the value of *Vasudhaiv Kutumbkam.* Exploring the content of language text books at senior secondary level

Class XI English: The Lesson: The Ailing Planet: The

Green Movement's role [from main reader, Hornbill] written by Nani Palkhivala raises issues regarding the declining health of the earth. The lesson brings out the relevance of a holistic and ecological view of the world, for which all nations need to cooperate and ensure a healthy and safe environment. The concept of sustainable development has been explained and the author has argued that human beings need to conserve the natural world of resources for future generations. The author has realistically presented the causes of the imbalance of earth's four principle biological systems which are fisheries, forests, grasslands and croplands. The lesson points out that the earth itself is a living organism whose health is declining and human beings need to remember that they are responsible trustees of the legacy to future generations. It is evident from this sentence, ***"The environmental problem does not necessarily signal our demise, it is our passport for the future."*** [Page 46] The lesson concludes with the words of Mr. Lester Brown, ***"We have not inherited this earth from our forefathers'; we have borrowed it from our children."*** [Page 47]

Thus, the lesson gives key message of protecting our environment and the need to check environment degradation [due to man's greed and selfishness]. In a nutshell, the lesson contends the need to establish ecological balance and harmony in nature, which has been disturbed by modern development.

The supplementary reader *snapshots* has lesson *The Address,* which is a poignant account of the repercussions of war and selfishness of human beings. In the lesson, the girl goes in search of has mothers' belongings after the war in Holland. She reaches at Mrs. Dorling's house, No. 46, Marconi Street, where the latter refuses to recognize her. At second time, she is able to enter the home as Mrs. Dorling's daughter invites her to come at home, however, she feels annoyed to see her belongings in an unfamiliar environment. When she finds the objects, they evoke her childhood memories. However, she makes a decision to leave them all behind and resolves to move on. As is evident, **"I *wouldn't go back there because the objects that are linked in your memory with the familiar life of formal time instantly lose their value when, severed from them, you see them again in strange, surroundings.*"** [Page 14] The story is divided into pre-war and post-war times and highlights the human predicament that follows war.

Class XII English: The main reader *Flamingo* has two lessons. *Lost Spring - Stories of stolen Childhood* and *Indigo,* which raise certain issues related to exploitation of human beings and provoke young minds to the relevance of establishing harmony and peace in life. These two lessons highlight the issues of marginalized sections in an effective manner. *Lost Spring-stories of stolen childhood* discusses the issue of child labour in India and its repercussions on the innocent children. The title of the lesson compels the reader to introspect as spring is the season of vigour, vitality, happiness, enjoyment and the children have been deprived of that happiness which is a salient feature of the stage of childhood. Their childhood is negotiated with the heavy burden of earning their living and becoming a helping hand to their family. Thus, childhood has an altogether different meaning for street children for whom rag picking is a means of their survival.

The first section of the lesson is concerned with the story of *Saheb*. His full name is *Saheb-e-Alam,* which is a satire on his present circumstances. The vicious circle, in which the life of rag pickers of Seemapuri is entrapped, has been aptly captured and documented by the author. These families have been migrated from Bangladesh and settled in Seemapuri, which is at the periphery of Delhi, yet miles away from it. These statements are indicative of the grim reality of street children, *survival in Seemapuri means rag picking, food is more important for survival than identity, garbage to them is gold.*

The second part of the lesson is a living commentary on the hazardous life of bangle makers in Firozabad. The lesson is a realistic account of the health hazards of the bangle makers. They are doomed to work in glass furnaces with high temperature, in dingy cells without air and light. Working in miserable condition culminates in making them blind in their early age. They often lose the brightness of their eyes. It throws light on the issues associated with child labour and asserts the need to establish harmony in the lives of poor children. The author contends that these children are unaware of child rights and the right against exploitation and they are living in a society which seems indifferent to their needs. The author points out that these children have an equal right to live a healthy and happy life. In a nutshell, the lesson portrays the lives of child labourers and enlightens the reader to come forward to the noble cause of extending support to poor children. The author has brought out the inequalities and injustice meted out to street children by meaningful sentences such as ***"stinking lanes choked with garbage, past homes that remain hovels with crumbling walls, wobbly doors, no windows, crowded with families of humans and animals co-existing in a primeval state." "Listening to them, I see two distinct worlds –one of the families, caught in a web of poverty, burdened by the stigma of caste in which they are born, the other a vicious circle of Sahukars, the middleman, the policeman, the keepers of the law, the bureaucrats and the politicians."***

Louis Fischer in the lesson 'Indigo' highlights the plight of indigo farmers in Champaran district in pre-independence era. It describes the role of Gandhi in initiating Champaran movement against British Empire. The issue of untouchability has been discussed emphatically by narrating an incident when Gandhi was discriminated due to misunderstanding. It addresses the pertinent question such as the true meaning and relevance of justice for poor people. For instance, ***"Where the peasants are so crushed and fear-stricken, law courts are useless. The real relief for them is to be free from fear."*** It gives meaningful message, i.e., asserting for one's rights and raising voice against injustice and oppression.

The lesson *Memories of Childhood* in vistas presents autobiographical narratives of two women who have been subjected to marginalization. The first section is concerned with *Zitkala-sa* whose hair was cut short against her wish in childhood. The second section deals with *Bama* who narrates how she experienced and conceptualized untouchability, her struggle for oppression and her indomitable will and strategy to make her way against social discrimination.

The two poems represent the circumstances of marginalized sections and one poem establishes the need of global peace and harmony. The poem – *An Elementary School Classroom in a Slum,* written by Stephen Spender, highlights the irrelevance of curriculum and education for slum children by presenting discrepancy between what is prescribed in text books and what happens in their life. The sharp contrast between what is taught in schools and what they feel and experience in their context is the key message of the poem. Thus, the disassociation and alienation from school education is discussed at length. The poet hopes that appropriate interventions need to be carried out to bring a ray of hope in the lives of downtrodden children. The last line of the poem, *History is Theirs Whose Language is the Sun,* is highly connotative and needs to be understood in terms of the emerging need of reviving and revamping the system and the call for social justice and a new order of equality.

The poem written by Robert Frost, *A Roadside stand* depicts the life of country folk who want to earn their living by selling fruits and vegetables. However, rich people are insensitive towards their condition and engrossed in fulfilling their own selfish motives. The poet urges rich people to pay their attention on poor people and contribute in noble cause of bringing harmony and hope in their lives.

The poem, *Keeping Quiet,* written by Pablo Neruda is concerned with the need of introspection, self analysis and promoting world peace and harmony. The poet urges all the people to become silent and engaged in self introspection to analyze their behaviour and action and understand the relevance of universal brotherhood, integrity, mutual understanding, social justice and peace in modern era of turmoil, anarchy and darkness. *There will be no victors as there will be no survivors,* is the key message inherent in the poem which provokes us to realize the futility of war. The poem *Aunt Jennifer's Tigers* lays bare the issues of suppression of women, a universal phenomena and the need to revolt against patriarchal society.

Hindi Text books: Class XI Hindi: In the book, *Antara* [XI Class], there are lessons and poems which depict the misery of downtrodden people, corruption and the need to establish a just and peaceful society. The lesson *Khanabadosh,* written by Om Prakash Valmiki depicts the grim reality of labour class. He portrayed very realistically the vicious circle of their exploitation and oppression.

The lesson, *Bharatvarsha Ki Unnati Kaise Ho Sakti Hai,* written by Bhartendu Harishchandara, very well presents the picture of pre-independence India and gives suggestions for the development of national goals which are quite relevant in contemporary scenario. He reiterates the crucial need of integration among various religious groups and the significance of shunning away the age old customs and superstitions to embrace the fruits of modernity in order to make India a progressive nation.

The poem *Hastakshep,* written by Shrikant Verma, is symbolic of the corruption prevailing in political system and asserts the need of democratic participation. The poet emphasizes upon the urgency to raise voice against atrocities and injustice and contribute in the development of nation by asserting human rights.

Integrating Peace Education in School: Integrating peace education through language textbooks is an effective way to develop the skills of critical thinking, debate and coalition-building and promote the values of freedom of speech, individuality, tolerance of diversity, compromise and conscientious objection. There is an urgent need to intertwine such topics through lessons and poems in text books so that young minds can understand this crucial aspect in a greater detail. Various co-curricular activities such as celebrating birth anniversaries of great people, project work, quiz, group discussions, workshops, debates, skit, poster making, slogan writing, essay writing, poem writing, peace march and observing silence can be held to sensitize students towards the issues of conflict resolution and peace education. In a nutshell, school education should be re-structured and re-designed to address the issue of peace education which is quite significant in contemporary scenario. School education should evolve to create an enabling and supportive environment which would enable students to learn, unlearn and re-learn the issues and develop capacities to question, debate and enquire about various dimensions and perspectives of peace in their contexts.

Concluding Remarks: National Curriculum Framework 2005 proposes the five guiding principles, i.e., connecting knowledge to life outside the school, ensuring that learning is shifted away from rote methods, enriching the curriculum to provide for overall development of children rather than remain textbook centric, making examinations more flexible and integrated into classroom life and nurturing an over-riding identity informed by caring concerns within the democratic policy of the country [Page 5]. In this regard, the role of text books needs to be examined. Text books have the potential to portray events in a meaningful way so as to enable learners to engage in construction of knowledge on their own. Peace education is a wider phenomenon which covers aspects of social justice, equality, peace, harmony, integrity, universal brotherhood, and elimination of subjugation, revolt against marginalization in peaceful and non-violent ways, asserting for one's rights and contributing in national development. The paper examines the content of language text books in promoting peace education. It is argued that text books need to be enriched with recent incidents so as to equip students with current issues. Moreover, multidisciplinary perspective needs to be given prominence. Teachers need to be oriented about integrating content across subjects. Social justice is the most important aspect of peace education. On analyzing the content of text books at senior secondary level, it is found that the issues related to marginalized sections have been discussed at length in class XII English book. It is suggested that the content of Hindi text books needs to be enriched with regard to issues related to peace education. Text books need to emerge as a means which could empower students to clarify their assumptions, beliefs perceptions and values and enable them to engage in meaningful deliberations and appropriate decision making in their life.

References:

- Antara. 2006. *Main Reader in Hindi for Class XI.* New Delhi: NCERT.
- Flamingo. 2006, *Main Reader in English for Class XII.* New Delhi: NCERT.
- NCERT. 2005. *National Curriculum Framework.* New Delhi: NCERT.
- Vistas. 2006. *Supplementary Reader in English for Class XII.* New Delhi: NCERT.

4. TEACHER AS CATALYSTS: ENSURING PREVENTION OF CONFLICTS AND PEACE-BUILDING

Kshama Pandey* and Neetu Singh**

Whenever two individuals opine in different ways, a conflict arises. It cannot be possible that two individuals can think alike and there is definitely a difference in their thought process as well as in their understanding. Conflict arises whenever individuals have different values, opinions, needs, interests and are unable to find a middle way. Conflict is

* Dr. Kshama Pandey is an assistant professor and **Ms. Neetu Singh is a research scholar at the faculty of education of Dayalbagh Educational Institute, Agra [UP], India.

defined as a clash between individuals arising out of a difference in thought process, attitudes, understanding, interests, requirements and even sometimes perceptions. A conflict results in heated arguments, physical abuses and definitely loss of peace and harmony. A conflict exists when two people wish to carry out acts which are mutually inconsistent. They may both want to do the same thing, such as eat the same apple, or they may want to do different things where the different things are mutually incompatible, such as when they both want to stay together but one wants to go to the cinema and the other to stay at home. A conflict is resolved when some mutually compatible set of actions is worked out. The definition of conflict can be extended from individuals to groups [such as states or nations], and more than two parties can be involved in the conflict. The principles remain the same. [M.Nicholson: Rationality and the Analysis of International Conflict. 1992:11]

Conflicts: Conflicts are of different types such as:

Personal Conflict: Personal conflict occurs on personal level. It arises when the ideals and aims of two individuals clash with each other.

Racial Conflict: Racial conflict is mostly due to the physical differences. The feeling of superiority or inferiority is the root cause of racial conflict. Conflict between the Whites and Negroes in the USA provides an example of racial conflict.

Economic Conflict: Economic conflict involves competing motives to attain scarce resources. Each party wants to get the most that it can, and the behavior and emotions of each party are directed toward maximizing its gain.

Value Conflict: Value Conflict involves incompatibility in ways of life, ideologies – the preferences, principles and practices that people believe in. International conflict [e.g., the Cold War] often has a strong value component, wherein each side asserts the rightness and superiority of its way of life and its political-economic system

Political Conflict: The main cause of this kind of conflict is power which they want to capture. The conflict between different political parties is an example of this type of conflict.

International Conflict: It may take place for political, religious economic, ideological or for any other reasons. The conflict between India and Pakistan is an example of such type of conflict.

Class Conflict: Class conflict takes place among classes with their differing interests. In the feudal society there was conflict between the landlords and the peasants.

In addition to the conflicts discussed above there are a few other forms of conflict. They are stated below:

Personal and Corporate Conflict: Personal conflict takes place within the groups. It arises on account of various motives, envy, hostility, treachery etc. Corporate conflict occurs among the groups within a society or between two societies. Race-riots, communal riots, war between nations are some of the examples of corporal conflict.

Social tension and dissatisfactions, before their expression in the form of hostile action, are two important kinds of latent conflict. On the other hand, the overt conflict is the conflict expressed by a part or parties. Latent conflict becomes overt conflict when an issue is declared and when hostile action is taken. The war between India and Pakistan is an example of overt conflict.

The Roots of Conflict: Conflict is defined as an incompatibility of goals or values between two or more parties in a relationship, combined with attempts to control each other and antagonistic feelings toward each other [Fisher, 1990]. Sigmund Freud and other psychologist hold the view that the innate instinct for aggression in man is the main cause of conflict. Thus, various causes lead to conflict. The main cause of conflict may be briefly stated as follows:

1. **Individual Difference:** In society, men are not alike in their nature, attitudes, ideal, interest and aspirations. Due to this difference, they fail to accommodate themselves which may lead to conflict among them.

2. **Cultural Difference:** The culture of one group differs from the culture of the other group. These cultural differences among the group, sometimes cause tension and lead to conflict.

3. **Clashes of Interests:** The clash of interests of different people makes conflict inevitable. The interests of the workers clashing with those of employers lead to conflict among them.

4. **Social Change:** Conflict also arises due to the difference between rates of social change. The change in the moral norms of a society and man's hopes, aspirations and demands leads to conflict. The conflict between the old and new generations is owing to social changes. Conflict is an expression of social disequilibrium.

Conflict is a fact of life, and the challenge for the educator is to channel this phenomenon into constructive responses and to construct in society the techniques and institutions to resolve conflict non-violently to deter large-scale aggression. Effective prevention and peacemaking is holistic involving the entire society, and the first step is to resolve the root causes of conflicts, which involve, among other issues, socio-economic and political factors. On a state level, absence of the rule of law and justice, denial of human rights, lack of political representation for minority groups, ideological position, unemployment, poverty and rise in food prices, lack of accountability, poor governance and weak judicial systems often lead to violence if not resolved in their early stages. [Machel, 2009, World Bank, 2011]

The Search for Global Peace: The present world is faced with many problems - social, political, economical, educational, and cultural and Environmental—due to deterioration in values. Human values are eroding at a very fast rate resulting in decline of the quality of education. It is a matter of great concern for all the people, particularly Educators and Social scientists. In this perspective Peace Education for sustainability plays an important role in building peace and harmony and also in developing non-violent global sustainable society. Thus Peace Education and teachers are key drivers for attainment of sustainable development.

Peace education only can extend a real peace in this world. It has been well said by Mahatma Gandhi that, "***If we are to reach real peace in this world we shall have to begin with the children.***"

Lasting peace may depend on educating future generations into the competencies, perspectives, attitudes, values, and behavioral patterns that will enable them to build and maintain peace. To understand how to make peace education effective and sustainable, it is first necessary to define the nature of peace and peace education. Finally, the steps of conducting an effective and sustainable peace education must be understood.

Peace Education: Peace education can be defined as the

process of promoting the knowledge, skills, attitudes and values needed to bring about behaviour changes that will enable children, youth and adults to prevent conflict and violence, both overt and structural; to resolve conflict peacefully; and to create the conditions favorable to peace, whether at an intrapersonal, interpersonal, intergroup, national or international level. It is problem-posing education that attempts to build in every person the universal values and behaviors on which a culture of peace is predicated, including the development of non-violent conflict resolution skills and a commitment to working together to realize a shared and preferred future. Peace education is aimed at teaching individuals the information, attitudes, values, and behavioral competencies needed to resolve conflicts without violence and to build and maintain mutually beneficial, harmonious relationships. It includes the cultivation of peace building skills [e.g., dialogue, mediation, artistic endeavors]. Peace educators, then, teach the values of respect, understanding, and non-violence, present skills for analyzing international conflict, educate for alternative security systems, and use a pedagogy that is democratic and participatory. Thus, peace education as a practice and philosophy refers to matching complementary elements between education and society, where the social purposes [i.e., why teach], content [i.e., what to teach], and pedagogy [i.e., how to teach] of the educative process are conducive to fostering peace.

The Secondary Education Commission [1952–53] had defined the purpose of education as ***"the training of the character and personality of students in such a way that they will be able to realize their full potentialities and contribute to the well-being of the community."***

Education for Peace through a School-Community linkage is a means of fostering this outlook in students. Fostering peace skills in children needs to be seen as an investment in building the foundation for life-long learning and enduring achievements. Schools can heal social illnesses if they engage their responsibilities from the enlarged perspective of peace. Peace education is multidimensional and holistic in its content and process. Education for Development is the term used in the UNICEF to describe an approach to teaching and learning which builds a commitment to global solidarity, peace, acceptance of differences, social justice and environmental awareness in young people [Fountain, 1995]. Peace education in the UNICEF refers to the process of promoting the knowledge, skills, attitudes and values needed to bring about behaviour changes that will enable children, youth and adults to prevent conflict and violence, both overt and structural; to resolve conflict peacefully; and to create the conditions conducive to peace, whether at an intrapersonal, interpersonal, intergroup, national or international level. According to RD Laing [1978], ***"Peace education is an attempt to respond to problems of conflict and violence on scales ranging from the global and national to the local and personal. It is about exploring ways of creating more just and sustainable futures."***

Fostering Peace Education: Implementing peace education can be achieved in the following ways:

- Using topics that raise issues related to peace and cultural understanding in the classrooms. This helps teachers to accord students the basic information to help them develop positive attitudes and values related to peaceful living; and
- Engaging in activities that encourage co-operation, consensus building and reflective listening gives students skills they need to meet and resolve conflicts.

Issues and problems related to the topics related to conflicts will undoubtedly provide opportunities for pupils and students to develop conflict solving and critical thinking skills alongside language skills to express themselves clearly and convincingly. At the center point of all this, is the desire to make learners negate their inbuilt biases against other groups.

Peace Learning Activities: To mention:

1. Debating- Debate promotes students' critical and logical thinking. It also helps to improve skills in public speaking and presentation. It can be used as a brief activity during a lesson at the classroom. Such debates help extensive exploration into the issue under discussion;
2. Colloquy- Colloquy is a formal discussion. As a part of lessons colloquies are useful in developing perception, awareness, and in-depth exploration;
3. Values clarification- This category of activities help students to reflect and reconsider their own values, attitudes and vision. When a student speaks out on attitudes, if the teacher feels that he/she needs to reconsider it, she asks a simple question, without expecting a reply in order to bring insight;
4. Brainstorming- Brainstorming is a method of encouraging students to come out with ideas, solutions, or views about the issue under study. It generates creative ideas and alternative solutions to problems;
5. Self-expression- Children like to express their feelings, wishes, fancies and ideas in various forms. They can be used as effective learning activities in the class;
6. Co-operative story-telling- To stimulate creative thinking, children can sit in a circle and build a story. The first child starts with a sentence to begin the story. The second one adds another sentence and it goes from one

after another in the round. The story gradually builds up adding new events. The teacher may intervene at difficult points to help the process go on the right track. Once it is completed it can be edited to assume an acceptable form;

7. Acting out- Acting out certain situations and events makes learning fun and entertaining. It specially helps to improve speech. There are several forms of acting that can be used in the classroom;
8. Icebreakers- These are activities that help to break down barriers between participants making them relaxed and interactive. They open up and create the social climate conducive to the session;
9. Co-operative games- There are activities designed to build up co-operation, group awareness and trust in the groups. Everyone has to work together in the activities, e.g. make a machine joining up together and rhythmically show how it works, with sounds;
10. Affirmation activities- These activities are effective in developing the self-esteem of children. Children express affection, positive remarks, appreciation and friendship for each other either verbally or non-verbally, in these activities, e.g: Children move around the classroom making pleasant comments to each one they meet; and
11. Guided fantasy- As we pointed out earlier, children are highly imaginative. This powerful faculty could be fruitfully used while learning in the class. Especially, imagination can appeal to deep positive feelings in children, such as kindness and peace. Guided fantasy could be used for meditation, which evokes deep, peaceful, pleasant and aesthetic feelings. Such activities help emotional development.

Need for Value-Based Education in the Twenty-First Century: A worthwhile education should target the total development of learner's personality. But in the present system emphasis has given to transmission of knowledge and cultivation of occupational skills. This has created a moral vacuum in the life of the individual. Inculcation of desirable values in the upcoming generation is felt essential for finding out answers to so many problems that humanity face today.

The need for value-based education is clear from the following points:

- It will help in developing positive social attitudes in new generation which prompt them to raise their voice against social evils;
- Meaningful education aims at the all-round development of the learner. The optimal development of the moral, spiritual and aesthetic aspects of personality needs enrichment and refinement in the form of value education;
- The humanizing role of the educational process is played by the value-based education; and
- The harmonious co-existence of different ideologies in society requires respect for moral and ethical values. Value education inculcates these virtues in a systematic manner;

Further, the need for value education is constantly increasing as we continue to witness increasing violent activities, behavioral disorder and lack of unity in society. Value education is essential for developing democratic qualities such as dignity of the individual, social justice, liberty, equality, fraternity etc. It education can strengthen students' self esteem, optimism and commitment to personal fulfillment, and help students exercise ethical judgment and social responsibility. Effective values education in schools and colleges will help students to understand and apply values such as care and compassion, doing your best, fair go, freedom, honesty and trustworthiness, integrity, respect, responsibility, understanding, tolerance etc. in their daily life. Value education is needed to give direction to one's social, moral and spiritual development, thus to bring quality to life. Value oriented education is needed to promote individual and social welfare, love, peace, goodwill and understanding.

Value-based education is needed for developing moral qualities such as humility, truthfulness, honesty, courtesy, tolerance, sacrifice etc. among the youth. Values are the greatest unifying force in life. Inculcation of these values through education is the necessity of the hour to check the disintegration of social relations. Value education is needed to strengthen social harmony, to encourage cultural development, to instill democratic qualities and to combat social evils and injustice. Value-based education inculcates sense of co-operation and fellow-feeling among people. Only value education would lead us to attain our ultimate goal of peace on earth.

Teachers as Peace-Builders: ***"Teachers are mirror of upcoming generations in the form of students and an effective element of establishing peaceful atmosphere."*** The role of teachers towards a child's education is to create a caring environment in the classroom. Teachers who listen to what the students have to say and develop a curriculum that is meaningful to the children have the most successful students. Teachers with a concern for the needs of the students and a student-oriented philosophy have co-operative students who look forward to learning. It is said that teaching profession is the best and constructive profession in all. The respect, regard and stature of teaching profession are very high. Teachers in India and elsewhere have always commanded great respect and regard from the society, because teachers are the builders of the nation. They prepare persons and create manpower for every sector of human activity. The quality of people and their level of thinking largely depend on the contribution made by the teachers. Mahatma Gandhi also supported this view. He said, ***"I have always felt that the true text book for the pupil is his teacher. I remember very little that my teachers taught me from books, but I have even now a clear recollection of things they taught me independently of books. Whose is the hand that has transmitted useless stone in to a sacred statue worshipped by many? It is the noble hand of the sculptor that has turned it in to a statue and has lent an immense value to it."*** Similarly, ***"it is the teacher alone just like the wise sculptor, who removes always, with careful handling, the drawbacks and weaknesses in a student and lifts him to sublime heights of teaching."*** Teachers should take their job seriously and work together so as to enjoy the challenge of teaching. Teacher can play an important role in imparting the peace education as:

- Value and model lifelong learning;
- Know the curriculum and communicate expectations to students and parents;
- Are approachable and have a positive relationship with students, colleagues, parents and community members;
- Provide a safe, supportive and inclusive environment in their classroom and school;
- Design and implement effective and meaningful instructional and assessment strategies;

- Challenge students to reach their potential and foster independent learning;
- Are firm, fair and consistent with discipline; and
- Assist their students in recognizing and understanding their role in a local and global community

Essential Traits for Teaching Peace Education: The first and foremost principle that a teacher should keep in mind in this respect is *unity in diversity.* Our curricular contents should draw freely upon the Indian traditions as well as the cultures of the world. Our curriculum has to inculcate among the students the value of paying equal respect to all. For this, the contents should be taken from the *Bhagawad-Gita*, The Quran and *The Guru Granth Sahib*, and *The Upanishads*. The curriculum should include religious stories, Legends myths and fables. Whenever possible, prayer, yoga and meditation camps should be organized to cultivate ethics and develop the quality of 'dignity of labour' among the students. We have to prepare them for future life. We have to make them men of characterizing above the considerations of country, caste, language and religion. Apart from it, some other necessary characteristics should also be considered:

First: The teacher must understand that multicultural, multiethnic, and multi-religious problems in society are not to be dealt with in isolation in bits and pieces of a good peace education program but, being interconnected with all other problems of peace and violence, are addressed in the whole program. For example, developing such qualities as compassion and service to others can help reduce racial, religious, or other prejudices, but students of all backgrounds must take part in the program.

Second: The teacher must be cognizant and wholly supportive of the basic nature and aims of peace education, one example given before from Dale Hudson being, ***"...education that actualizes people's potentialities in helping them learn how to make peace with themselves and with others, to live in harmony and unity with self, humankind and nature."*** The principles upon which this statement rests include:

- The cardinal prerequisite for world peace is the unity of humankind; and
- World order can be founded only on the consciousness of the oneness of humankind. ***"It follows that, in this view, the teacher of peace education in an apparently diverse society must keep certain basic aims in mind: the achievement of a unified, peaceful society both globally and within the nation, where world citizenship is fostered and unity in diversity"*** is recognized and practiced.

Third: the teacher should constantly keep in mind that the attainment of any aim is conditioned upon knowledge, volition, and action. Unless these three are forthcoming, nothing will be accomplished. The power needed to accomplish a peaceful world is the unification of humankind. To this end, the teacher must use his own volition and will-power. In the words of Sarvepalli Radhakrishnan, we...***"... will peace with our whole body and soul, our feelings and instincts, our flesh and its affections."*** Then we should act intelligently to reduce intercultural, interethnic, and inter-religious violence, bringing a greater degree of unity and harmony in society. To accomplish this, the teacher should develop qualities such as tolerance, respect of appreciation of others, being fair and open-minded, and being able and willing to consider other points of view looking beyond his or her own self-interest. In other words, the teacher must be sincerely attempting to be free of prejudice.

When a teacher becomes deeply and regularly involved in teaching peace education, this can cause that teacher to take a long, deep look at his or her values and beliefs. Clearly, it can center a person on one's own thoughts, words, and deeds. In order to be a model for the students, the teacher has the opportunity of transformation and change of the inner self. Then the students can be helped to understand and feel what is a peaceful person who is a peacemaker, and the teacher will have a powerful, positive influence on hundreds and thousands of children and youth. Teachers are the torch bearers of the society. Their role is to bring perfection in the society and perfection in the field of education, science, art, literature, and in all walks of human life. Precisely the role of the teacher is as follows:

- Teachers should take each members of society for what they are and look for the good in them;
- Teachers should bring spiritual culture in the society;
- Teachers should teach genuine love and respect for all;
- Teachers should inculcate moral and ethical values in the society;
- Teachers should update society with latest scientific and technological knowledge and allow each student to become a good scientist, good economist, a good philosopher;
- Teachers should bring environment consciousness in the society and remove inferiority and superiority complexes among the members of the society;
- Teachers should teach cosmic brotherhood in the society; Teachers should make each member self reliant;
- Teachers should allow each member of the society to become rational, logical and inventive in nature;
- Teachers should teach good culture, customs and traditions to the society;

- Teachers should motivate reading habit among the students and provide good counseling;
- Teachers should find out individual's talent and him/her guide accordingly;
- Teachers should teach living style to the society; and
- Teachers should be well-versed in all subjects and specialized in some subjects.

Living in harmony and good coexistence implies having developed a certain degree of personal and social maturity. With regard to co-existence and harmony, the following contents should be included in the Teacher Education curricula:

1. Self-actualization for teachers;
2. Sociology of education;
3. Psychology in teaching and learning;
4. Skill oriented contents;
5. Contents related to ICT;
6. Cultural programmes;
7. Physical activities;
8. Social manners and code of behavior for administrators;
9. Foundation of related country culture;
10. Local tradition;
11. Religion and culture;
12. Scout basic unit leader training course [BBTC];
13. Four or five periods on peace education in a week during whole school year;
14. One or two national or international seminar/conferences/ workshop/symposia;
15. Geeta darshan; and
16. Moolya chetna vikas shiksha etc.

It can be deduced from this that there is little course work which is directly related to harmony and human rights, but all these courses will have as one of their objectives the inculcation of values relevant to harmony and human rights.

Life Skills Needed in Teacher Education Programme for Peace Education: Thus, different types of life skills need to be included in the teacher education programme for peace and harmony. Life skills can influence the way and one feels about oneself and others. The students will develop the skills necessary to be effective peace makers. Skills significant for the education for peace are:

- Critical thinking: ability to analyze information and experiences in an effective manner;
- Creative thinking: ability to generate new ideas by combining, changing or reapplying existing ideas;
- Problem solving: identifying the problem, exploring the available alternatives and deciding on the possible solution;
- Decision making: to choose from the varied options based on the existing knowledge of the topic under consideration keeping in mind the positive or negative consequences of each of the option;
- Interpersonal relationship: ability to establish positive relationships in positive ways;
- Effective communication: ability to express, verbally through spoken or written language and non-verbally through gestures and body movements; and
- Coping with emotions: being aware of the predominant emotion that preoccupies the mind at any point of time, knowing how emotions influence behaviour, and being able to respond to emotions appropriately.

Conclusion: Education aims at all-round development of the individual. But, unless the student is at peace within himself and with the external world or his environment, he/she cannot progress in various fields. Therefore, in the present society, education should foster eternal and universal values oriented towards the unity and integration of our people. It should develop the feelings of respect for human rights, justice, tolerance, co-operation, social responsibility and cultural diversity in addition to a firm commitment to democracy and non-violent conflict resolution through various curricular and co-curricular programmes. Success of such programmes largely depends on the competence of the teacher – his/ her knowledge, understanding, attitude, interests and critical thinking etc. Therefore the teacher is the catalytic agent for realizing the desired objectives and for translating the dreams into realities. Thus, it is a great need of this hour to be aware for organizing peace education for the all round development of the children and peaceful society.

References:

- Aggarwal, JC. 2005. *Education for Values, Environment and Human rights*. New Delhi: Shipra Publication.
- Danesh, H B. 2006. *Towards an integrative theory of peace education* in the Journal of Peace Education [3-1, 55–78].
- Galtung, J. 1969. *Violence, Peace, and Peace Research* in the *Journal of Peace Research [*6-3: 167-191].
- Jane, Sahi. 2000. *'Education for Peace*. Pune: Akshar Mudra.
- Singh, YK. 2009. *Value Education*. New Delhi: APH Publishing Corporation.
- Smith, A. and Vaux, T. 2003. *Education, Conflict and International Development*. London: Department for International Relations.
- UNESCO. *Non-violence education*. http://portal.unesco.org/education November 2002Development (DFID).
- UNESCO. Human Rights Education. http://www.unesco.org/education/hci/index. html.November, 2002
- Retrieved 19 December 2011 from: www.gsdrc.org/docs/open/sd29.pdf
- UN General Assembly. 1998. *International decade for a culture of peace and nonviolence for the children of the world, 2001-2010. Resolution 53/25*. http://www3.unesco.org/iycp/uk/uk_sum_decade.htm as accessed on April 5, 2009

5. ROLE OF LANGUAGE IN PEACE EDUCATION

Punam Beniwal*

All over the world, a great deal of emphasis is currently being placed upon peace education, as the quest for peace necessitates extensive knowledge and unfailing assiduity. The widespread interest in preparing individuals for peace on earth makes us resort to the teaching-learning process. The inevitability of this emphasis upon education for peace has arisen not only from the need to educate the public opinion of the scourges of war, its prodigality or the danger of total annihilation etc, but also from the necessity to promote understanding, acceptance and friendship among all peoples and nations, and to strengthen respect for human rights and fundamental freedoms.

Learning to make a living is not the sole reason for getting education; there is another, equally important byproduct: learning to make a life, a life that is beneficial, useful and peaceful. After all, humans are social animals; their success in life is largely a matter of successful social relations. Quite evidently, student age is the crucially important period which enriches one's personal life, nurtures social adjustments, fosters friendship and understanding and affects one's whole life pattern. Seen from this perspective, one could very well understand the critical necessity of teaching students, youth

* Ms. Punam Beniwal is a research scholar at the JT University of Jhunjhunu [Rajasthan], India.

and young leaders the art of living together, in mutual respect, justice, love and peace.

Alfred North Whitehead calls education, ***"the acquisition of the art of the utilization of knowledge."*** We need to tell our students, youth and young leaders about our world and its problems. We need to explain to them their part in the solutions. We need to instill in them a genuine appreciation of, and a profound liking towards, our humanitarian traditions and values such as non-violence, tolerance, understanding, co-operation and peace. To quote HG Wells, ***"human history becomes more and more a race between education and catastrophe"*** and hence, we must educate the youth for peace. However, will any kind of education, given by anybody to anybody under any circumstances, bring about these results? It is highly unlikely.

Peace education itself is as abstruse a notion as peace. Any attempt to define peace education in strict terms, or to typify a set of programmes for the purpose of generalization would prove futile, as the most important features that characterize the notion of peace education are many and varied. The aims and objectives, the perspectives of the subject, the working methods and other theoretical and practical approaches are decisive variables. Furthermore, place, period, local environment and other internal variations are major affective components in deciding the kind of peace education, its scope, its nature and the values one would attach to it. Owing to these factors, peace education varies from country to country, and even between regions within one country. However multifarious the approaches are, all educational programmes and activities collected under peace education would seek to prepare the students for peace. To put it in a nutshell, peace education sees to the construction of defenses of peace and fences of justice in the minds of the younger generation, and to making the youth hold to peace individually in life.

Peace education covers a wide territory, and has many subsidiaries. Mitsuo Okamoto argues that disarmament education, international education, development education and the like can, by broad definition, be included as programs in peace education. The contents denominated by the various titles like world order education, global education, education for international understanding, education for justice, ecological education etc., have been categorized by Okamoto into four types of peace education.1 The first sees peace education as criticism of war. The basic view here is that peace is the absence of war. Content of this type includes teaching concerning the legacy of war experience, a scientific explanation of the causes of war and conditions of peace, the promotion of international understanding as a preventive to war, etc. The second type considers peace education as liberation.

Here, a new concept of peace, positive peace, is presupposed. Liberation from poverty, ignorance, discrimination and oppression etc. is seen as the objective goal for peace education here.

The third type regards peace education as a learning process. In this type, peace education is grasped as a learning process towards inter-personal maturity on the basis of the unity between theory and practice on the one hand, and a critical understanding of history and society on the other. The fourth type holds peace education as life-style movements: it rests upon the realization that warfare and war preparations are intimately tied to the fact that the over-production and extravagance of the nations at the center have been gained at the expense of the wealth and development of nations at the periphery. Here, we can refer to a standard of values emphasizing a simple life, human scale, self-determination, ecological awareness and personal growth.

Disarmament education is a major development in the field of peace education. It implies education both for and about disarmament. All who engage in education or communication may contribute to disarmament education by being aware of and creating an awareness of the factors underlying the production and acquisition of arms, of the social, political, economic and cultural repercussions of the arms race, and of the grave danger, to the survival of humanity, of the existence and potential use of nuclear weapons. Development education explores development issues and focuses on the development process. Obviously, the content of development education in a developing country like India is entirely different from that of a developed country. Given the present situation in India, creating a deeper consciousness and awareness of our development problems among our students, and designing programs of personal involvement in development activities will open up new vistas in our development process. We can also find a very strong correlation between development education and environmental education. The wider view of the meaning of peace gives rise to several innovations in the domain of peace education, viz. the teaching of human rights and fundamental freedoms, education for international understanding, education about the UN, its other non-formal peace education programs, such as the UN students' association, the UNESCO clubs, the UNESCO Associated Schools Project and so forth. Both the conceptual and the practical approaches must be quite conspicuously delineated.

Having developed a theoretical framework and drawn up policy prescriptions for carrying out peace education programs and activities, we should attend to curriculum change. Indeed, peace education demands the modification of the existing educational system, rather than mere expansion of it.

In the case of India, although caste oppression, Untouchability, gender discrimination and other cruelties existed, the culture has been marked by acceptance, catholicity and an innate inclusiveness which refuses to be taken away by doctrinal divergences. All these factors have facilitated the commingling and constant cultural exchanges of tribes, races, religions and ethnic groups with grave doctrinal, philosophical and ideological differences. Islam, which came to conquer, compromised and became Indianized in the form of Sufism, and Islam influenced Hindu reformation thoughts of the nineteenth century. Indian culture, characterized by a profound understanding of the nature of humans and their relations with other beings and the universe, is absorbing all the essentials in the Western scientific civilization, and the inherent Europeanism in it has made it possible to understand the Christian culture. This ancient culture of India was taken to many contiguous lands in Asia. When improved means of communication like the printing press and the rail road were about to hasten cultural communication, the advent of political changes and aspirations, the movement for independence, fears of dominance and dependence and all such sorts of influences gave rise to an insistence on cultural independence and actual divide. The South Asian scene, which was once described as a *harmony of contrasts,* gave a different picture. The contrasts with strong political and psychological undercurrents became violent and caused recurrent divisions.

Role of Language in Peace Education: Recently, however, there has been a rejuvenated will to see harmony through regional co-operation efforts, and bilateral transactions and dialogues. After all, there are many cross-cutting alliances and allegiances. One of the main philosophic-religious schools of Indian culture, Buddhism, reigns supreme in Sri Lanka, where the minority Tamils share their language and religion with the people of Tamil Nadu in India. Besides the Tamils, there is other *language- culture* group represented by the Urdu-speakers in Pakistan and India, Bengali-speakers in Bangladesh and West Bengal [India], and Sindhi, Punjabi and Nepali speakers across the borders of Pakistan, India and Nepal. If Pakistan, Bangladesh, or the Maldives claims a preponderance of Islam, India too possesses eminence in Islamic culture as it has the second largest Muslim population in the world. Signaling India's unique identity, Hinduism and Buddhism offer a basis of understanding with the Himalayan kingdom of Nepal and Bhutan.

Furthermore, there is ample scope to define commonalities on the foundations of philosophy, ethics and religion, literature, theater, music, dancing, painting, sculpture, architecture and even minor arts such as wood-carving, copper and cloisonné work, carpet making, earthenware etc. The wind and the limbs, the brush and the chisel, the trowel, the pen and the very spirit itself strengthen the fabric of the rich cultural milieu of South Asia with some basic character, emphasis on melody in music, traditional and stylized form in dance, free variations in painting, monumentalize in sculpture, lyricism in poems, and realism in stories.

Religious fervor, fervent wedlock, strong affinity to family, respect for elders, and a host of other cultural habits and customs, too, contribute to the spinning of the regional cultural web. In spite of all these, South Asian countries cannot be simply lumped together culturally; it is even less likely, under the present circumstances marked by divided politics, diverse allegiances, differing perspectives and cultural policies etc. Maybe a good compromise would be engaging in peace education activities in one's country without overlooking the larger regional backdrop.

The peace education we plan should be carefully adapted in kind, in amount and in distribution. The major point we have to reckon with, while deciding the quality of teaching to be given, is to understand the subcultures of India as a prerequisite to develop world-mindedness. It is highly difficult to specify the exact amount of peace education. But it is worth taking note of some of the basic questions in distribution. First, too few teachers are capable of meeting the requirements and values dictated by peace education which are crucial for favorably affecting the awareness and behavior of young minds. Second, a trite description and vague discussion will prove as useless as mere cramming up details, unless a solution is specifically mentioned and the means of implementation are spelt out. Third, the form and content of peace education is quite unique and so it does not go with conventional treatment. Evaluation, for example, is a rather difficult process as the teaching aims at the essence of individuals. There are many more related things which demand our prudent concern.

It is important to remember that peace education is not an additional academic subject we add to the existing system. Instead, it is the general orientation that we introduce in the existing subjects, textbooks and teacher discourses. For instance, the Sociology textbooks could underscore the fact that peaceful co-existence is an objective requirement for peaceful development, and vice versa. In the Physics textbooks, emphasis could be laid on the need to fight for a ban on Nuclear weapons and other weapons of mass destruction, and international agreements in this field. Biology books could explain, among other things, the deadly effects of exposure to radioactivity on human beings. Needless to say, one who wills the end wills the means. Though international comparisons are difficult, general lessons and indicative suggestions can be taken from international experiences also.

The challenge for educators all over the globe is to choose between going ahead with the present effete educational system, or preparing our younger generation for the kind of life each and every one of us aspires towards. To use Swami Vivekananda's categorization, should we teach them just *to know* or *to be*.

*****

E: <u>Miscellaneous</u>

1. CLASSICAL OPPORTUNITIES FOR CULTURE OF PEACE EDUCATION

Asha Thokchom*

Peace education is more effective and meaningful when it is imparted taking into account the social and cultural context and the needs of the country. It should be globally relevant. It should be enriched by cultural and spiritual values and with the universal human values. Peace education is a remedial measure to protect children from falling into the ways of violence in society. It aims at the total development of the child. It tries to inculcate higher human and social values in the mind of the child. In essence, it attempts to develop a set of behavioral skills necessary for peaceful living and peace building from which the whole of humanity will benefit.

---

* Dr. Asha Thokchom is an associate professor at the GP Women's College, Imphal [Manipur], India.

Children need self-development, one of the important needs is building an effective, integrated personality in the child with positive self-esteem. To live peacefully, an individual has to have many skills, like those related to affirmation, positive thinking, empathetic listening and communication, assertive behaviour, decision making and critical thinking.

Teacher should help children to develop such skills so that they are empowered as individuals in the society.

At the school level, the predominant need is to have a peaceful climate that is peace culture. In such a culture, children will naturally absorb the spirit of peace. There is a popular saying that peace has to be caught rather than be taught.

Peace education is the best method of education now. It is one means to find out the needs of the society. In today's world, one can see conflict all round. We should give peace a chance and there will be love, respect, understanding and prosperity for all.

Peace education must be included in the school curriculum by including one period in the class each week, conducting workshop for youth periodically, forming peace groups, emphasising on the role of teacher as counselor, role model, and a stickler to punctuality. A learning atmosphere must be created to bring quality education and community participation.

Designing Peace Education: In designing a peace programme for the whole school, it is necessary for the members of staff to be involved to assure the validity and relevance. Parents also can provide good insight. The existing values programmes need to be analyzed in order to find their strengths and weaknesses. Reviews of research on effective school-based skill-oriented conflict resolution programmes [which have been, to date, carried out primarily in western countries] suggest that important elements may include:

* Conducting a situation analysis prior to designing the programme, and planning for monitoring and evaluation prior to beginning any intervention [WHO, 1998];
* Allowing ample time to train staff/teachers, so that they can both internalize concepts and skills of peace education themselves, and be adequately prepared to convey those concepts and skills to others [Metis, 1990];
* Using co-operative and interactive methods that allow for active student participation and practice [Stevahn, et. al., 1996];
* Teaching generic problem-solving skills through the use of real-life situations [Tolan and Guerra, 1994];
* Consistent reinforcing of conflict resolution skills learned at school in non-school contexts, for example, through educating parents and community groups in the same skills taught in the school [Metis, 1990];
* Ensuring gender and cultural sensitivity in programme design and implementation, as well as appropriateness for the age group [Blakeway, 1997];
* Incorporating analysis of conflicts in the community and/or the wider society, as well as of interpersonal conflict, in the programme [Institute for Conflict Analysis and Resolution, 1994];
* Providing young people with the opportunity to engage in constructive, peace-building activities in their school and community [Tolan and Guerra, 1994]; and
* Enlisting broad-based community support for the programme from the outset, among politicians, educators, community leaders, public health professionals, religious groups and business leaders [WHO, 1998].

Action Research: Teachers in every country have the opportunity and capacity to undertake some research. Such research carried out in the day-to-day work of the school should be concerned directly with the problems of that school. It can properly concern itself with such matters as child development, class organization, teacher –pupil relationships, interaction with the community, curriculum matters, teaching techniques and many others.

The head of the institution has to do many things to encourage, support and assist teachers who want to do research, to experiment, to improve themselves. Important points in this direction are:

* Creating of an atmosphere in the school that would make experimentation by teachers easier; and
* Acting as a research consultant to his teachers, providing advice and counsel at each step in the research process.

Action research is distinguished from conventional scientific research by its goal of improving a social situation through an understanding of it [Hart, 1997]. Rather than confine research to the activities of experts, action research involves the subjects of a study in investigating themselves, looking critically at their social conditions in order to change them. It is an approach that is thus uniquely well suited to research and evaluation processes in peace education. Teachers and other facilitators can carry out action research as a way of reflecting on their own personal and professional development with respect to peace education. Children and young people can also be involved in researching the development of their knowledge, skills and attitudes in their own social contexts. Over the last two years step, through peace education programme has conducted several Workshop and consultancies in Churachanpur district [flash point for 1997 violence] of Manipur. Over three students, fifty teachers and ten schools Principals have participated in these workshops. Since the W/S provide knowledge, skills, behavioural change needed for conflict transformation.

Practice of Peace Education: Schooling and other educational experiences that reflect UNICEF'S approach to peace education should:

- Uphold children's basic right as enumerated in the CRC;
- Develop a climate, within the school or other learning environment, that models peaceful and rights- respectful behaviour in the relationships among all members of the school community; teachers, administrators, other staff, parents and children;
- Use teaching and learning methods that promote participation, co-operation, problem-solving and respect for differences;
- Allow opportunities for children to put peace-making into practice, both in the educational setting and in the wider community;
- Integrate an understanding of peace, human rights, social justice and global issues throughout manner that respects the rights and dignity of all involved; and
- Draw on the knowledge of peace-building that already exists in the community, including means of dealing with conflict that are effective, non-violent, and rooted in the local culture.

This vision of peace education is consistent with the UNICEF concept of rights-based, child- friendly learning environments. [UNICEF 1999, E/ICEF/1999/14] This concept includes [among others] elements such as the realization of the rights of every child, gender sensitivity, responsiveness to diversity, the promotion of quality learning outcomes such as life skills and successful problem solving, and the enhancement of teacher capacity.

Life Skills Education: The Ministry of Education and UNICEF have collaborated on a holistic approach to AIDS education that focuses on learning a range of life skills, rather than only medical information about preventing transmission of HIV. The programme is planned around the actual needs and suggestions of Zimbabwean young people themselves.

Activities explore issues such as self-esteem, coping with stress, gender roles, communication skills, decision-making with peer pressure through the use of role play and small group discussion. For example, in a section on preventing rape and sexual abuse, groups of students act out ways of coping with potentially dangerous situations.

For example: A stranger knocks on your door saying he is hungry and is in need of help. You are alone at home; you are doing very badly in science. Your unmarried teacher offers to give you extra lessons in his house in the afternoons after school. Through the course, students are encouraged to put their skills to use doing action projects such as carrying out surveys and interviews on the needs of the people with HIV/ AIDS, their families, and young people at risk in their own community.

Curriculum development: A number of countries have developed peace education curricula, usually consisting of activities around themes such as communication, co-operation and problem solving.

Manuals have been produced to guide teachers in using

these curricula with children in Burundi [1994], Croatia, and Liberia [1993]. In the Federal Republic of Yugoslavia, a series of workshops on peace education themes has been created for primary school children [1996]. Teachers' manuals in Sri Lanka demonstrate ways of integrating peace education into the traditional subjects of the existing curriculum [National Institute of Education, Sri Lanka, undated, a, b, c]. A series of readers has been developed in Rwanda for primary school children and adult literacy classes with stories and poems on peace themes. Sport and physical education have also been used in Rwandan schools as a vehicle for developing skills and attitudes of peace. Operation Lifeline Sudan has developed activity kits for schools that build co-operation and respect for differences through sports, art and science projects. Community service that is facilitated by the school is another feature of some programmes. The United Kingdom Committee for the UNICEF has produced a pack of teaching materials entitled *Children Working for Peace* [United Kingdom Committee for the UNICEF, 1995] introducing children to conflict resolution efforts through activities developed in Lebanon, Liberia, Northern Ireland and Sri Lanka.

Conclusion: Peace Education has become a strategy for peace building. The goal of peace education is to imbibe in the population a culture of peace, values, attitudes, respect for life and end to violence. Peace education is not a part of formal course work. There would be no examination and certification. Its foundation is conviction, understanding and appreciating its need in the individual, community, national and global life. There are several sources from which students can acquire knowledge. Peace education cannot restrict its objective to understanding the concept of peace. Just as was is in the minds of men, peace has to be installed in the minds of young men and women. In this new pedagogy, teachers' role undergoes massive change. Teacher is no more the reservoir and sole dispenser of knowledge. She is the planner, facilitator and guide, mediator, knowledge organizer, and evaluator. Peace education being essentially an applied subject, passive pedagogy would not serve the purpose. In the new pedagogy, both teachers and learners are active; indeed it is a joint venture. Lastly, peace education is an essential component of quality of good life.

Bibliography:

- Anand, CL, Ruhela, SP, Panda SN et al. 1983. *The Teacher and Education in Emerging Indian Society*. New Delhi: NCERT.
- Fountain, Susan, *Peace Education in UNICEF, UNICEF Staff Working Paper*. New York: UNICEF, pp 52 http:/www.unicef.org/education/files/peace education. Pdf
- Metis, Association. 1990. *The Resolving Conflict Creatively Program* of 1988-9: Summary of Significant Findings. New York: Community School District 15/New York Educators for Social Responsibility/New York City: Board of Education.
- Singh LC. 1990. *Teacher Education in India: A Resource Book*. New Delhi: NCERT, pp 42-53
- UNICEF. 1994. *I Dream of Peace*. New York: Harper-Collins.
- UNICEF. 1993. *Lebanon Learning for Life Programme*.
- UNICEF. 1996. *The state of the World's Children Report*. UK: Oxford University Press.
- World Health Organization. 1989. *Violence Prevention: An Important Element of a Health-Promoting School* [WHO Information Series on School Health Document 3]. Geneva: WHO.
- www.loc.gov.researchers on 10.7.2013
- www.thesangaiespress.com.

2. CURRICULUM FOR PEACE EDUCATION: CONSTRUCTIONS WITH STANDARDS AND GUIDELINES

Candice C Carter*

India made policy to support the formal education of your poorest children and you are planning to alleviate their hunger. The Right to Education Act demonstrates your desire to improve opportunities for all young citizens in your great nation. The National Food Security Act 2013 also establishes support for survival of even the nation's poorest children. The wellbeing of a state reflects the intellectual tools and skills it has provided its youth for success as cultural, national and global citizens. Indeed, the social contract of statehood demonstrates the responsibility of the state to provide for its citizens, and their responsibility to serve their state. As an interdependent body, the state and its citizens work together for their good. This body has an obligation to maintain the wellbeing of the global community as well as it own. In modern times, awareness of human fragility in the web of life that Earth supports forefronts another responsibility in the social contract. Humans must take care of their planet, including other forms of life in it. The interdependent body has biological along with social and political parts. These three components comprise a system that influences and responds to human

* Dr. Candice C Carter is a professor at the University of North Florida, Jacksonville, USA.

activities. For the sake of current and future survival, those activities most focus on wellbeing. The conditions of life in the state determine the security of that political collective. Perceptions of wellbeing and a good life are important factors for curriculum design as well as government policies. Hence, it is imperative to clarify the conception of a good life and wellbeing in it. With an awareness of human dependence on and ability to manage natural resources this planet can provide, a good life includes sustainable practices. For that purpose, humans must convert their cultural, economic and political norms. While sustainable use of resources is one determinant of wellbeing, another factor is justice. The right to food and safe drinking water is essential for wellbeing. There are many considerations for management of resources to meet the life-sustaining needs of every population, including the reproduction rate of humans.

Intentional living, in which people make conscious decisions about the impact of their behaviors on others and the planet, necessitates awareness. Knowledge of planetary and societal needs is not enough to change behaviors. People need to learn the skills of sustainable living and they need the support of their state for that accomplishment. Further, they must be motivated to change their lifestyles. Modeling by and accountability of their leaders to achieve the good for everyone is one source of motivation. Informal learning and motivation to emulate respected leaders result from observations in public, media and institutions.

Educators have the first responsibility to be respected role models for their students. In reality, teachers are animated curriculum. They informally teach how to pursue the good and demonstrate interest in wellbeing. As role models, educators embody lessons. Their informal instruction occurs through their communication and behaviors. Hence, there are professional and societal standards for teachers. Through the choices they make, teachers affect the wellbeing of students and their community. One professional decision is the curriculum they will use. Non-violence and peace education, highlights the responsibility of the state to support its citizens in pursuit of the good. For satisfaction of the state's responsibility in the social contract, it must support its teachers. Successful educators have preparation for their profession. They must develop knowledge of and skills for curriculum design, as well as dispositions that support student wellbeing and success in the learning process. This discussion will focus on resources for teachers that influence their design and provision of curriculum.

Standards and Guidelines: States have been producing guidelines and standards for instruction. These documents represent the state's interest in the education of its population. Discernable in those guidelines are the aspirations of the state. Government-generated standards need analysis for their alignment with current notions of the good. Content analysis enables that inquiry through examination of communicated ideas [Hsieh and Shannon, 2005]. The standards' statements have indicators that illustrate what students must learn to do. For example, California has Health Education Standard 5 for Decision Making with the following indicator, ***"Analyze the benefits of using non-violent means to resolve conflicts."*** [California Department of Education, 2008, page 21] Florida's Social Studies Standard 5.C.2.5 has an indicator that states the students will, ***"Identify ways good citizens go beyond basic civic and political responsibilities to improve government and society."*** [Page 11] Standard 1 of Washington's Environmental and Sustainability Learning

Standards states, ***"Students develop knowledge of the interconnections and interdependency of ecological, social and economic system. They demonstrate understanding of how the health of these systems determines the sustainability of natural and human communities at local, regional, national and global levels."*** [Washington State, 2009, page 4]

A recent content analysis of standards in the USA highlighted aspects of peace education that the standards of its states promoted through their curriculum directives. [Carter, 2013] Peace-related topics those standards prescribed were: health, social awareness, communication, conflict management, citizenship, civics, global awareness and sustainability. Health promoted knowledge about oneself, self-care and management of emotions. Social awareness featured perspectives of others and respect for different cultures. Appropriate and effective statements were communication goals. Conflict management focused on decision-making and interpersonal resolutions. Citizenship extended from school to community, state and nation. Political participation and service were goals of civics. Global knowledge included history of nations, institutions and cultures. Sustainability overlapped with social, economic and civic responsibilities. While these standards support some of the aspects of peace education, there are components of it that still need development in the standards states provide.

Peace Education Standards: Identification of components that need inclusion in state standards occurred through use of the standards for peace education. During 2004-2006, peace educators from different world regions collaborated in meetings of the Peace Education Special Interest Group of the American Educational Research Association to develop the initial Standards for Peace Education. They subsequently suggested more peace-oriented competencies for use in curriculum. The Standards for Peace Education responsively undergo revision from the feedback of researchers in on that pedagogy and its outcomes. As an inclusive and dynamic set of curriculum guidelines, the recommendations for peace education will continue to change. Currently, knowledge of *inter-subjectivity* and the disposition of *humility* are competencies that need addition to those recommendations. They are aspects of peace derived from Gandhian philosophy and its applications in education. [Shira, 2013] Participants in the Non-violence and Peace Education Seminar at Shridhar University may clarify evidence of those competencies and possible inclusion of others for global advancement of peace education. The evidence statements would explain what students do as demonstrations of understanding *inter-subjectivity* and displays of *humility*. Members of the school where students learn informally as well as through formal lessons would need to display such competencies as co-constructors of peace in addition to their role as informal teachers. All school members are informal peace educators for their students through the behaviors they display and their preparation of a peace-focused environment in the school.

Beyond recommendations for the education of students, teachers and school administrators need support for the achievement of multi-dimensional peace pedagogy. The omnipresence of conflict and opportunities to build peace that exist in every field allow for peace-oriented instruction in multiple dimensions. India has recognized the importance of preparing teachers for peace education. [De Paul, 2010; Mukhopadhyay, 2005] Instructors in higher education have the responsibility of tooling their students for peace. To support that endeavor while building *Conflict and Peace Studies* as a new discipline, specialists in that pedagogy are writing needed guidelines. A goal in the draft of the Model Higher Education Guidelines is provision of programs that develop student ability ***"...to analyze conflict, its sources and causes and non-adversarial methods for its prevention, management, and/ or resolution."*** [Association for Conflict Resolution Higher Education Standards Task Force, 2013, page 3]

While those guidelines are in refinement as a draft, educators can use the Standards for Peace Education [SPE] that provides competencies for teachers, administrators and their educators.

The SPE guidelines for teachers prescribe pedagogy. For example, one recommends that teachers ***"Cultivate and support the student's responsibility for their own peaceful-problem solving while you stay aware of, and responsive to, their needs."*** [Carter, 2013, page 251] Constructivism, whereby instruction incorporates students' own experiences and ways of knowing, begins with teachers' own conceptions of peace as they learn how to facilitate their student's learning. SPE Standard 1 advises teachers to ***"Facilitate student construction, from their collective experiences and new information, their concepts of peace and positive processes for increasing it."*** [Carter, 2013, page 250] Initiatives and guidelines exist for preparation of teachers to educate about diversity, conflict and communication. [Hagbok, 2005] However, instructors in higher education typically miss that support, unless they are in the field of peace education. This fact highlights the need instructors in higher education have for assistance with peace education. Regardless of their instructional discipline, they need support in provision of constructivist and transdisciplinary learning about peace. Inclusion of conflict transformation as an instructional strand is one way of providing peace-oriented instruction in higher education. [Carter, 2010]

Changing interactions and improving relations in an organization, which are core goals of conflict transformation, are the purview of school leaders. Administrative support is a foundation of peace education for every level of school and discipline in it.

Guidelines and theories for school administration abound. However, there is a need for peace as a specific goal of educational administration. While the word peace variably appears in mission and vision statements as well as in other goal statements of education, there are scarce guidelines for educational leadership that delineate peace. Identified in leadership literature are mere aspects of peace, including diversity, social responsibility, social justice, sustainability, conflict management, etc. However, theories of educational administration for comprehensive peace need articulation and publication. Peace education, and its administration, is comprehensive when it includes all domains of life and processes that occur in them. [Hantzopoulos, 2011] While administrators committed to advancement of peace have access to information that can support their behaviors that model peace, there is at least one set of corresponding guidelines for leading a school? The interactions and processes that school leaders administer is an informal curriculum for future leaders. Consequently, everyone in the school has an interest in refinement of their organization's tacit curriculum.

The SPE has recommended standards for school administrators. Several of the recommendations provide specific ways for advancement of peace by all school members. In line with modeling by Mohandas Gandhi, one recommendation is for maintaining peaceful interaction with oneself, ***"A man is but the product of his thoughts. What he thinks, he becomes."*** [Gandhi, 2013] This suggestion recognizes the intrapersonal aspects of management. A leader, and everyone else, must monitor and manage inner thought processes and immediate emotions with a focus on peaceful treatment of self as well as others. For example, intrapersonal peace involves listening to and revising inner thoughts that do not evidence a peace process. Let us say a school leader hears the inner voice exclaim, *He is so slow he must not be trying to get the project ready! I am going to get someone else to do the job.* With monitoring, the leader can recognize the inappropriate assumption and judgment in that inner thought and revise them. Subsequently, the inner voice can clarify, *I feel frustrated by the slowness of this project. I will find out why it is at this pace and if it is possible to expedite the project.* By recognizing the feeling and need, the leader rehearses the appropriate expression that will not be divisive or destructive in the organization.

The SPE standard, ***"Use congenial and equitable problem solving; Theory Y"*** addresses this need to avoid potentially harmful management decisions [Carter, 2013, page 253] Theory Y holds positive views of employees and that perspective supports their ability to accomplish goals [McGregor, 1960]. This is analogous to the self-fulfilling prophecy. It is a very influential factor in many aspects of education, for students, staff and faculty of a school. Expectations held of a person will be evident and influence both peoples' behaviors. Another directive the SPE provides for administrators expresses the expectation that non-violence will be evident in all aspects of the school. This clear focus enables examination of curricular contents in each discipline and subject area, as well as the interactions at school.

There are several resources for educators to use in development of the informal and formal curriculum. The Center for Non-violent Communication offers free online guides as well as small books for each of the different participants. Its list of vocabulary useful for expression of feelings has no cost for access at the organization's website. [Centre for Non-violent Communication, 2013] There is an opportunity to translate that Feelings Inventory to Hindi for use by speakers of that language. Nonprofit and non-governmental organizations have been supporting curriculum development through provision of guidelines.

Guidelines for curriculum exist in the Internet where organizations provide cost-free resources. These guidelines represent the particular interests of each organization. Every establishment features their specialization that is a component of peace education. Table 1 provides examples of current organizations and links to their curriculum guidelines that pertain to peace education. The guidelines of the many organizations worldwide supporting peace education and non-violence in schools fill some of the gaps in directives that governments provide. For example, The Dalai Lama Foundation provides the concept of non-violence as a *weapon of the brave.* [Nagler, 2013, para 3] There is no specific standard for instruction about the notion of non-violence as a method for government response to conflict. This, and other components that organizations provide to missing components of government standards demonstrate curricular issue.

Table 1. Organizations in USA Providing Curriculum Guidelines

Organization	Website [2013]
Anti-Defamation League	www.adl.org
Teachers Without Borders	www.teacherswithoutborders.org
Educators for Social Responsibility	http://esrnational.org
Human Rights Education Association	www.hrea.org
National Association for Multicultural Education	http://nameorg.org
North American Association for Environmental Education	www.naaee.net/
The Earth Charter Initiative	www.earthcharterinaction.org/content/pages/Read-the-Charter.html
Collaborative for Academic, Social and Emotional Learning	http://casel.org

Governments need to specific peace as a curricular topic in all domains of education. This includes instruction across and between subject areas. Students can learn in each class about knowledge and skills that people have or might use for developing and maintaining peace. Educators have already demonstrated their ability to infuse peace as a concept within traditional subject areas of modern education. While standards states provide justify curriculum, each discipline needs an explicit directive for teaching about peace. Additionally, states must provide peace-focused directives for school leadership. With mandates to manage an organization through processes that maintain and enhance institutional peace, school cultures would contribute to societal peace. If peace within and between nations is a goal of the state, there is a need to critically examine current curriculum and directives for it.

This discussion will focus on one subject area for illustration of the opportunities India has for developing curriculum that supports peace education. Social studies incorporates many disciplines as curriculum content, including geography, anthropology, sociology, psychology, history, economics, political science and humanities. Each discipline supports knowledge and skills people need for managing their world now and in the future. Yet, they are not neutral. They have contestable information and political agendas. For example, the study of history often limits contents that will orient students towards patriotism and ethnic pride by the dominant culture. [Guyver and Taylor, 2012: Kumar, 1991] War is a common topic in history textbooks with very limited information about the rationale, processes and outcomes of that violent response to political conflict. [Leahey, 2009] Hence, student inability to critically analyze historical events and understand different perspectives of it hinder development of mental capacities needed for peacemaking in the present and future. [Yogev, 2010] Discernable from narrow presentations of history and the minimal inclusion of peace as a topic is the promotion of militarism. [Howlett and Harris, 2010] That curriculum legitimates violence. It fails to develop wellbeing through education about harm-free responses to conflict: non-violence. Commendably, there has been a proactive response to this shortcoming in the curriculum of social studies.

Responses to this situation have been development of auxiliary or replacement curriculum. For instance, a nonprofit organization in the USA publishes curricula teachers develop as supplemental or replacement text for learning from multiple perspectives and through democratic action in response to conflict. [Rethinking Schools, 2013] Setalvad [2010] recognized and responded to this situation in India with development of a supplemental curriculum. Clearly there is an opportunity for curriculum revision in social studies. Although India's 2005 edition of the National Curriculum Framework stipulated peace in its syllabus and textbook recommendations, specifically for the study of social sciences/political science, there is a need for a broader revision of curriculum. [National Council of Educational Research and Training, 2012, page 14] For that reason, it is essential to use existing guidelines for peace education until India and many other nations provide standards or guidelines that broadly specify peace as a learning goal.

Conclusion: Vital for wellbeing is visionary education that fosters students' expectations, knowledge, skills and dispositions for peace in global as well as local contexts. When states use standards to influence curriculum and instruction, there is a need for analysis of those guidelines. Examination of directives for curriculum can reveal conflicts to avoid in the preparation of students for present and future success. Curriculum throughout the world needs inclusion of peace as a learning goal. When states do not clearly provide that, educators make a decision whether or not to support the goals of the state or teach with an alternative curriculum. The latter choice represents a political conflict. It weakens the legitimacy of a state that reinforces violence as a response to conflict. That is an unwanted structural conflict in addition to a distraction for school leaders and teachers.

India can be a leader in curriculum design. It has theoretical tools, motivated educators and an entire population of its children ready for instruction about peace in the past, present and future. Its prospects are good for peace education, especially when the government and school leaders clearly identify and support that learning goal.

Notes and References:

- Association for Conflict Resolution Higher Education Standards Task Force. 2013. *Model higher education guidelines: draft.* Author. Reston, VA.
- Carter, CC. 2013. Standards for Peace Education in IM Harris and ML Morrison [Eds.] *Peace education* [Third Edition], pp. 247-53. Jefferson, NC: McFarland.
- Carter, C. C. 2013, June. *Government Standards for Peace Education: Puzzling the Pieces of Prescribed Pedagogy* a paper presentation at the XV Comparative Education World Congress. Buenos Aires, Argentina.
- California Department of Education. 2008. *Health Education Content Standards for California Public Schools: Kindergarten through GradeTtwelve* as Retrieved August 25, 2013 from http://www.cde.ca.gov/be/st/ss/documents/healthstandmar08.pdf
- Center for Non-Violent Communication. 2013. *Feelings Inventory* as retrieved on August 30, 2013 from http://www.cnvc.org/Training/feelings-inventory.
- De Paul, SV. 2010. *Peace in Tamilnadu's Teacher Education* in CC Carter and Ravindra Kumar [Eds.], *Peace Philosophy in Action,* pp. 140-59. New York: Palgrave Macmillan.
- Florida Department of Education. 2008. *Next Generation Sunshine State Standards* as retrieved on August 25, 2013 from http://www.cpalms.org/Standards/FLStandardSearch.aspx
- Gandhi, MK. 2013. Gandhi quotes. Goodreads as retrieved on August 30, 2013 from http://www.goodreads.com/author/quotes/5810891.Mahatma_Gandhi
- Guyver, R and Taylor, T. 2012. *History Wars and the Classroom: Global perspectives.* Charlotte, NC: Information Age.
- Hagbok, M. 2005. *Action Report: Constructive Conflict Management in all Swedish Teacher's Training* in the *Journal of Peace Education, 2* [2], 212-213
- Hantzopoulos, M. 2011. *Institutionalizing Critical Peace Education in Public Schools: A case of Comprehensive Implementation* in the *Journal of Peace Education, 8* [3], 225-242
- Howlett, CF and Harris, IM. 2010. *Books, Not Bombs: Teaching Peace since the Dawn of the Republic.* Charlotte, NC: Information Age.

- Hsieh, H and Shannon, S. 2005. *Three Approaches to Qualitative Content Analysis* in the *Qualitative Health Research, 15*[9, 1277-88
- Kumar, K. 2002. *Prejudice and pride: School histories of the freedom struggle in India and Pakistan.* New Delhi: Viking Penguin.
- Leahey, CR. 2009. *Whitewashing War: Historical Myth, Corporate Textbooks and Possibilities for Democratic Education.* New York: Teachers College.
- McGregor, D. 1960. *The Human Side of Enterprise.* New York: McGrawHill.
- Mukhopadhyay, M. 2005. *Peace Education Framework for Teacher Education.* New Delhi: United Nations Educational, Scientific and Cultural Organization.
- Nagler, M. 2013. *Weapon of the Brave: Many Paths to Peace.* Dalai Lama Foundation as retrieved on August 30, 2013 from http://learning.dalailamafoundation.org/moodle/mod/resource/view.php?id=72
- National Council of Educational Research and Training. 2012. *A Report of the Committee Constituted for Reviewing the Textbooks of Social Sciences/Political Science, for Classes IX-XII.* New Delhi: Author. Retrieved on August 30, 2013 from http://www.ncert.nic.in/announcements/notices/pdf_files/NECERT_SKT_%28final%29.pdf
- Rethinking Schools. 2013. *Milwaukee, WI*: Available at http://www.rethinkingschools.org/
- Setalvad, T. 2010. *Pluralism and Transformative Social Studies Us and Them: Challenges for the Indian Classroom.* in CC Carter and Ravindra Kumar [Eds.] *Peace philosophy in action,* pp. 105-39. New York: Palgrave Macmillan.
- Shira, K. 2013, April 2. *Ahimsa and Humility in/for Philosophy of Education Discourse.* [Unpublished Doctoral Dissertation]. Canada: University of Toronto.
- Washington State. 2009. *Washington State K-12 Integrated Environmental and Sustainability Learning Standards* as Retrieved August 26, 2013 from http://www.k12.wa.us/environmentsustainability/pubdocs/ESEStandards.pdf
- Yadav, SK. 2011. *National Study on Ten Year School Curriculum Implementation.* Department of Teacher Education and Extension. New Delhi: National Council of Educational Research and Training as retrieved August 30, 2013 from http://www.ncert.nic.in/rightside/links/10YRSNCERT.pdf
- Yogev, E. 2010. *The Challenge of Peace Education in Israel* in CC Carter and Ravindra Kumar [Eds.] *Peace philosophy in action*, pp. 80-103. New York: Palgrave Macmillan.

3. RAISING PEACE IS TANTAMOUNT TO RAISING WOMEN

PK Willey Diwan*

Daily we are inundated with news of social violence, particularly from within the USA, the admired world model for social, political, educational, and technological development. We hear of wars, violent video games, pornography, male teens and adults going on suicidal rampages and shooting incidents in schools, drug use, raping. Somewhere from within us, comes a wondering question: What happened to their mothers? Why were not the children trained right?

Peace, with Nature, within society, begins with the acknowledgement of the powerful and beautiful force within women, to create and sustain society, beginning in the family unit. Holy Mother Amma —Mata Amritanandamayi, the Great World Teacher, Woman Saint and Humanitarian of Kerala, has mentioned how, ***"Statistics show that men—not women—commit by far most of the crime and murder in this world. There is also a deep connection between the way men destroy Mother Nature and their attitude towards women. Nature should be accorded the same importance in our hearts as our own biological mother."*** In the race and urge for `development' the most crucial element, the future generations, are being myopically and suicidally neglected. Present education and society prepare youth to fit into the same social, cultural and economic structures that are

* Ms. PK Willey Diwan is an independent researcher from the USA.

undeniably bringing about our planetary, societal, and self-destruction.

The sexual objectification through media images of women in societies under consumer economies and an increasing monoculture is destabilizing societal peace by negatively impacting women's perceptions of themselves. Damaged self-confidence creates weak mothers, unable to guide the development of their children with Earth Ethics. Low self-esteem directly impacts women's ability to bring the intelligence of the feminine principle into all social relations. Women's participation in society is further devalued by a false objectivity which seeks to neutralize the intrinsic characteristics of gender.

The emerging globalised philosophy and psychology have not matured into ways of life that are environmentally, socially or psychologically sustainable. What solutions exist for us today?

The psychological ethos of globalization environment is stronger than will power in most circumstances. Gandhi noted, ***"I have not come across any human being who remains unaffected by his surroundings. I for one think there can be no such person. If there is any such person in a million, he must be a vatapi, that is, one who lives only on air."***

Since the early 1960's, the dominant North American and Western European monoculture of our world have chosen models for children's socialization that sexually objectify the female body, with a corresponding crippling effect upon the ability of many mothers to become strong mothers for their children. These idealized images, internalized, are destroying the hope for sustainable peace.

With advertising media dancing grotesquely and screaming loudly into our ears, even common sense understandings are being uprooted. The decades long work [1950's-80's] of US psychologist John Bowlby, acknowledged the effects of maternal deprivation in infant and child development. His work emphasized the necessity of the tender loving relationship and attachment between mother and child as crucial for not only the emotional, but also the physical well being and thriving of both baby and mother. For nearly 30 years, Bowlby's views were accepted; courts, educational and medical systems in the USA and Western Europe honoured this natural and basic understanding. Bowlby's views were counter to the mainstream psychoanalytic theories, based in Freudian thought which hold the human being as being most concerned with sensory gratifications – food, sex, and shelter. However, within the last 35 years, Bowlby's findings have been increasingly discredited by 'new mainstream psychology' which finds a child of tender years, under two years of age, ***"too young to have developed a relationship with either parent."*** The US courts are now reflecting acceptance of these findings, adding to further destabilization of the child's home environment.

These findings fly in the face of all common sense. And of course there are counter findings; scientific studies which shows how biological mother's mere smile can relax her stressed baby. Research on these findings and similar facts; however, seek to understand the neural connection, rather than its sociological import for female education and development, family life and society. There is a blind refusal in mainstream science to connect the dots, to be guided by Earth ethics. Concerned people and world leaders are raising their voices. On the world stage now we hear His Holiness the Dalai Lama extolling again and again, the necessity of maternal love and care in youth in order to develop the warm heart, which brings inner and outer peace.

We are at the point now in industrialized and technologically advanced nations, where legally and medically, the self-identification of being either male or female, is increasingly considered a result of social construction, not reality, which is to say, by Nature. Human beings are becoming seen to be without any intrinsic or inherent nature, without any specific role in the wider and grander schema of life. Men and women are becoming interchangeable components in the basic unit of society –family life.

Since the late 1990's, there has been a significant drop in academic and scholarly studies on the effects of self-esteem in parenting, in society, and in female development. Through scientific studies, perceptions of self-esteem are becoming divorced from personal actions. This signifies a dangerous trend in research.

Destroying Self-Confidence in Girls and Women: the Facts: Along with this has come an extremely disturbing trend in media to sexually objectify and degrade women. Blasting images of unnatural looking women, from the time young eyes can focus, is resulting in traumatic directions in the monoculture: subsequent low self-esteem in women is affecting their ability to care for infants, to be strong mothers. This type of brainwashing through the media has been continuing since 1960, and we are looking at, and dealing with several damaged generations of motherhood and parenting in the USA and Western Europe today.

Girls are being taught by media, medical, and educational systems, to be promiscuous, and to depersonalize their sexual connections with others, seeking to use their bodies as recreational vehicles for sexual pleasure. The internalized effects of promiscuity are not part of self-confidence and esteem studies, which are focused largely on appearance perceptions alone.

The profound psychological effects of constant bombardment by distorted images and displays of the female form are causing many women to value having a slim body more than love and life itself. Research in the last decade in the US and Europe is finding that 90% of eating disorders are found in girls. The Rudd Centre for Food Policy and Obesity at Yale University, USA, in their 2006 survey found that: out of 4,000 respondents in varying numbers, between 15% and 30% said they would rather walk away from their marriage, give up the possibility of having children, be depressed, or become alcoholic, rather than be obese. Further, 18% would rather give up 10 years of their lives than be obese. 5% and 4%, respectively, said they would rather lose a limb or be blind than be overweight.

A UK study by Dove Research [2004] on perceptions of beauty and self esteem, found that: low self-esteem affects how girls think and feel about their future careers, with just one in three feeling confident that they will have a successful career in the future. If the status quo remains, the UK could be deprived of 200,000 female business professionals and 42,000 successful female entrepreneurs by 2050.

The discontentment felt by young girls about their appearance is at the heart of the issue. Almost half of those involved in Dove's study describe themselves as average, ordinary, plain, unattractive and ugly. Too many girls believe that happiness and success come from looking a certain way.

A girl is bombarded by approximately 6000 images every day, either in magazines, on TV, over the internet. Everywhere she goes, there will be images, displaying the perfect woman, and this is having a much wider impact than most realize.

In addition, there are new forms of self-mutilation appearing in our youth in America and Western Europe, known as cutting, in which the child slices their body, causing blood to flow, not with the intent to suicide, but to hurt them. Studies show in the most developed, educated, well-fed and technologically advanced societies that ***"each year, 1 in 5 females and 1 in 7 males engage in self injury."***

Others put the figure at 1 in 12. With an estimated 6 percent to 10 percent of all teenagers engaged in self-harm, ***"the numbers are huge. It represents much distress."***

The effects of the sexual objectification of women through thousands of images daily upon girls and women are no longer restricted to developed nations. The Dove Campaign for global studies revealed that ***"92% of teen girls would like to change something about the way they look, with body weight ranking the highest. 75% of teenage girls felt 'depressed, guilty and shameful' after spending just three minutes leafing through a fashion magazine. 70% of girls ages 15 to 17 avoid normal daily activities such as attending school, going to the doctor, or even giving their opinion "due to feeling badly about one's looks."*** Moreover, ***"61% of all women and 69 % of girls (15 to 17) feel that their mother has had a positive influence on their feelings about themselves and their beauty. Nearly 1/4 [25%] would consider undergoing plastic surgery."***

Studies demonstrate the devastating relationship between low self-esteem and parenting. A mother with low-self esteem is more likely to enter into, or allow, exploitative relationships, that are marked with violent behaviours. Children, growing up in homes with violence, suffer low self-esteem, which is enhanced by media pressures, and likewise, results in relationships that perpetuate the cycle.

Steffenhagen and Burns [1987] found the underlying cause of low self-esteem creates a psychodynamic mechanism that facilitates deviant behaviours.

Nowadays, a pregnant woman is held against the idealized image of a super slim model with a *baby bump.* Her mammary glands are *boobs.* More alarming, is that this is how young women refer to their own bodies as well. The influence of *Barbie Doll* and similar phenomenon, has been found to have long term if not life-long effects upon the minds of female children, resulting in *body dimorphic disorder* in which older women mentally obsess about specific parts of their anatomy, as not being *right* or needing correction. In the USA, the rate of cosmetic surgery for girls ages 13–19, was over 236K in 2012.

"For young children, fantasy and play are vital parts of socialization in which they internalize ideals and values, and dolls provide a tangible image of the body that can be internalized as part of the child's developing self-concept and body image."

Children whose mothers had negative self-images, were less academically successful, less able to reach out, to defend themselves, as well as being prone to drug and sexual experimentation and use, precursors to violence, upon the self, and consequently in society. Mothers with low self-esteem are not able to be attentive to the ethical development of their children, their inner struggles and frustrations preclude their ability to be aware enough to positively intervene in their children's development.

Different psychological trends now, globalized by media and market forces, enforce a continued destruction of the feminine perspective and devalue the role of the mother within the home. A woman's worth in society, her viability in the market and employment arenas, is closely tied to her sexualized physical appearance.

The family unit is no longer strong, and children are prone and pressured by media to become victims of increasing low self-esteem and violence within the home, and without. Not knowing, nor having a place of peace in their lives and youth, members of society are handicapped in meaningfully working towards peace.

Strong mothers on the other hand were found to have children with positive self-esteem. America's beloved talk-show host Oprah Winfrey encapsulated the findings well, ***with "You can't fix the girls and the self-esteem until you fix the mothers. As Naomi Wolf said so beautifully, 'A mother who radiates self-love and acceptance actually vaccinates her daughter against low self-esteem."***

Immature Ethics in Globalised Societies: There are theological persuasions present in the psyche of consumer economies of the North America and Europe, which tend to see the human being as inherently *sinful* with an evil nature that needs redemption; a view that sees human beings as beings *naturally* selfish and greedy. Such an outlook necessarily mandates a more violent approach to life, the self and the environment.

Consumer manipulation through media *plays the fiddle*

to greed, lust, and desire, as being pleasure, and pleasure is equated with the goal of human life experience, as happiness. Correlations are implied that sources of pleasures are therefore human rights of action. Combined with a theological shadow of *sinfulness*, esteem conflicts internalize.

Consumer based economies have psychological understandings that tend to see the human being as a *needing and wanting organism* physically, emotionally, and intellectually. A need is perceived for the individual to be in close association with another person in order to be whole and complete.

In contrast, Indian psychology finds the *totality of being* already present in the individual self. This self-identification is one that fills the person with an expansive peace. India's Earth ethics are necessarily ecological in nature as they are all embracing, all inclusive of the internal man and his relationship to his external environment. Holy Mother Amma addresses this, ***"Their [current psychology and philosophy of consumer economies] conception is that the refuge for man is woman and vice-versa. It would be difficult for them to live abandoning this idea as the guiding factor in their way of life....It is difficult to change their opinion as long as they remain in that state. They will learn when they develop more spiritually..."***

As far as a spiritual person is concerned, neither man nor woman is his place of refuge. Human beings are not a refuge for human beings. All human beings are imperfect and an imperfect person cannot protect another imperfect person. Both will struggle like a small snake swallowing a big frog. The only perfect being is God or a God-Realized Soul. Therefore the real place of refuge is God or one's own self.

Indian psychology holds that all beings have instincts of hunger, fear, sex and possessiveness, which we share in common with the animal kingdom. Yet, the human being is also endowed with an ethical and moral instinct, which allows us to rise above our primitive nature to behold ourselves as an indivisible part of the Creation, imbued with an immortal life force that is inherently love and truth itself. The veracity of this has been proved by all saints regardless of religious persuasion. Gandhi noted:

"That is the fundamental conception of Sanatana Dharma which has years of penance and austerity at the back of discovery of this truth. That is why, whilst we have had saints who have worn out their bodies and laid down their lives in order to explore the secrets of the soul, we have none, as in the West, who laid down their lives in exploring the remotest or the highest regions of the Earth."

It is this attention to man's supreme duty, the deeper reason for our having the *experience* of being a human being that is the hallmark of Indian psychology, philosophy, civilization, and culture. Seeking truth, the underlying reason for our existence and putting that search into action in one's life is what makes the human life worthwhile, bringing an expansive peace to oneself and to society.

Today, India's Irom Sharmila Chanu of Manipur, now entering her thirteenth year of an indefinite Fast with involuntary force feeding, in an appeal to end the terrors upon civilians by the Armed Forces Special Powers Act, stands as a singular demonstration of the power of a woman's moral force within her. The efforts of human beings like Dr. Martin Luther King, Jr., Dr. Vandana Shiva, Mother Therese, Sunderlal Bahuguna, Helena Norberg Hodge, Dr. Joseph Elder, Medha Patkar, and

Damayani Bharla, to name only a few, have all shown that a transcendent personal ethos based upon Earth Ethics is essential to have a productive and socially beneficial life, engendering peace.

Philosophically, the monocultures in North American and western European have outlooks on the individual which take a big cue from the French philosopher, Descartes, who surmised, ***"I think, therefore, I am."*** This understanding firmly unites man's self-identification with his mind. Indian thought sees the normative use of the mind as supporting the root of the ego. The perception of an individual *I* out of an ocean of oneness, absolute monism, causes differentiation, duality, schism, it disturbs the peace.

The problems confronting women's rising low self-esteem, like the immoral economics that are tromping across the planet, have no national or cultural boundary today. In history, Gandhi stands as perhaps the greatest champion for the societal necessity to accord women equality in all spheres of life. In a conversation with a guest, recorded by his granddaughter Manu in 1947, Gandhi described his understanding of the reverence for the feminine principle by Indian cultural traditions, ***"The underlying intent in our ancestors' introducing in our daily routine the custom to offer worship to goddesses is simply this—that we accord our womenfolk a high place in our society. Look at their spirit of sacrifice. What sufferings does a woman willingly go through in order to bring up her young child!"***

In moral courage, women far surpass men. The woman is the very embodiment of non-violence, patience and endurance. But what do we see today? People do not shrink even from violating their modesty! What scripture sanctions such heinous deeds? Know for certain that the home, the society or the nation which does not give due respect and honour to her womenfolk is doomed.

Gandhi saw that *the hand that rocks the cradle rules the civilization.* Speaking in terms of the vast majority of women, the fundamental fact that natural motherhood is gender bound, he stated, ***"Whilst both [men and women] are fundamentally one, it is also equally true that in the form there is a vital difference between the two. Hence the vocations of the two must also be different. The duty of motherhood, which the vast majority of women will always undertake, requires qualities which man need not possess. She is passive, he is active. She is essentially mistress of the house. He is the bread-winner; she is the keeper and distributor of the bread. She is the caretaker in every sense of the term. The art of bringing up the infants of the race is her special and sole prerogative. Without her care the race must become extinct."***

Gandhi noted the great need for women to lead the way, based upon their intrinsic strengths, ***"To call woman the weaker sex is a libel; it is man's injustice to woman. If by strength is meant brute strength, then, indeed, woman is woman less brute than man. If by strength is meant moral power, then woman is immeasurably man's superior. Has she not greater intuition, is she not more self-sacrificing, has she not greater powers of endurance, has she not greater courage? Without her, man could not be.***[1] ***If nonviolence is the law of our being, the future is with woman. Who can make a more effective appeal to the heart than woman?"***

Yet, times have changed. Modern India did not heed

Gandhi's advises for development. Through the sexual objectification of women, the rise of low self-esteem and social devaluation, and now gender neutralization, women, particularly young women, are losing awareness of their power to effect change in society through the moral power that is in touch with truth, within them.

Governments appear to be unable to serve the interests of society, unable to think in terms of saving nature for future generations. We are in a situation where our children must lead us back to reality, and they also cannot. The hope of this Earth, our children are being weakened by drugs, sex, for which they have received parental and social licence, their minds distorted by grotesque aspects of media that is well versed in psychological manipulations.

Solutions: Earth Ethics for Culturing Girls into Strong Mothers for a Peace Filled Society –Moving Towards a Global Philosophy and Psychology of Harmony and Peace.

The challenge facing humanity is to evolve into a world philosophical view that will allow us to develop a *humane* civilization. Globalization has the potential to philosophically unite humanity. At this time, driven by the media, promoting market forces of unbridled greed, the ideals that guide humanity towards peace have been silenced, or distorted for the economic ends of the *development* model.

Through our ideals and the qualities they give us, we wield powerful and dynamic forces that can change our destiny and the fate of our planet. Intrinsically universal, the home of the Earth ethics of Gandhi and Holy Mother Amma is in India.

Holy Mother Amma has often given this parable to

illustrate the power and responsibility of the maternal figure to the ethical development of the child, ***"There was a man, who, having committed a string of heinous anti-social crimes, was sentenced to death by hanging. As the hour approached and he was taken to the gallows, he was asked for his last wish. He requested to see his Mother. She was brought to the scene. The condemned man asked her to come close so that he could hug her goodbye. As he embraced her, he bit her ear ferociously with his teeth."*** The Mother screamed in shock and pain and the guards pounced upon him. Of course, he was immediately subdued. He was hauled off in his chains again to the Judge. The Judge asked him, ***"Why did you do this to your mother?"***

The convicted man replied, ***"As a child, whenever I started to go wrong, to tell lies, to steal small things, she never stopped me. She never told me what I was doing was wrong. As I got bigger, I did worse and worse things, still she kept silent. Her silence encouraged me. It is because of her lack of guidance that I will be hung today."***

Today, Amma speaks to the great need for women's ways of knowing and being, their unique capacity to direct their intelligence in ethical ways, to influence political and social arenas, to come forth, ***"In general, today's women are living in a world fashioned by and for men. Women have no need of that world; they should establish their own identities, and thus recreate society."***

More than half of the world population are women. It is a great loss when women are denied the freedom to come forward, and when they are denied the high status that should be theirs in society. Society loses the contribution of women by regulating and enfeebling them.

To date, the strongest opponents to the corporate state destruction of nature have been women. The effects of denying women genuine respect are seen in the wide-scale planetary destruction; the senseless ravage and pollution of Nature. Women have the duty to be true to themselves. Amma has said, ***"In today's world, everything is being contaminated and made unnatural. In this environment, women should take extra care that her qualities of motherhood—her essential nature as a woman—don't become contaminated and distorted. Whether you are a woman, or a man, your real humanity will dawn and come to light only when the feminine and masculine qualities within are balanced."***

Humanity as a whole and all of the natural creation with us is suffering from the loss of the contribution of the feminine principle and its integrated intelligence.

The Holy Mother Amma has said, ***"Men have also suffered greatly as a result of the exile of the principle from the world. Because of the oppression of women and the suppression of the feminine aspect within men, men's lives have become fragmented, often painful. Men, too, have to reawaken to their feminine qualities. They have to develop empathy and understanding in their attitude towards women, and in the way they relate to the world."***

We have to strive for the awakening of this latent principle, which informs all life with love, morality, and ethics. Amma tells us, ***"Women are the power and the very foundation of our existence in the world. When women lose touch with their real selves, the harmony of the world ceases to exist, and destruction sets in. It is therefore crucial that women, everywhere, make every effort to***

rediscover their fundamental nature, for only then can we save this world."

Both Mahatma Gandhi and Holy Mother Amma acknowledge the sacred relationship between the individual and the natural Creation. Amma speaks about this necessary unity through harmony, ***"Life becomes complete when humans and nature move together, hand in hand, in harmony. When melody and rhythm come together beautifully, the music will be pleasing to hear. Likewise, when people live in accordance with the laws of nature, life will flow like a melody."***

There is an order for, everything in the cosmos. There is a rhythm for everything; the wind, rain, waves, the flow of breath and the heartbeat. Similarly, there is a rhythm in life. Our thoughts and deeds should become the melody and rhythm of our lives. Should the rhythm of our thoughts become tripped up, that disturbance will be reflected in our deeds. This will in turn disturb the very rhythm of life.

The rhythm of nature depends on people. It is necessary to maintain the rhythm of the mind and body for the sake of our health, lifespan, humanity and nature. But we see this rhythm being disturbed. This is reflected in nature and society as natural disasters like the tsunami.

India has a planetary responsibility to uphold the wisdom that she has been bequeathed with, through her Mahatmas, to restore a vision of the ideals that will light a path for people to walk towards sustainability and harmony with nature, and peace with themselves and one another. Her educated elite must model awareness of Earth Ethics, and demand that her ways of knowing and being, her women, be truly honoured. Once the message has reached the masses, pressure can be placed upon the engines of media to serve the interests of true peace and harmony in society, over any other cause.

Holy Mother Amma tells us, ***"Our character will be the cause of both good and evil in the world. Knowing that, you should live cautiously. The actions of human beings are the basis of nature's goodness.***

"People, especially the younger generation, are becoming addicted to drugs and other intoxicants, thus losing their vitality, creativity and capacity to benefit themselves and the world. The younger generation, which is meant to blossom and give fragrance to the world, is instead withering away in the bud stage. One generation has already strayed from the path of righteousness. In order to rebuild a healthy and wholesome society, the children must be taught moral and spiritual values. This emphasis should be integrated into the world's educational systems."

Education through anthropology and sociology, particularly, from the untold 'south-north' view, can help youth develop critical and analytical skills with which to view and understand the motives behind the sexual objectification of girls, women, and now boys as well. This will be of some relief to our youth.

Raising awareness of Earth Ethics among people of all ages will enable the election of leaders that will work for the benefit and preservation of Nature, and of human society, with especial attention to women, as the first teachers of peace to our children.

The support of community in divesting minds of false ideals is invaluable. To this end, it is suggested that communities, as pocket neighbourhoods, form wherever they can. Led by strong mothers, the ability to question, to critically analyze, and then to see personal choice in acceptance of media views or not will be fostered. As early as possible, young girls should be made aware of their moral power through discussion of Earth Ethics. This awareness of the moral power inherent in the human being will assist in moving self-concepts from the body image, to the power within. Once our children recognize their own moral power, they will be able to effect change in themselves and society for peace.

Added to this is the necessity for children to be able to compassionately understand the misconceptions their own parents have inculcated and to seek to help them to rise above drug and alcohol use, and to become aware of their own ethical strengths.

Increasing the frequency of open discussions on these topics will assist in helping women to shake themselves free of the psychological hold that societies, under the grip of economic models based upon greed, have had over their minds.

India has the unique and genuine spiritual authority of Holy Mother Amma, presently giving Her teachings. With such wise teachers, the government would benefit the populace and the planet immeasurably, if it were to ardently seek to spread awareness of Her message to humanity, on how to live sustainably and in harmony and peace with Nature, one another, and one's self.

Throughout millenniums, India evolved a philosophical world view, around which the basic building block of society, the family unit, organized itself.

Holy Mother Amma tells us, ***"The advice that***

Mahatmas living in different times and places gave their disciples and followers on how to attain God—that is, realizes the supreme Truth—later became the religions that prevail today. In contrast, the eternal principles, values and injunctions revealed through personal experience to the many Mahatmas from Bharat came to be known as Sanathana Dharma. Later it came to be known also as Hinduism....It gives seekers the freedom to choose the path they prefer from among those the Mahatmas laid down, or the option of creating a new path. It also respects the personal choice of believing or disbelieving in the existence of God."

India's philosophical thought and psychology, with millenniums of continued refinement, honing and elucidation, exists today, ripe, for all humanity to partake of. Holy Mother Amma stresses that what the world sees as a religion, Hinduism, is really a way of being, unconfined to the conditioning of even India's cultural ethos, ***"...the eternal Sanathana Dharma is not confined to certain individuals; it is a pure subjective experience of great importance to every human being. Everyone is the embodiment of this great Truth. Sanathana Dharma does not pertain to any particular caste, creed or sect. The world should know this. Truly, Sanathana Dharma is a great source of power and inspiration for all of mankind. As such, its followers should constantly work for the peace and harmony of the world. Only then will the sankalpa [resolve] of the Rishis become a reality."***[2]

References and Notes:

- Amritanandamayi, Mata. 2003. *Awaken Children* [Volumes 1–7]. Kollam, Kerala: M.A. Mission Trust.
- Amritanandamayi, Mata. 2003. *Awakening to Universal Motherhood.* Kollam, Kerala: M.A. Mission Trust. Amritanandamayi, Mata. 2003.

Eternal Wisdom [Volumes 1–2]. Kollam, Kerala: M.A. Mission Trust.

- Amritanandamayi, Mata 1994. *Immortal Light.* Kollam, Kerala: . M.A. Mission Trust.
- Amritanandamayi, Mata. 2002. *Lead us to the Light.* San Ramon, California: M.A. Centre.
- Amritanandamayi, Mata. 2000, August 29. *Living in Harmony:* An address given at the Millennium World Peace
- Amritanandamayi, Mata. 2004. *May Peace and Happiness Prevail: Address at the Parliament of World Religions* [Barcelona]. Kollam, Kerala: M.A. Mission Trust.
- Amritanandamayi, Mata. 2002. Summit of Religious and Spiritual Leaders, the UN General Assembly. Kollam, Kerala: M.A. Mission Trust.
- Baldwin SA and Hoffmann JP. 2002. *The Dynamics of Self-Esteem: A Growth-Curve Analysis* in the Journal of Youth and Adolescence.
- Bean RA, Bush KR, McKenry PC and Wilson SM. 2003. *The impact of parental support, behavioral control, and psychological control on the academic achievement and self-esteem of African American and European American adolescents* in the Journal of Adolescent Research.
- Battle, J. 1990. *Self-Esteem: The New Revolution.* Edmonton, Alberta, Canada: James Battle and Associates.
- Beane, J. and Lipka, R. 1984 *Self-Concept, Self-Esteem, and the Curriculum.* New York: Teachers College Press.
- Bhatti et al. 1989. *Association Between Child Maltreatment and Self-Esteem: The Social Importance of Self-Esteem.* Berkeley, CA: U.C. Press.
- Blyth DA, Traeger C. 1988. *Adolescent Self-Esteem and Perceived Relationships with Parents and Peers* in Selzinger S, Antrobus J and Hammer M [Eds.] *Social Networks of Children, Adolescents, and College Students.* NJ: Hillsdale.
- Bowlby, J. 1951. *Maternal Care and Mental Health.* Geneva: World Health Organisation.
- Lama, Dalai. 1999. *Ancient Wisdom, Modern World: Ethics for the New Millenium.* UK: Abacus.
- Dittmar, Suzanne Ive and Emma Halliwell. 2006. *Does Barbie Make Girls Want to Be Thin? The Effect of Experimental Exposure to Images of Dolls on the Body Image of 5-to 8-Year- Old Girls* in the Developmental Psychology [Second Edition] Vol. 42, Brighton: 283-92

- Elder, J. 1970. *Chapters in Indian Civilization: A Handbook of Readings to Accompany Lectures in Indian Civilization.* Dubuque: Kendall Hunt Publishing Co.
- Freud, WE. 1973. *Prenatal Attachment and Bonding* in the Greenspan, SI and Pollock, GH [Eds.] *The Course of Life* [Volume I] *Infancy.* Madison, CT: International Universities Press.
- Gandhi, MK. 1955. *Ashram Observances in Action.* Ahmedabad: Navajivan.
- Gandhi, MK. 1956–1983. *Collected works of Mahatma Gandhi* [100 Volumes} 1956–1983. Navajivan: Ahmedabad.
- Gandhi, MK. 2007. *An Autobiography or The Story of My Experiments with Truth.* Gandhi, MK. 1956–1983. *Collected works of Mahatma Gandhi* [100 Volumes} 1956–1983. Navajivan: Ahmedabad.
- Gandhi, MK. 1987. *Essence of Hinduism.* Gandhi, MK. 1956–1983. *Collected works of Mahatma Gandhi* [100 Volumes] 1956–1983. Navajivan: Ahmedabad.
- Gandhi, MK in Hingorani, AT [Ed.]. 1998. *Gandhi For the 21st Century* [24 Volumes)] Mumbai: Bharatiya Vidya Bhavan.
- Gandhi, MK in Prabhu, RK. 1949. *Mohan Mala: a Gandhian Rosary.* Ahmedabad: Navajivan.
- Gandhi, MK in Prabhu, RK [Ed.]. 1947. *India of My Dreams.* Ahmedabad: Navajivan.
- Gandhi, M.K in Narayan, S [Ed.]. 1968. *The Selected Works of Mahatma Gandhi.* Gandhi, MK. 1956–1983. *Collected works of Mahatma Gandhi* [100 Volumes] 1956–1983. Navajivan: Ahmedabad.
- Hoskins, Stephanie. 2012, May. *The Negative Effects of Barbie on Young Girls an the Long Term Results.* http://www.divinecaroline.com/life-etc/momhood/negative-effects-barbie-young-girls-long-term-results. 2013, August.
- Kaplan, HB. 1975. *Self-Attitudes and Deviant Behavior.* CA: Goodyear, Pacific Palisades.
- Kalarthi, M [Ed.]. 1962. *Ba and Bapu* [xii–xiii]. Ahmedabad: Navajivan.
- Mansingh, S. 1988. *Historical Dictionary of India.* New Delhi: Vision Books Pvt. Ltd.
- Nehru, J. 2004. *Glimpses of World History.* India: Penguin Books.
- Nikhilananda, S. 1946. *Essence of Hinduism.*, New York: Ramakrishna-Vivekananda Centre.
- *The Real Truth about Beauty: A Global Report.* 2004, September. Findings of the Global Study on Women, Beauty and Well-Being.

• Yukteswar, J. 1972. *The Holy Science*. Los Angeles: Self-Realization Fellowship.

Footnotes:

1 Author's emphasis.

2 The Rishis, the ancient reformers and social architects of India, did not form a separate religion. They gave importance to different human values and spiritual truths. That is why their prayers included the entire universe. The following translation of a Sanskrit prayer chanted daily in Holy Mother Amma's ashram exemplifies this: ***"May the whole world live in happiness. May contentment prevail in all. May peace prevail in all. May perfection prevail in all. May auspiciousness prevail in all. Peace, Peace, Peace."***

4. NON-VIOLENCE FOR PEACE AND CONFLICT RESOLUTION AMONG STUDENTS

S Arulsamy*

The whole world is increasingly affected by violence, social problems, and a lack of respect for each other. Even in these modern times it is clear that one's precious life is not safe. When we listen to the radio or read the newspaper, we are confronted with the same sad news: violence, crime, and wars. The escalating rate of violence occurs in many countries in the world. But, the problem of violence is not restricted to any one city or country. All people today are affected by the violence that pervades our society. As a result, the healthy development of our society and nation is in serious jeopardy.

* Dr. S Arulsamy is an assistant professor at the department of education in the Bharathiar University, Coimbatore [Tamilnadu], India.

The present day education system lays a great deal of stress on intellectual development. Our colleges and universities are producing excellent teachers, scientists, lawyers, administrators, educationists and businessmen. But they are unable to produce high quality ethical, religious and spiritual men and responsible citizens. The left lobe of our brain has become overactive and the right lobe has become inactive. This imbalance has made the whole human personality unbalanced and an unbalanced personality becomes the cause of violence. Only a balanced personality can bring about non-violence. For solving the problem of violence it is necessary that our education system should aim at a balanced development of the intellectual and emotional aspects of the personality. Both the lobes of the brain have to be activated so that the right soil is created for sprouting the seeds of non-violence.

"Education about non-violence can help to counter the culture of violence that reverberates throughout the media, the entertainment industry, politics, national policy, the schools, the community and the family. It provides images of peace." [Harris 1999] The methods of practicing non-violence such as non-resistance, active reconciliation, moral resistance, selective non-violence, passive resistance, peaceful resistance, non-violent direct action, Satyagraha and non-violent revolution can be and should be explored in any peace education programme. We, teachers have a civic duty to promote **non-violence as a viable method of social change.**

Relationship between Peace and Violence: There is a very common misconception about the relationship between peace and violence. This is that peace is the absence of violence. Peace is not the absence of violence. The reality is quite the other way around. Violence is the absence of peace.

Violence is much like darkness. One can neither produce, manipulate, nor destroy dark. The idea we call dark is in actuality the absence of light. Light, on the other hand, is entirely real. We can easily produce, manipulate, and destroy light. In this way, light is much like peace.

Peace, like light, is not an absence but a presence. Peace is the presence of awareness. Or, more accurately, peace is the awareness of Presence. Peace is the awareness of the sacred [by whatever name... God, Beauty, Wholeness, Life, or whatever symbol you prefer]. Violence is the painful state of being in ignorance of the divine. In the awareness of Presence, violence is not overcome or defeated, it simply does not exist. With this realization, if we want peace, we must not seek to end violence. We must create peace. If we want peace, we must shine like a beacon in the darkness so that others may see the holy in all they behold.

Role of Violence in Our Lives and Lives of Others: Violence has affected our life and the lives of others in our generation in many ways. We suffer because of increased crime and violence against mankind. Violence has affected the way we live, play and go about our daily lives. Increased violence has forever changed the way we live. There are many things that violence affects in society. Children and adolescents are exposed to violence in increasing numbers each year. Children and adolescents repeatedly exposed to violence tend to accept violence as an acceptable way to resolve even complex problems.

Violence touches the life of every one, some more directly than others. The effects of violence are many and varied. The emotional effects of violence are, low self-esteem and self-confidence; feeling that you in some way deserve or are to blame for the violence and abuse; feeling guilt, feelings of self-doubt; feeling that no one else will ever want you; feelings of hopelessness and despair; feelings of depression and anxiety; feeling suicidal; feeling totally isolated from friends and family and any other support networks; wondering if anyone will believe your story; feeling low in energy and unable to make a decision/s.

Some other effects can include: Onset of stress related illnesses; Exhaustion; Eating issues; Headaches; back pain or abdominal pain, Gastrointestinal disorders and/or using alcohol or drugs to cope.

The violence that plagues our nation has many sources, and its elimination will require systematic attention at many levels. Most importantly, the citizens of our nation must become outraged at the victimization and must turn this outrage into positive action and increased resources toward preventing violence.

Factors Influencing Non-Violence: Nobody is born as violent One becomes violent because of the kind of environment and circumstances that he/she is facing. Children and youth learn a lot from their environment and it plays an important role in shaping their future. If the environment in which they are living is exhibiting large amount of violence then they will learn it too. Parents, schools, media and films are equally responsible for violence in children. A large amount of action, killing and fights are being showed in the films and media. This boosts the violence among kids. They learn new ways of fighting and killing from these TV shows and films and practice them in schools over other children. Today everybody is quite busy with their work. Parents and teachers do not have time for the children. They are not getting proper love, affection, support and guidance. This increases their violence. Friends who are having violent nature will make the other children violent too.

The non-violent ways only can resolve these issues. There are certain factors which influence non-violent behavior among children.

The home environment plays a crucial part in changing a child's behavior. Parents who show their constant love and affection towards their children help them to grow up with love and affection. So it is very important to look and keep an eye on the children at an early age without telling them. Parents should provide better attention, care and love their children and also teach them certain manners at an early age. Good characteristics can be achieved by children more motivating advices from parents. Smooth and lovable acts between parents help the child to develop a non-violent attitude. Another major factor is the school itself as it is where the child spends most of its time in the mornings. Teacher's love and concern towards children has very good effect on them. A teacher should carefully select his/her punishment types as severe corporal punishments have major effects on children. Constant love and affection of the teacher may drive a student to have permanent change.

Parents and teachers should also monitor the children's friend circle as it also plays a part in the sudden change of behavior. Neighborhood friends should also be advised as to which kinds should be selected. A good friend will obviously have a positive result and the same can also happen with a bad one.

These are some factors which plays a part in a child behavior development. Steps should be taken to ensure that the children of the future with good things and also develop non-violent behavior. Adequate love, affection and care should help to change a child's behavior but still professional help should be applied if necessary.

Role of Peace Education in Resolving Conflict: Conflict is a daily reality that comes from differing needs, values, goals, resources, scarcity, and competition. Conflict seems to be increasing in our modern world. It is ubiquitous and it is inevitable. The ability to resolve conflict without using force is probably one of the most important skills an individual can learn. There has been in the last decade a rapid growth in the number of programs teaching these skills from nursery school through college. Various organizations are also appearing in both the public and private sectors that offer mediation services and teach the skills of conflict resolution to a wider audience. In order to be dealt with constructively, conflict has to be faced. Peace education seeks to avoid power confrontation and rests on compromise and negotiation to resolve conflicts. Peace educators see that education provides an important strategy to achieve peace, because it provides awareness about different peace strategies, including peacekeeping [or peace through strength], peacemaking [or peace through communication], and peace building [or peace through a commitment to nonviolence].

Peace educators focus on peacekeeping strategies and try to get students to think of themselves as concerned global citizens willing to transcend national and ethnic differences in order to promote peace. They hope, through the study of security system, to teach how to construct laws and institutions, like United Nations, that will help humans avoid the terror of war.

Peace educators teach peacemaking strategies to help children avoid violence by resolving international conflicts constructively. School personnel bring conflict resolution programs into schools to address aspects of interpersonal violence and to teach peacemaking skills such as mediation, empathy, and alternative dispute resolution methods. School-based peer mediation tries to resolve conflicts between students that may not be overtly violent. Mediation provides a vehicle for de-escalating violent behavior in schools. One study showed that fights were reduced as much as fifty percent in a school that adopted mediation. [Lantieri and Patti, 1996]

Peace educators who teach peace building strategies are concerned about building, in children's minds, a desire for peace. Often this type of peace is referred to as positive peace, as opposed to negative peace, which tries to stop some form of violence. Positive peace education tries to build peaceful communities by promoting an active democratic citizenry interested in equitably sharing the world's resources. These approaches to the problems of violence are controversial because they seek to struggle against injustice and replace structural inequities with institutions that create a more equal world order.

Reducing Conflicts Among Students: Conflicts are relatively common in classrooms. Overt student behaviours are a common source of classroom conflict and include actions that teachers find immature or irritating, such as students talking during lectures, eating and drinking noisily, *or* arguing with the teachers. Covert student behaviors also precipitate conflict, but these actions appear more passive or inattentive, such as students sleeping during class, missing classes, acting bored or apathetic, and leaving class early. [Apple-by 1990: Kearney and Plax 1992]. Fur-thermore, disruptive behavior and conflict can spread and ultimately include numerous students. Such classrooms are characterized by a pervasive sense of negativity among students, overt hostility or disrespect expressed by many people in the course, class-wide resistance to completing assignments or participating in discussion, and the expression of contempt between students. [Boice 1996]

Regardless of their academic discipline or amount of teaching experience, many teachers encounter conflict in the classes that they teach. They perceive classroom conflict to be distressing and disruptive; they are often reluctant to take active measures to resolve the disputes [Amada 1994]. They are not effectively prepared to handle these situations. In the worst cases, frequent or intense encounters with unruly or uninvolved students result in teacher disillusionment or even dread of teaching. [Boice, 2000]

Cultivating a positive classroom climate often prevents student apathy, hostility, and conflict. However, there are times when teachers must directly engage with students' negative emotions to contain conflict after it has occurred. This process is not only necessary to ensure successful classroom management but can ultimately provide an opportunity for students' growth and development.

Conflict Reduction Strategy I: The initial step in restricting the potentially deleterious impact of student disruptiveness and conflict is for the teacher to acknowledge explicitly students' feelings and communicate empathy. Hill and O'Brien [1999] commented the following basic format so that listeners identify the speakers' feeling and its rationale, ***"You feel because... "*** A teacher responds with empathy to a student who is plaintive about a low mark on a test by stating, ***"It seems like you're very disappointed and upset about your mark, especially because you studied for several hours and felt well-prepared beforehand. It also sounds like you feel that I'm being insensitive and not understanding the points that you made in this essay."*** The teacher's acknowledgement surprises the student; validating the student's emotional responses reduces the intensity of the conflict because he feels understood by the teacher.

Although reflecting students' feelings seems to be a simple process on the surface, there are many subtleties that influence whether students will actually perceive the teacher as empathic. First, teachers should be aware of their nonverbal communication during these times. They should display an open body posture, maintain eye contact, and appear attentive and comfortable. A compassionate statement will seem insensitive if a teacher simultaneously looks at his/her watch or clenches his/her jaw. Second, teachers can use brief, encouraging remarks to allow their students to express fully their thoughts and feelings. Statements such as ***"I see"*** or ***"Tell me more about this"*** express interest and allow them to gain greater awareness about students' classroom problems. Third, teachers should listen intently at these times to absorb students' mood; they should concentrate on the text and the subtext of students' statements. Although reflections can be brief [e.g., ***"You're really upset about this"***], they convey greater empathy when the statements are detailed, communicate an understanding of students' feelings and their situations, and avoid simple repetition.

Conflict Reduction Strategy II: Help students evaluate their alternatives. Teacher can empower students by helping them look for alternatives and evaluate the consequences for each possible solution. [Popkin, 1993]

During school/college hours, a student complained that members of his/her learning group were not contributing equitably to a course project. The teacher helps the student evaluate his/her alternatives by first empathically stating, ***"You seem really frustrated and angry at other members of your learning group because they're not putting in as much effort as***

you. It also sounds like you feel helpless because they have been unwilling to work harder even though you talked with them about the situation." The teacher then encourages the student to examine different alternatives by asking questions including. ***"What can you do about that?" "What else can you try?"*** or ***"What do you think would happen if you did that?"***

The student decides to confront his/her peers again, but now chooses to propose a more concrete plan for dividing up the project work. He/she also asks the teacher to help arbitrate the situation if his/her plan is unsuccessful. When the teacher followed up a week later and asked him/her how the solution worked out, he/she was happy to learn that his/her assertiveness with his/her peers had effectively reduced conflict within his/her group.

Conflict Reduction Strategy III: Use comprehensive problem-solving methods. In contrast to student-owned problems, teacher-owned classroom conflicts involve the teacher in a more direct and inextricable way. Teacher-owned problems often require comprehensive management techniques that integrate and extend the strategies described above. [e.g., Bodine and Crawford, 1998; Holton, 1998; Kuhlen Schmidt and Layne 1999; and Tiberius and Flak 1999] This approach typically involves three phases: setting the stage for effective conflict resolution, clearly defining the problem, and developing mutually acceptable solutions.

Problem solving is most effective when teachers detect conflict at an early point and promptly initiate dialogue with students. Because problem solving discussions are often lengthy and may be personal in nature, teachers should carefully choose an appropriate time and location to meet with students. The teacher is very annoyed and distracted by the student because he/she frequently talks to students sitting next to him/her using a relatively loud voice. The teacher views his/her behaviour as disrespectful and believes that he/she does not want to be in the class. The teacher has attempted to curb his/her talkativeness by relatively benign methods [e.g., asking the class if there are any questions and standing closer to the particular student while he lectures], but the teacher feels that the problem is actually getting worse. He decides to address this conflict directly and discretely asks the student to speak with him immediately following class.

Teachers should define problematic behavior in concrete and objective terms. They should also be able to pinpoint when the conflict occurs as well as its antecedents and consequences. Students are most likely to be committed to the problem-solving process if teachers demonstrate empathy, tact, and concern when broaching issues of contention.

The teacher initiates a conversation with the student by stating, ***"I'm concerned about whether you're enjoying class. Over the past two weeks, I've noticed that you frequently talk to people who sit near you when I lecture. Although I understand that students' attention will wander at times, I'm worried that other people find your conversations distracting. I also feel that it is more difficult for me to explain concepts clearly and remain focused when students talk during class lectures. I want to make sure that the class is a positive learning experience for you and for all students, so it is important that we talk about this."***

Students play an important role in defining the problem during the conflict resolution process. Students often have different interpretations of the facts and are in the position to provide otherwise inaccessible information about their thoughts, expectations, motivations, and feelings. [Tiberius and Flak, 1999] Rather than *informing students about their problem*, skillful teachers ask students about their perception of the problem. These teachers then verify their understanding of students' perspective by periodically paraphrasing students' view of the situation and reflecting their feelings. In general, an accurate definition of the problem is the product of a collaborative dialogue rather than the teacher's monologue. The particular student did not dispute that he/she talks during lectures, he/she did not view his/her behavior as rude or inappropriate. The teacher responds, ***"I often don't agree with what you're saying in class and I've just got to let someone know. I also think that you blame all the problems of the world. That's not fair or right."***

Teachers should be aware of their own heightened emotions when discussing classroom conflicts with students. For example, a teacher may be angered by the student's behavior, anxious about confronting the student, or defensive in response to die student's complaints and accusations. Teachers should monitor their emotional reactions to ensure that they can constructively define and remedy the problem. [Kuhlen schmidt and Layne, 1999] After clearly identifying their needs and interests, teachers and students then propose as many different ideas as possible for resolving the problem. Teachers and students should initially refrain from critiquing these suggestions during brain-storming. Rather, they should evaluate options only after many possibilities have been generated. Effective solutions often involve modifying and combining several suggestions. Teachers should monitor the effectiveness of the solutions and revisit the situation at a later point in time if it is necessary.

Successful conflict management may therefore be accomplished when teachers modify their interpersonal behavior, their attitudes toward students and the classroom experience, or their teaching style. Students' responsibility to create a positive class room environment is also more important. In actuality, students and teacher both affect the tenor of the class. Teachers are in an influential position to change the social and emotional climate of the class.

Conclusion: The pursuit of peace and justice is not embodied in any particular piece of our curricular or extra-curricular program. Instead, every realm of school life is involved in teaching young people about war and violence, ethnocentric/ nationalist content rather than understanding of human relationships and interdependence and peace. Perhaps true peace education cannot be mandated or fully tested, at least in a package that would work in any local cultural and political context. Young people cannot be expected to promote and encourage the peaceful resolution of conflicts if they do not see conflict resolution principles and strategies being modeled by adults in all areas of their lives, such as in business, sports, entertainment, and personal relationships. Adults play a part in making the environment more peaceful by practicing nonviolent conflict resolution when minor or major disputes arise in their daily lives.

Notes and Bibliography:

Afzalur, Rahim. 2000. *Empirical Studies on Managing Conflict* in the International Journal of Conflict Management [Volume 11]

Amada. G. 1994. *Coping with the Disruptive College Student: A Practical Manual.* Asheville: NC College Administration Publications.

Appleby, DC. 1990. *Faculty and Student Perceptions of Irritating Behaviors in the College Classroom* in the Journal of Staff, Program, and Organization Development 8:41-46.

Balasooriya, AS. 2001. *Learning the Way of Peace a Teachers' Guide to Peace Education.* New Delhi: United Nations Educational, Scientific and Cultural Organization.

Bodine, RJ and Crawford, DK. 1988. *The Handbook of Conflict Resolution Education: A Guide to Building Quality Programmes in Schools.* San Francisco: Jossey-Bass.

Boice. B. 1996. *Classroom Incivilities* in the Research in Higher Education 37:453-86

Boice. R. 2000. *Advice for new faculty*. Nihi nimus, Boston: Allyn and Bacon.

Harris, I. 1988. *Peace Education.* Jefferson, NC: McFarland and Co.

Hill. CE and O'Brien, KM. 1999. *Helping Skills: Facilitating Exploration, Insight, and Action.* Washington D.C: Mexican Psychological Association.

Keaney, P and Plax K. 1992. *Student Resistance to Control* in Power in the Classroom: Communication, Control, and Consent by VP Richmond and JC McCroskey [Eds.] 85-100. Hillsdale: NJ, Erlbaum.

Kulilen Schmidt S. L and Layne, LE. 1999. *Strategies for Dealing with Difficult Behavior* in Promoting civility: A Teaching Challenge by SM Richardson [Ed.] 45-57. San Francisco: Jossey-Bass.

Lantieri, Linda and Patti, Janet. 1996. *Waging Peace in Our Schools.* Boston: Beacon Press.

Prasad, SN. 1998. *Development of Peace Education in India* [since Independence] in the *Peace Education Mini Prints* 95: 1–14

5. EDUCATION FOR A SUSTAINABLE DEVELOPMENT OF PEACE

Meeta Verma* and Sonam Mehta**

Both peace and environmental educators have a common goal of stopping violence, but in human communities there will always be conflicts and humans must consume natural products. The challenge is to learn to resolve conflicts non-violently, to share limited resources equitably, and to live within the limits of sustainability. This will become increasingly important as the Twenty-First Century unfolds with increasing human

* Ms. Meeta Verma and **Ms. Sonam Mehta are research scholars at the faculty of education in the Dayalbagh Educational Institute of Agra [UP], India.

populations all seeking a better life. Peace will require environmental sustainability and environmental sustainability will require peace.

Distinctive dimensions of Futures Education: Futures education has much in common with other areas of educational innovation, such as peace education and environmental education. Whether in schools, colleges, universities or in community education, these areas of teaching and learning attach major importance to not only what is but what might be.

Introduction: Despite peace education's early focus being on disarmament and the prevention of war, scholars have also in the past two decades considered sustainable development, and environmental education to be a central goal of peace education. While peace is not always discussed vis-a-vis environmental education, and environmental issues aren't always included in peace education. There is an increasing awareness of the symbiotic relationship between the two approaches and the relevance of education in inculcating values to promote peace and environmental sustainability.

Peace Education and its Co-Disciplines: Peace education has largely developed as a scholarly field over the past 40 years and emerged out of its "parent" field of peace studies. Peace education is broadly defined as the educational policy, planning, pedagogy, and practice that develops awareness, skills, and values toward peace. Peace education is comprised of multiple subfields in which scholars and practitioners work, but often are not considered part of peace education. These subfields, such as global security and human rights education, have often developed in their own right and hence are referred to here as *co-disciplines* of peace education. One such field is environmental education.

It is noted that contemporary conceptions of positive peace have extended to include a more holistic approach, including human rights education, development education, and environmental education. While there are different approaches to educating about and achieving peace, there nonetheless exists the unifying concept that peace education seeks to achieve human rights for all by transforming students into agents of change for greater equity and social justice.

This overarching theme of working toward a better future has allowed peace education to manifest in a multidisciplinary way, yet retain its core characteristics. These subfields, or co-disciplines, take different conceptual and methodological approaches—from anti-nuclear efforts to interreligious dialogue—but fall under the umbrella of peace education because of their shared purposes. A framework can thus be constructed whereby peace education, with its aim to achieve human rights for all, is understood alongside its co-disciplines. Each co-discipline has certain constituents who align themselves with the goals and values of peace education as a field, and others who prefer to develop on their own terms and without stated connection to the field of peace education. While these co-disciplines continue to emerge and evolve, for the purposes of this article, the most oft-discussed ones vis-a-vis peace education are included. Peace education may serve as the nucleus, but each co-discipline interlinks and interconnects with others directly. For example, teaching about nuclear disarmament not only works toward peace, but it also requires resolving conflicts and engaging in mediation efforts. Similarly, both co-disciplines affect and are affected by ecological and environmental factors. The conceptual framework presented in Figure-1 has its roots in literature on peace and ecological education. The idea of education for social responsibility is not a new idea, but an increasingly urgent one among educators and communities alike, as evidenced by the many educational organizations seeking to effect change through what is learned in the classroom. Given the unprecedented speed of global change, from political decisions that have accelerated environmental destruction to the increasing inequity among the world's rich and poor, educating for peace has come to be seen as an interdisciplinary effort rather than being isolated to one approach or disciplinary school of thought.

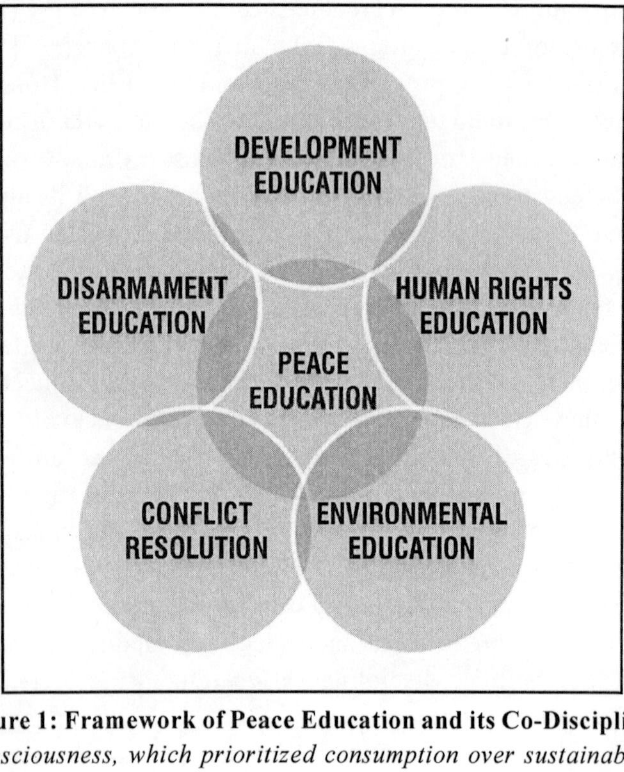

Figure 1: Framework of Peace Education and its Co-Disciplines: *Consciousness, which prioritized consumption over sustainability, and have noted the laudatory move toward a post-ecological consciousness.*

Peace and Environmental Education: Both peace and environmental educators have a common goal of stopping violence, but in human communities there will always be conflicts, and humans must consume natural products. The challenge is to learn to resolve conflicts non-violently, to share limited resources equitably, and to live within the limits of sustainability. This will become increasingly important as the twenty-first century unfolds with increasing human populations all seeking a better life. Peace will require environmental sustainability and environmental sustainability will require peace. In the 1990s, the idea of global security within peace education extended to that of ecological security as ***"environmental issues give rise to actual and potential international conflicts."***

In the 1990s, the idea of global security within peace education extended to that of ecological security as ***"environmental issues give rise to actual and potential international conflicts."*** Since then, an emerging and more accepted pedagogy has embraced the holistic nature of ecological thinking and learning that underscores the idea of interconnectedness and co-operation. With the "vision of a transformed global society" where the younger generation perceives itself as an integral part of a shared planet, education for peace cannot be separated from education for ecological responsibility.

The framework of peace education and its co-disciplines—including environmental and ecological education—introduces the emerging call for and acceptance of peace pedagogy that sees learning as a collective and experiential process aimed at empowering and creating agents of change. The selection of literature reviewed by peace educators offers evidence to Lothar Brock's claim that ***"the environment has now become firmly established as an item on the agenda*** *of peace research.*" Environmental degradation threatens global security in an indirect, but nonetheless real and critical, manner.

Elaborated by authors such as Brock, the established link between the peace problem antique and the environment can therefore engage and promote co-operation and peace building at an international level. Moreover, the inclusion of environmental security and sustainable development as benchmarks for international development in the Millennium Development goals evidence their inclusion as important components of a comprehensive rights-based approach to human development.

The UN Decade of Education for Sustainable Development: Education is not only an end in itself. It is a key instrument for bringing about the changes in knowledge, values, behaviors, and lifestyles required to achieve sustainability and stability within and among countries and ensure democracy, human security, and peace. Education at all levels and in all its forms constitutes a vital tool for addressing virtually all global problems relevant for sustainable development, in particular poverty, HIVD AIDS, environmental degradation, peace and stability, knowledge formation and sharing, rural development, and changes in production and consumption patterns.

Future Education and Intergenerational Equity: To get beyond narrowly egocentric ethics is in part a matter of how we may begin to negotiate a sense of inter-being or interdependence, including notions such as a *global ethic*, *peace with environmental justice* and *intergenerational equity*. In an increasingly globalized world, this entails particular challenges and many contradictions. Rather than one identity, we may have plural identities [e.g.as a teacher, a student, member of a local community, member of a global community]. How these identities play out may have significant implications for the future.

As teachers, we usually feel a strong sense of responsibility to our students. There is within such a professional and moral framework an implied futures perspective. We are not just concerned with what happens here and now in a particular classroom context, but much more. We are concerned with what will happen when our students finish school and, if they have the chance, go on to college or university. If I run into former students and they tell me that they are doing well and are engaged in doing socially valuable work, I am delighted.

Yet, such an implied futures perspective arguably needs to be made explicit both within the formal curriculum and how we teach. In so doing, there is an important invitation to rethink our moral imagination in ways that include not only responsibilities to the present generation but to future generations. Our sense of inter-being and active hope would then be part of an emergent global civic culture. Foresight and a compassionate regard for future generations, both human and other species, would be integral to visions of good teaching for this century and beyond.

An Integrated Approach to Peace, Environment/ Sustainability and World Future: There is still too much of a tendency in curriculum development and design to focus on narrowly disciplinary frameworks rather than encouraging active cross-disciplinary dialogue and an explicit futures dimension. As part of the push of the past with the ways in which the major Western academic disciplines have come to be constituted, we tend to ignore interconnections.

Figure-2. Flower-petal Model of Peace Education

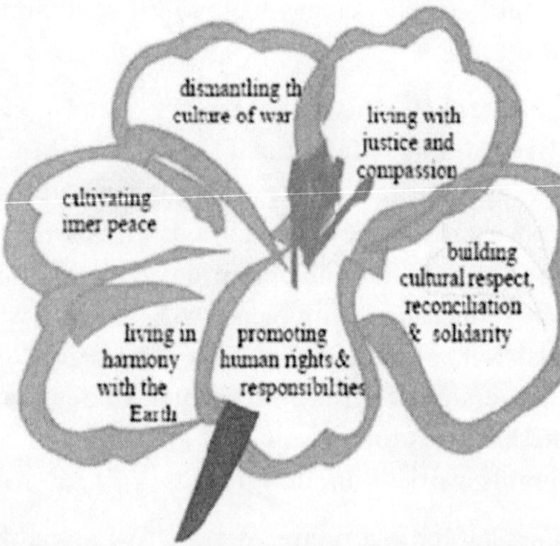

Conclusion: The holistic approach to contemporary positive peace has expanded the notion of structural and direct violence to include violence inflicted on the natural environment, as Wenden outlined. While peace education and environmental education each exist independently with their respective subthemes and concerns, the intersection between the two is also emerging as education for sustainable development as a valid and critically important field. As the literature has shown, this intersectional space places emphasis on how peace—both positive and negative—cannot be achieved without environmental security and ecological responsibility. It also underscores the need for an integrated approach to education that will encourage the development of a set of values and behaviors to empower each individual to take personal responsibility for his or her interaction with nature, use of natural resources, and connection with the environment. This responsibility directly and naturally affects one's sense of respect for neighbour and stranger alike, promotes larger goals of conflict transformation, and ultimately supports the movement toward greater respect for human rights.

Notes:

Adams, M, Bell, LA and Griffin, P [Eds.] 1997. Teaching for Diversity and Social Justice: A Sourcebook. New York: Routledge.

Alaska Library Association. 2001. *Culturally Responsive Guidelines for Alaska Public Libraries*. Fairbanks: Alaska Native Knowledge Network, www.ankn.uaf.edu/standards/library.html

Andrzejewski, J and Alessio J. 1999. *Education for Global Citizenship and Social Responsibility* [Monograph]. Burlington, VT: John Dewey Project on Progressive Education.

Assembly of Alaska Native Educators. 1998. *Alaska standards for Culturally-Responsive Schools*. Fairbanks: Alaska Native Knowledge Network, www.ankn.uaf.edu

Francis P. Hutchinson. 2009, March. *Reflections on the Connections between Peace Education and, Environmental Education* in the futures education.

Julie, Andrzejewski. 2005. *The Social Justice, Peace, and Environmental Education Standards Project*. St. Cloud State University: Department of Human Relations and Multicultural Education.

Universal Declaration of Human Rightshttp://www.ohchr.org/EN/UDHR/Pages/Introduction.aspx

United Nations Educational, Scientific and Cultural Organization [UNESCO]: www.unesco.org

European Commission [EU] Education and Training section: ec.europa.eu/education/index_en.html

UN Children's Fund (UNICEF): http://www.unicef.org

UN High Commissioner for Refugees - http://www.unhcr.ch

UN High Commissioner for Human Rights - http://www.unhchr.ch

6. ICT INFORMATION AND IDEA SHARING THROUGH TECHNOLOGY: A PERSUASIVE WAY OF FUTURISTIC PEACEFUL SOCIETY

Richa Agarwal* and Savita Agarwal**

The extensive availability of Information and Communication Technologies has led to the globalization process and continues to have a large influence on social, economic, political and cultural structures around the world. These same technologies are however still struggling to find place in the developing countries. Technologies have been integrated in the daily activities of the World as well as peace building efforts. The growing boom and expending dimensions of telecommunications offers various new opportunities and guidelines for the promotion of peace and humanistic peace culture. These new opportunities have not as yet been fully explored or used enough. Television, press, radio and internet play a vital role in forming are views, values and relations. Action and behaviour begin in the mind, and the stories we show, write and tell should be peaceful and constructive and not violent and destructive as we unfortunately often see on television today. Awareness is power, when people are well informed they are empowered and ICT has made this possible

* Ms. Richa Agarwal and **Ms. Sarita Agarwal are research scholars at the faculty of education of the University of Agra [UP], India.

in many countries especially in developing countries. Information reaches people through cell phones, internet, and satellite television and radio stations which can help to improve decision making skills, the ability to see the critical information and likely results of decisions, and the environment in which decisions are made. We are nowadays in the greatest global cultural crisis in human history and it is therefore necessary to mobilize technology in all its form to improve and help solve this dangerous crisis. ICTs can be used for peace building but on the other hand it has also negative effect on society as cybercrime, cyber-warfare, and surveillance, the spreading of extremist propaganda, the suppression of democratic processes and other destructive purposes. For peaceful society it is important to use ICT carefully.

Key Benefits of ICT in Information and Idea Shearing: ICT has become a persuasive force in transforming social, political and economic life globally as well as created both new opportunities and threats for humankind. One of the most important features of the digital age is the use of new communication technologies to construct digital citizenships. Technologies can certainly contribute to a society where people can more easily communicate, understand the current situation, visualize the implications of their actions, understand each other's point of view, and form meaningful relationships with people who are geographically or culturally distant. The key features of ICT are following:

Sharing experiences and voicing out their salient issues.

- Inter-operability of information access has pulled down all digital barriers;
- Exchange information seamlessly, securely and sustainably;
- It is viewed as an *intrinsic part of nation building* [Hattotuwa, 2003];

- Carry *the new global knowledge based economy* [Huyer and Sikoska, op cit];
- It can afford various education modalities such as distance and online training;
- ICT is a tool for the transformatory empowerment;
- Internet can make distant situations more understandable;
- It can facilitate various services for establishing global friendship;
- Ability to communicate through written word, photos, sound clips, video clips, and web cameras can keep people connected regardless of how far apart they are geographically;
- My space, face book, tagged etc. can give opportunity to develop social contact;
- Blogs can help to understand people who are different than us;
- In addition to helping to process information, *Online Dispute Resolution (*ODR) tools can facilitate better decisions;
- The possibility to quickly access a huge amount of information; and
- Open Debate Engine, allows to openly discussing many aspects of space weaponization.

ICTs ***"may reshape, reorganize, and restructure working methods"*** through its ***"generic advantages of efficiency, information sharing, storage, faster knowledge accumulation, dissemination which can permit new and collaborative work methods."*** Social, political economic and cultural change is inevitable based on the development and diffusion of technology.

Need for Global Peace and Harmony for Society: Now-a-days we are living in era of cultural crisis. People are emotionally far from each other which increase violence, conflicts, division. Many conflicts and violence between and within nations are in one way or the other rooted in cultural differences, the lack of respect for cultural diversity, and the resulting misunderstandings and tensions between peoples. If one's identity is threatened or denied legitimacy or respect, conflicts can quickly arise and become intractable, i.e. very difficult to resolve. If we know enough about each other, we are more likely to understand, respect, and perhaps even enjoy each other's identity, and less likely to engage in conflict and violence with each other. And if we recognize each other as humans instead of engaging in mutual processes of dehumanization, we will be able to solve conflicts before they unfold their destructive character. It is important to remember the value of cultural diversity, as well as the beneficial potential of intercultural dialogue for a Culture of Peace. So we need to create a peaceful society.

Peace means a fully developed life, where one lives in harmony with oneself, with society and with nature. To be genuine, peace must manifest itself at all levels of society and in all aspects of life. It cannot define itself solely by the absence of the most extreme form of conflict settlement between states. Peace rather stands for the opposite of all forms of violence, exploitation or injustice. It is characterized by the presence and active realization of positive human values such as justice, freedom, equality, equity, solidarity, respect, tolerance, co-operation, compassion and dignity. Peace refers to the process of promoting the knowledge, skills, attitudes and values needed to bring about behaviour changes that will enable children, youth and adults to prevent conflict and violence, both overt and structural; to resolve conflict peacefully; and to create the conditions conducive to peace, whether at an intrapersonal, interpersonal, intergroup, national or international level. Peace not only is the absence of conflict, but also requires a positive, dynamic participatory process where dialogue is encouraged and conflicts are solved in a spirit of mutual understanding and co-operation. There are many reservations and barriers that may hinder the utopian vision of establishing a global culture of peace. First- is in today's globalized world in which cultures interact in highly dynamic ways, there might be an increased risk of processes of cultural violence. The second one is cultural and religious identities can be major sources for conflict, and culture can often be a source of conflict rather than of synergy. The state of peace or conflict is often greatly influenced by a single decision. To deal with its daunting challenges, developing countries will need more candid and vigorous dialogue between ordinary citizens and their leaders. Interestingly, when it comes to technology, diversity is often less desirable. In breaking the barriers of cultural crisis, digital divide and conflicts technology may be helpful through its feature of connectivity and shearing information. Technology can provide an important context and channel for peace culture and the respect and love of humankind and of life. In the light of the increased cultural conflict that we are witnessing in the various parts of the world, the promotion of the unconditional love of peace, life and of humanity, through technology, is of central importance. In the context of peace and conflict studies, ICTs can play an important role in many ways. ICT is most effective when it is standardized and uniform, content is most valuable when it is varied and unique. ICT infrastructure strives to be culture-neutral, content is most powerful when it intermingles with local cultures.

A Critical Role of Technology in Shaping Futuristic

Peaceful Society: Ronald and Teresa [2007] note that Information and communication technologies can be a huge aid in the effort to build lasting peace, by helping people communicate, view information, make decisions, and to understand each other better.

Barring several obstacles that have to be considered, modern communication technologies are a powerful asset for fruitful discussion between cultures. International organizations have long recognized that ICTs can play a great role in achieving this goal. For example, in 1990, UNESCO has established the new operational sector ***"Communication and Information"***, which since then has become equally important as the three traditional sectors *education, science* and *culture.* ***"Considering that the process of globalization, facilitated by the rapid development of new information and communication technologies, though representing a challenge for cultural diversity, creates the conditions for renewed dialogue among cultures and civilization."***

A 2010 report of Foundation Culture of Peace, 2010 states, ***"With access to the Internet and greater global movement people are connected with different cultures, ideologies, ethnicities, etc. that helps break down barriers."***

According to the Global Movement for a Culture of Peace, website15 started by Culture of Peace architect David Adams, ***"Early on, we recognized that Internet could play an important role in the development of a global movement."***

UNESCO's website on the Culture of Peace program11 mentions [as one of the cornerstones of the program] the need to ***"support participatory communication and the free flow of information and knowledge."***

Technical Considerations: Dialogue between two or more

individuals requires a medium. This is generally the most effective form of communication, capable of transporting large amounts of information in a short time. Compared to face-to-face communication, any electronic medium is necessarily more limited and less able to efficiently convey all the semantics that are typically found between humans.

Identity Online: The medium properties vary a lot, the way identity functions also varies and depends on the concrete application being used, e.g. identity on Facebook is different from identity on Skype. It is useful to distinguish between personal, social and cultural identity, and to examine how they are expressed online.

There are several examples of ICT applications and services that are specifically relevant to the vision and ideals of a Culture of Peace. Several groups and initiatives promoting the concept of a Culture of **Peace Exists on Social Networking Services Such as Face-book:**

1. Culture of Peace Campaign: http://www.facebook.com/group.php?gid=135306216564758;
2. Culture of Peace Press: http://www.facebook.com/group.php?gid=119792618049606; and
3. Youth Team for a Culture of Peace: http://www.facebook.com/group.php?gid=196437314231

Prospective of ICTs for Building Peaceful Society: From a high-level perspective, ICTs can play an important role for promoting peace in the following ways:

1. Increasing the Effectiveness of Traditional UN and NGO Activities: ICTs can facilitate many day-to-day tasks for companies and individuals, in long-time endeavors, in daily work and in co-operation with other organizations, in order to perform tasks with higher productivity;

2. Empowering Disadvantaged People through Capacity Building: Access to information is an important part of capacity building, and the UNDP is a pioneer in using ICTs in development projects in order to work towards the UN Millennium Development Goals;

3. Empowering Disadvantaged People through Education: E-Learning and on-line libraries can improve education in a variety of ways and make specialized knowledge available in areas where it would be hard to obtain otherwise. In some projects, ICTs even help teachers acquire knowledge which they then pass to others;

Non-Violent Struggle: Several categories of using ICTs in non-violent struggle can be distinguished. The following list is partially based on Gene Sharp's 1973 classic list of non-violent methods, the politics of non-violent action:

* **Protest and Persuasion:** Communicating a political message to an audience using ICTs; and
* **Public Speeches:** Podcasts, Youtube videos, Soliya, participants can engage in a moderated video conference, discussing specific topics, posing questions, and exchanging personal views, ideas and opinions;

Group or Mass Petitions: Online petitions:

Letters of Opposition or Support: Blog posts, comments, Smart mobs organized via SMS have had impact across the world. Reading informal accounts of events or lives through a blog can be a powerful way to understand different cultures and ways of life;

Newspapers and Journals: Online newspapers;

Displays of Flags and Symbolic Acts: Use of banners, icons, ribbons, buttons, widgets etc. on a movement's website;

Wearing of Symbols: Custom browser skins, wallpapers, screensavers, etc. with the symbols of the movement;

Destruction of Own Property: Campaigns to stop using certain online services, e.g. http://www.quitfacebookday.com;

Fraternization: Web rings, hypertext links, blog rolls; and

Protest meetings: Online meetings in chat rooms, discussions forums, skypecasts etc. allow a large audience to participate in discussions that can be on any topic.

2. Rebelliousness: Using ICTs to inactively take out from or resist against unjust societal processes. This approach is also meaningful in the context of ICTs and can take concrete forms in two ways: the installation and use of proxy servers and similar systems in order to circumvent firewall and control technologies; the installation and use of private wireless, LAN networks and other low-level communication devices to circumvent mainstream infrastructures.

3. Peaceful Intercession: Using ICTs to actively interrupt unfair political conditions and instruments of power. In the context of ICTs, this can mean in particular the conscious breaking of online security systems, e.g. by the two means: hacking into networks, websites and other services, i.e. the direct exploitation of security deficiencies; and denial-service attacks, i.e., overpowering a system's communication channels in order to prevent it from fulfilling legal requests. Virus attacks, i.e. the infection of systems with malicious code in order to disrupt or manipulate their functionality.

4. Self-Organization: The use of ICTs for this purpose can range from gathering information useful to the movement to the online organization of gatherings, protests and other events. To quote as:

Example 1: Iran Green Movement In this struggle, Facebook, Twitter, blogs and photo/video hosting services all played a major role for publishing information and political messages to the movement's members and international supporters;

Example 2: Anti-FARC Protests in February 2008, an online article by BBC News describes how the march was organized to a large part through the use of the social networking service Face-book;

Example 3: In the Philippines, large scale demonstrations organized via SMS are credited with bringing down President Joseph Estrada. In South Korea, groups of students organized using SMS to protest the intense entrance exams for elite universities;

Example 4: During the fighting in Burundi, online discussion groups hosted by Burundinet and the Burundi Youth Council allowed Burundi of different backgrounds to discuss the situation, debate root causes, and figure out ways to move forward, after it became difficult to physically meet; and

Example 5: In the Philippines, large scale demonstrations organized via cell phones and SMS were a major factor in forcing President Joseph Estrada to resign, thus bringing about change without large-scale violence.

The view implicit throughout this paper is that a Global Culture of Peace can be promoted through the use of ICTs, if the respective online applications and services are designed in a way that accurately represents cultural identity, that encourages respect for cultural diversity, and that enables the free and beneficial exchange of thoughts and ideas.

Challenges for ICT in Peace-Building: There are challenges for ICT in peace building in spite of its phenomenal potential to supplement the interventions of individuals in many areas of peace building process like renewal of trust between communities, creating dialogues within and between ethnic groups, giving voice to the marginalized women and youth, and enabling grassroots participation in the dialogues related to peace building. What discourages wide and regular use of ICT are the high capital and recurrent costs which most of the person and their organizations cannot meet. This dovetails into the problem of access. By elbowing people out of ICT through bad policies, this disempowers them from having a voice in the peace building processes when in fact, ICT must be able to facilitate the building of social capital that can empower human and ***"local communities to grapple with conflicts in a non-violent way."*** [Hattotuwa, 2004]

Trust the Next Person: People can conduct critical discussion in virtual spaces while being assured of confidentiality of shared content. This is important in countries where terror and violence is heavily embedded and people cannot afford to trust the next person. How would it be possible to trust a worldly technology that one does not control? Next is sustainability of the ICT in a world where equipment can be novel today and obsolete the next day.

The lack of technological ownership: The lack of technological ownership is a huge challenge to be overcome if peoples are going to take a lead in peace building. A sense of ownership is an important precondition for overcoming the barriers to people's access to and use of ICTs.

Inaccessibility of the Internet: Many people think that this is a source of wrong information and harmful for children and teenagers, So most of the time they avoid accessing internet.

Information Overload: It is the phenomenon that information can become a problem in itself if available in amounts too large to process and in a structure too hard to search.

Digital Gap: The term *Digital Divide* [or *Digital Gap*] refers to the phenomenon that basic access to ICTs is distributed unequally, both between different world regions, and between different parts within **societies.**

The Education and Knowledge to Effect the Use: Interaction on the Internet can actually reinforce prejudices, rather than help overcome them. According to Hsu, 2009, people are likely to consume sources on the Internet that match their already existing views. Also, the Internet makes it easier for us to find and join groups that we already agree with, which might, in turn, make our views even more extreme, rather than advance the vision of a Culture of Peace.

Conclusion: It is the view of this paper that if ICTs are to be used for promoting the values of a Global Culture of Peace, then especially the expression of cultural identity in online platforms must be greatly enhanced, so that it may become possible to learn the value of cultural diversity and to actively engage in intercultural dialogue. It is important to keep in mind that intercultural dialogue, tolerance and understanding cannot be achieved through technology alone. They require respect for cultural diversity, an open mind, as well as political and social precondition that support peaceful dialogue. Peace is not created with a one-time act, True peace is built over time, with many different processes and approaches that move conflict into lasting, peaceful relationships. It requires action at many different levels, by different people, in different ways, and at different points in a conflict. The role of ICT in peace building can never be over emphasized but there are impediments to effective utilization of ICT for peace building especially in developing countries.

Bibliography

Adams, D. and True, M. 1997, March. *UNESCO Culture of Peace Programme: An Introduction.* International Peace Research Newsletter [35: 1].

Akhtar, S. 2001. *Internet Technologies in the Himalayas: Lessons Learned During the 1990* in the Journal of Information Science [27: 1, 9-17].

Boulding, E. 2008. *Peace Culture* in L Kurtz [Ed.] Encyclopedia of Violence, Peace and Conflict [Second Edition]. Amsterdam: Elsevier.

Castells, M. 2000. *The Information Age: Economy, Society and Culture: The Rise of the Network Society* [Second Edition, Volume 1]. Cambridge, MA.

Chenoweth, E and Maria, SJ. 2008. *Why Civil Resistance Works: The Strategic Logic of Nonviolent Conflict* in the International Security [33: 1, 7-44].

Curle, A. 1971. *Tools for Conflict Transformation* as cited in Peace building Bulletin, 1-3

Foundation Culture of Peace. 2010. Report on the *Decade for a Culture of Peace* in the Foundation Culture of Peace.

Gumisai, M. 2005. *New Information Technologies Change the Lives of Those in Reach.* New York: United Nations.

Hofstede, G. 2001. *Culture's Consequences: Comparing Values, Behaviors, Institutions.* Thousand Oaks, CA: SAGE Publications.

Hsu, J. 2009, June 7. *People Choose News That Fits Their Views* as retrieved from Live Science: http://www.livescience.com/3640-people-choose-news-fitsviews.html

Morozov, E. 2009, July 18. *God Bless This Gadget* as retrieved from Newsweek: http://www.newsweek.com/2009/07/17/god-bless-this-gadget.html

Ronald C and Crawford T. 2008, June. *Campaigning Against Conflict* in ACP ICT Update Bulletin No. 43

Scherrer, C. 2008. *Prevention of Violent Conflict through Structural Accommodation* in L. Kurtz [Ed.] Encyclopedia of Violence, Peace and Conflict [Second Edition]. Amsterdam: Elsevier.

Servon, Lisa. 2002. *Bridging the Digital Divide: Technology, Community, and Public Policy.* Malden, MA: Blackwell.

Shaules, J. 2007. *Deep culture: The Hidden Challenges of Global Living.* London: Multilingual Matters Ltd.

United States Institute of Peace. 2007. *ICT For Peace Report.* New York: USIP.

World Summit on the Information Society. 2005, November 18. *Tunis Agenda* as retrieved from http://www.itu.int/wsis/docs2/tunis/off/6rev1.html

7. SOCIO-CULTURAL ASPECTS OF NON-VIOLENCE AND PEACE EDUCATION

Pradip Giri* and Shyamasree Sur**

"In war torn societies, women often keep societies going......We must ensure that women are enabled to play a full part in peace negotiations, in peace processes, in peace missions." –Kofi Annan, United Nations Secretary General

Violence against women is a common and serious problem in India. It is any act of gender – based violence, which results in physical, sexual or arbitrary deprivation of liberty and violence of human rights of women. There are various types of violence against women in India like child marriage, female feticide and infanticide, sexual abuse, female child labour, domestic violence, dowry harassment and bride burning, sexual harassment at work, eve teasing, violence against elderly women, violence against widows and women trafficking etc. Violence against women can be categorized under three broad headings of:

* Mr. Pradip Giri and **Shyamasree Sur are research scholars at the department of education in the University of Kalyani [West Bengal], India.

- Criminal violence as rape, abduction or murder;
- Domestic violence which includes dowry – deaths, wife battering, sexual abuse, maltreatment of widows or elderly women and lastly; and
- Social violence which forces a wife or daughter in law to go for female feticide eve-teasing, refusing to give a share to women in property, forcing a woman to commit sati or harassing a woman for any other cause. Since the very primitive time, the condition of women was pathetic.

If we look towards the statistics about crimes/violence against women and educational development [Literacy] in India, we can simply conclude that cases of violence against women are rapidly rising with educational development. The correlation between above both variables should be negative but it is positive in India. Education is an empowering tool for women and it is the crucial criteria of social development. Current peace education does its utmost to be considered a unique educational practice, a field of research and a discourse that has its own philosophical, social, rhetorical and political aspects. Peace education, however, has no theoretical framework. The promotion of peace through education is at the heart of UNESCO's mission. Two fundamental concepts of peace education are respect and skills. For sustaining and achieving peace, the need for peace education is felt more and more. Peace does not simply mean the absence of war but the absence of fear, and structural inequalities. Justice is integral to peace – so peace with justice is what women fight for. The only lasting peace is just peace based on respect for human rights. Women should come forward to protect themselves by empowering themselves. Women are expected to work for peace building by peace Education. Women are half of every community and they can shoulder the responsibility of the tasks of peace building. We should provide the Zone to empower women to overcome threats and obstacles that may interrupt or prevent their peace building.

Concept of Peace Education: Peace building is a relatively new term, but the ideas and practices behind peace building have deep roots in all cultures. All cultures and communities have ways of building peace. The tasks of those who desire to be peace building are; to help uncover the traditions of peace building within each culture, to borrow peace building ideas from other cultures, to adapt them to local contexts, and to empower people to engage in peace building processes. In simple terms, peace building is all activity aimed at improving the quality of life. Peace building prevents, reduces, transforms, and helps people to recover from violence. Peace building includes a set of values, relational skills, analytical tools and processes to create sustainable, just and peaceful communities. Peace building is found in every community and in every culture, but many of our communities need help to explore and strengthen their capacity to building peace. Men and women in every community are already engaged in building peace, but their tasks are almost always different. Women and men both have their role to place in peace building. But empowerment of women is a challenge in building culture of peace in India.

Peace Education Policy: The UN Resolution 1325 recognized the relevance of gender and peace and security matters, and mandated all United Nations member-states to ensure full participation of women at all levels of decision making in conflict resolution and peace processes. It also called for the protection of women and girls against violence during and after conflict, and for the adoption of a gender perspective to prevent and mitigate impacts of conflict on women. While progress has been made at policy levels, translating the goals of Resolution 1325 into reality in conflict- affected countries remain a challenge.

In the education sector, more efforts must be made by Government to identify and strengthen the right methodologies for empowering both male and female teachers to create a safe and secure school environment for girls and boys. Synergies must be created between experience and policies.

In 1995, the Beijing Platform of Action recognized education not only as a human right but also as an essential tool for achieving the goals of equality, development and peace. ***"Literacy of women is an important key to improving health, nutrition and education in the family and to empowering women to participate in decision – making and society."*** The issues raised at the UN Beijing conference remain relevant. The conference identified twelve critical areas of concern. Each concern revealed that women's human rights are very much compromised and discriminated against solely on the basis of gender. Equality between men and women could not be achieved unless the rights of women are fully respected.

The 2011 European conference on the move for equality highlighted that women's civil society organizations are an important vehicle for the promotion of women's participation and gender friendly policies, both important for long term peace and democracy. Burundi and Nepal are two post-conflict countries that are notable for the large number of women engaged in civil society. In these countries, women's organizations have been a driving force behind women's engagement in public and political life, for the adoption of laws protecting women's rights. Yet, the impact and sustainability of these organizations are hampered both by a lack of political will, and by insecure and inflexible funding regimes.

Men-Women Empowerment: Gender equality is a human right, but our world faces a persistent gap in access to opportunities and decision making power for women and men. Globally, women have fewer opportunities for economic participation than men, less access to basic and higher education, greater health and safety risks, and less political representation. Guaranteeing the rights of women and giving them opportunities to reach their full potential is critical not only for attaining gender equality, but also for meeting a wide range of international development goals. Empowered women and girls contribute to the health and productivity of their families, communities and countries, creating a ripple effect that benefits everyone.

The word gender describes the socially constructed roles and responsibilities that societies consider appropriate for men and women. Gender equality means that men and women have equal power and equal opportunities for financial independence, education and personal development. Women's Empowerment is a critical aspect of achieving gender equality. It includes increasing a women's sense of self worth, her decision making power, her access to opportunities and resources, her power and control over her own life inside and outside the home, and her ability to effect change. Yet gender issues are not focused on women alone, but on the relationship between men and women in society. The actions and attitudes of men and boys play an essential role in achieving gender equality.

Education is key area of focus. Although the world is making progress in achieving gender parity in education, girls still make up a higher percentage of out of school children than boys. Approximately one quarter of girls in the developing world do not attend school. Typically families with limited means who cannot afford costs such as school fees, uniforms, and supplies for all of their children will prioritize education for their son. Families may also rely on girls labour for household chores, carrying water, and childcare, leaving limited time for schooling. But prioritizing girl's education provides perhaps the single highest return on investment in the developing world. An educated girl is more likely to postpone marriage, raise a smaller family, have healthier children, and send her own children to school. She has more opportunities to earn an income and to participate in political processes, and she is less likely to become infected with HIV.

Women's health and safety is another important area. HIV/AIDS is becoming an increasingly impactful issue for women. This can be related to women having fewer opportunities for health education, unequal power in sexual partnership or as a result of gender based violence. Maternal health is also an issue of specific concern. In many countries, women have limited access to pre-natal and infant care, and are more likely to experience complications during pregnancy and childbirth. This is a critical concern in countries where girls marry and bear children before they are mature; often well before the age of eighteen. Quality maternal health care can provide an important entry point for information and services that empower mothers as informed decision-makers concerning their own health and the health of their children.

A final area of focus in attaining gender equality is women's economic and political empowerment. Though women comprise more than fifty percent of the world's population, they only own one percent of the world's wealth. Throughout the world, women and girls perform long hours of unpaid domestic work. In some places, women still lack rights to own land or to inherit property, obtain access to credit, earn income, or to move up in their work place, free from job discrimination. At all levels, including at home and in the public area, women are widely underrepresented as decision makers. In legislatures around the world, women are outnumbered four to one, yet women's political participation is crucial for achieving gender equality and genuine democracy.

The world Economic forum recently ranked the United States as nineteenth in the world on its gender gap index. With women comprising less than one fifth of elected members of congress, the report identifies political empowerment as the greatest gender equity issue for the United States. The US ranked higher in economic empowerments, but women's earning power remains approximately twenty percent lower than men's. Women in the United States have a very high ranking of educational attainment, though, with high levels of literacy and enrolment in primary, secondary, and university education. At present, there are more US women attending college than men.

Globally, many countries have fully attained gender equality. Scandinavian countries like Iceland, Norway, Finland, and Sweden lead the world in their progress towards closing the gender gap. In these countries, there is relatively equitable distribution of available income, resources and opportunities for men and women. The greatest gender gaps are identified primarily in the Middle East, Africa and South Asia, However, a number of countries including South Africa, Sri Lanka etc. outrank the US in gender equality.

Around the world Peace Corps and volunteers are working with communities to address gender equality and empower women and girls. In 1974, Congress signed the

Percy Amendment requiring Peace Corps Volunteers to activity integrate women into the economic, political and social development of their countries. Many Peace Corps Volunteers implement the camp GLOW [Girls Leading Our World] programme, to help girls develop self-esteem and leadership skills. Recognizing that men and boys must be equal partners in achieving gender equality, volunteers also teach leadership and life skills to boys through Teaching Our Boys Excellence [TOBE] camps. Peace corps volunteers promote gender equality and women's empowerment through health education, business development, and by raising awareness of women's rights and their contributions to communities.

Gender Equality in Education: Gender based discrimination in education is both a cause and a consequence of deep-rooted disparities in society. Poverty, geographical isolation, ethnic background, disability, traditional attitudes about their status and role all undermine the ability of women and girls to exercise their rights. Harmful practices such as early marriage and pregnancy, gender-based violence, and discriminatory education laws, policies, contents, and practices still prevent millions of girls form enrolling, completing and befitting from education.

Gender must therefore be integrated at all levels of education, from early childhood to higher education, in formal and non-formal settings and from planning infrastructure to training teachers.

A culture of peace and non-violence goes to the substance of fundamental human rights; social justice, democracy, literacy, respect and dignity for all, international solidarity, respect for workers' rights and core labour standards, children rights, equality between men and women, cultural identity and diversity, indigenous peoples and minorities rights, the preservation of natural environment to name some of the more obvious thematic.

Education is a key tool in combating poverty, in promoting peace, social justice, human rights, democracy, cultural diversity and environmental awareness. Education for peace implies an active concept of peace through values, life skills and knowledge in a spirit of equality, respect, empathy, understanding and mutual appreciation among individuals, groups and nations. By educating women, society would be striving to get them out of the deep levels of illiteracy the world over. It would give them a chance to engage competitively in various issues that will invariably have a positive impact on sustainable peace.

Peace education would enable the girl child to have an equal platform in contributing to addressing form of structural and cultural violence and actively participating in seeking effective and sustainable ways of resolving the situation and enhancing all rounded peace.

Conclusion: It is only by critically addressing the cultural and structural hindrances that exist against women that sustainable peace and development can be achieved. In order to override these problems, we need to act to empower women by taking steps to eliminate inequalities by the promotion and fulfillment of women's potential through education, skill development and employment hence giving paramount importance to the elimination for sustainable development and positive holistic peace.

Education is the first building block of development upon which everything else, health care, social care, employment – must be founded. It is the key to holistic development in the economic, social and political spheres. The role of education in development and in the enhancement of positive peace cannot be overlooked. Thus, the education of the girl child can be used as an empowerment tool to address practices that institutionalize discrimination, injustice and equality. By educating the girl child, the society as a whole would have come one step further in addressing human security and ensuring better future for all its citizens. In order to grow as nation, we must realize the importance of bringing women and most specifically girl child to the same level as the men and boy children, then and only then, can we realize positive peace.

The hard action and law and regulations are made by the judicial committee. It is true that this heinous act was the outcome of narrow-mindedness of the people. But it seems that women are responsible for this type of activity. The harassing and exploitation of women by women. The girls commit suicide because of dowry, but the question is who force them for doing so? The answer will come only as women. Today who is making a girl fashionable? The answer will be only women. How can a man be responsible for this type of activity? In the male dominated society, women are dominated. The incidents are increasing day to day because women have themselves vulnerable persons of the society. They must understand that their role is important to prevent this type of act which happened to them. For this, they will have to raise their voice and start the movement against those who consider women a weak character. The time has come that we all should work together to maintain our safety and security even if we have to start the movement against ourselves and our system because our system is handicapped and corrupted. Hence we should not believe in the system but try to change or amend it so that we may ensure our girls or women security.

The promotion of peace education is the way out of cultural and structural violence against women. Women also need to be represented at the decision and policy making level within the education sphere. Educating women will farther societal expectations in various ways including improved health and better socio-economic status. This is in striving towards the attainment of equity through education and in giving both genders the same opportunities to access education. Peace education for the women and girl child affects all spheres in society be it political, economic or social. If well implemental, it has the potential to promote sustainable development and positive peace.

Notes/Bibliography:

* Basiga, Brenda. 2004. Article: *Globalization and peace Education* in the University of Alberta [Canadian Social Studies, Volume 38, Number 3].
* Brecher, J and Castello, T. 1994. *Global Village or Global Pillage.* Boston: South End.
* Brock–Utne, B. 1989. *Feminist Perspectives on Peace and Peace Education.* New York: Pergamon.
* Carnoy. M. 1999. *Globalization and Educational Reform : What Planners Need to know.* Paris: UNESCO: International Institute for Educational Planning.
* Eisler, Riane. 1997. *Human Rights and Violence in:Turpin* in Jennifer and Lester R Kurtz [Eds.] *The Web of Violence.* Chicago: University of Illinois Press [pp 16-187].
* The Times of India. 2013, February 6.
* UNDP. 1997: *Human Development Report.*

8. THE ROLE OF EDUCATOR IN ENHANCING SOCIAL RELATIONS THROUGH PEACE EDUCATION IN LEARNERS

Archana Rajput* and PS Birla**

Peace education covers a wide territory, and has many subsidiaries. Mitsuo Okamoto argues that disarmament education, international education, development education and the like can, by broad definition, be included as programs in peace education. The contents denominated by the various titles like world order education, global education, education for international understanding, education for justice, ecological education etc., have been categorized by Okamoto into four types of peace education. The first sees peace education as criticism of war. The basic view here is that peace is the absence of war [negative peace]. Content of this type includes teaching concerning the legacy of war experience, a scientific explanation of the causes of war and conditions of peace, the promotion of international understanding as a preventive to war, etc. The second type considers peace education as liberation. Here, a new concept of peace, positive peace [which is defined as that social condition characterized by economic independence, a stable order, social justice, human rights and welfare], is presupposed. Liberation from poverty,

* Ms. Archana Rajput and **Mr. PS Birla are research scholars in Education at the Dayalbagh Educational Institute of Agra [U.P.], India.

ignorance, discrimination and oppression etc. is seen as the objective goal for peace education here.

The third type regards peace education as a learning process. In this type, peace education is grasped as a learning process towards inter-personal maturity on the basis of the unity between theory and practice on the one hand, and a critical understanding of history and society on the other. The fourth type holds peace education as life-style movements: it rests upon the realization that warfare and war preparations are intimately tied to the fact that the over-production and extravagance of the nations at the center have been gained at the expense of the wealth and development of nations at the periphery. Here, we can refer to a standard of values emphasizing a simple life, human scale, self-determination, ecological awareness and personal growth.

Peace education operates differently in various global contexts. What does it mean in globalization and particular regional interests? Questions were raised about practical strategies that link theory and practice, especially in the context of countries experiencing war or having recently experienced war. What different peace education content is addressed in societies that are not at war but still experience high levels of crime, ethnic conflict, and domestic violence? How can insights gleaned from these different contexts be used to help each other? Are our key concepts universal? How are they interpreted by separate cultures in specific contexts?

Peace educators establish democratic classrooms that teach co-operation and promote positive self esteem among their students. Teachers serve as peaceful role models to help to counteract images of violent behaviour young people receive through popular culture and in their homes. Their teaching style adjusts to the developmental needs of their pupils, respecting the various identities and concerns about violence students bring to the classroom.

At the school level, the predominant need is to have a peaceful climate, i.e. a peace culture. In such a culture, children will naturally absorb the spirit of peace. There is a popular saying that peace has to be caught rather than be taught. Initiating a peaceful culture in school should start from within the staff, by developing attitudes and behaviour of appreciation, co-operation, belongingness, trust and spirit of learning. By way of developing a friendly and mutually respectful teacher-pupil relationship, a peace culture will bloom naturally in the school. To ensure it, the school has to introduce a living system of peace values, norms and practices into the daily life of the school. It would be necessary to change the *teacher-centred* classroom approach to *child-centred* learning. When there is active and participative learning in the classroom using interesting teaching and learning methods in a friendly and lively atmosphere marked by creative expressions of potentials and self discipline, peace will emerge naturally. Teachers have to identify effective strategies and practices that could transform the school into a place of harmony.

Other issues concerned the difference between teaching separate peace education classes versus integrating peace themes into existing curricula. In many different countries, teachers are starting programs that don't use the terms *peace education* to describe them. Rather, they are calling their programs conflict resolution, violence prevention, anger management, etc. What is the source of this reluctance to use the terms *peace education?* How can we overcome it? In general people want immediate solutions to the problems of violence they fear. Peace education, because it provides a long term solution, is not seen as necessary and is not grabbing the kind of support as does conflict resolution which helps put out fires.

A key issue is: How can educators contribute to making a peaceful person? This would include feminist insights into peace theory as well as a certain orientation towards peaceful values, beliefs, and behaviours. A peaceful person should display a certain *groundedness* that implies not being in a constant state of anger and frustration. What does it mean in social skills and democratic participation? What kind of contribution can peace education make to build *a culture of peace*?

What does it mean to be *transformative*? How can peace educators empower their students to take action to end violence? Peace keeping may be a valuable ingredient especially in keeping bullies from disrupting classes and in keeping warring parties from each other's throats. Otherwise, threats of violence can undermine attempts at peaceful pedagogy. What skills should peace educators teach in order that their students become effective peacemakers? How can we help students embrace the values and behaviour of nonviolence? How can we get broader acceptance for peace building approaches to violence?

What is the difference between peace studies and peace education? How do these two concepts overlap? Earlier within the International Peace Research Association, peace education was seen as a means for propagating the findings of peace researchers. Peace education is quickly becoming a field of its own as teachers all over the world are looking to insights from peace theory to help them make their schools more peaceful and resolve bloody disputes in civil societies. Students in peace studies classes learn about the causes of war and alternatives to violence. Peace educators figure out how to teach those concepts to different age levels in different contexts. Insights into the international sphere provided by peace studies may not seem relevant to educators whose schools and communities are experiencing violence and whose students are being shot. How do the micro issues of violence relate to the broader macro cultures that glorify violence throughout the world?

Peace Education is about empowering people with the skills, attitudes, and knowledge:

- To build, maintain, and restore relationships at all levels of human interaction;
- To develop positive approaches towards dealing with conflicts -from the personal to the international;
- To create safe environments, both physically and emotionally, that nurture each individual;
- To create a safe world based on justice and human rights; and
- To build a sustainable environment and protect it from exploitation and war.

Peace education is based on a philosophy that teaches non-violence, love, compassion, trust, fairness, co-operation and reverence for the human family and all life on our planet. Skills include communication, listening, understanding different perspectives, co-operation, problem solving, critical thinking, decision making, conflict resolution, and social responsibility. Peace education leads to peaceful living.

Notes:

Arnow, J. 1995. *Teaching Peace: How to Raise Children to Live in Harmony without Fear, without Prejudice, without Violence.* New York: The Berkeley Publishing Group.

Bickmore, Kathy, J Looney and Goldthwaite, P. 1984. *Alternatives to Violence: A Manual for Teaching Peacemaking to Youth and Adults*. Cleveland, OH: Cleveland Friends Meeting.

Heater, D. 1984. *Peace through Education: The Contribution the Council for Education in World Citizenship*. London: The Farmer Group.

Mukhopadhyay, M. 2005. *Peace education: Framework for Teacher Education* [IN/2005/ED/6]. New Delhi: UNESCO.

Navarro-Castro, L and Nario-Galace, J. 2008. *Peace Education: A Pathway to a Culture of Peace*. San Francisco, CA: Scribd Inc.

Page, James. 2008. *Peace Education: Exploring Ethical and Philosophical Foundations*. Charlotte, NC: Information Age Press.

Stomfay-Stitz, AM. 1993. *Peace Education in America, 1828-1990: Sourcebook for Education and Research*. Metuchen, NJ: Scarecrow Press.

*****

INDEX

[I]

[J]

[K]

[L]

[M]

[N]

[O]

[P]

*****